1964

This book may be kept

FOURTEEN DAYS

A fine will be charged for each day the book is kept overtime.

MR 3 '66			
MR 3 0 '67			
DE 10 70			
MAR 14 '74			
6-3-76			
GAYLORD 142			PRINTED IN U.S.A.

THE
CULTURAL MILIEU
OF
ADDISON'S
LITERARY CRITICISM

THE
CULTURAL MILIEU
OF
ADDISON'S
LITERARY CRITICISM

Lee Andrew Elioseff

UNIVERSITY OF TEXAS PRESS · AUSTIN

Chapter 6 appears as an article in the *Journal of Aesthetics and Art Criticism* (XXI, No. 4, Summer, 1963) under the title "Pastorals, Politics, and the Idea of Nature in the Reign of Queen Anne."

Published with the assistance of a grant from the Ford Foundation under its program for the support of publications in the humanities and social sciences

Manufactured in the United States of America

TO MY PARENTS

CONTENTS

ACKNOWLEDGMENTS

"Gens sans aveu" is Boileau's damning epithet for the philosophers who had denied the authority of Aristotle. A young scholar rarely deserves such a title. Indeed, he is more likely to have too many masters, whom he thanks with pleasure, optimistically hoping that he has forgotten none of them and is worthy of some of them.

Those whom one knows only through their works are hardest to thank. Yet, without the books and articles of Marjorie Hope Nicolson, Clarence DeWitt Thorpe, and Richard Foster Jones, this book could hardly have been written. I am indebted to Arthur Oncken Lovejoy not only for his *Great Chain of Being* and *Essays in the History of Ideas,* but, also, for the memory of his presence at the History of Ideas Club meetings at Johns Hopkins University, where he gently reminded members and guests of that club that there is much that they did not know and had not read. To Professor Earl R. Wasserman I owe the awakening of my interest in the possibilities of relating the study of the history of ideas to Addison's literary criticism.

Professor George Winchester Stone, Jr., directed both my master's thesis, "English Empirical Philosophy and Addison's Literary Criticism" (New York University, 1957), and my doctoral dissertation (New York University, 1960), an earlier version of the present work. Professor Stone gave unstintingly of his time, intelligence, and good humor in his supervision of "The Cultural Milieu of Addison's Literary Criticism." After rereading and revising this work, I am no longer certain what is his and what is mine. He has saved the reader from more errors and omissions than I should care to remember.

I owe Professor Edward L. McAdam, Jr., two debts. He has been most generous with his collection of seventeenth- and eighteenth-century periodicals and newspapers, and his detailed criticism of an earlier version of this work has been invaluable.

The staffs of the New York Public Library, the Library of Congress, and the libraries of New York and Harvard Universities have been most helpful. I recall with special pleasure the time spent at the Sterling Memorial Library of Yale University, whose librarians made the stacks and Rare Book Room my home for six weeks during the spring of 1959.

I offer my thanks to the graduate faculty of New York University's Department of English for its interest in this project and encouragement of it, and to the Graduate School of Arts and Science of that university for the award of a Penfield Fellowship which made this work possible.

The greatest debt of all, one which can never be repaid, I mention last. Three teachers and one friend of long standing have done more to stimulate and direct the organization of my thought than the meagre references to published evidence of their intellectual activity can possibly indicate. Professors Kathrine Koller, Lewis White Beck, and Robert B. Hinman, of the University of Rochester, have proved themselves—in seminar and conversation, by precept and example—to be the three best teachers I have had the pleasure to study with. Robert Rosen, whom I have seen less often than I would like since we first met eleven years ago, is now with the Committee on Mathematical Biology at the University of Chicago. Not even his inherent modesty can obscure his broad critical intelligence.

If the reader of this book finds that it has helped him to better understand the structure of Addison's critical thought, his thanks should go to all of these masters.

Lee Andrew Elioseff

Austin, Texas

ABBREVIATIONS FOR REFERENCES

Eighteenth-Century Periodicals and Newspapers

Athenian Gazette .. *Athenian Gazette; Or Casuistical Mercury,* 20 vols. (London, 1690–1697).

G. .... *The Guardian* (1713), 3rd ed., 2 vols. (London, 1747).

Review .... *A Review of the State of the British Nation* (1704–1711) ; *Defoe's Review,* reproduced from the original editions, with an introduction by Arthur Wellesley Secord, 22 vols. (New York, 1938).

S. .... *The Spectator* (1711–1714), ed. G. G. Smith, 4 vols. (London, 1907). Checked with the original folio sheets by S. Buckley and J. Tonson, and the first octavo edition (1712–1713) of the first seven volumes (Nos. 1–555), printed for S. Buckley and J. Tonson.

T. .... *The Tatler* (1709–1711), ed. George A. Aitken, 4 vols. (London, 1898–1899).

Works of Addison

Letters .... *The Letters of Joseph Addison,* ed. Walter Graham (Oxford, 1941).

Works .... *The Works of the Right Honourable Joseph Addison,* ed. Richard Hurd. A new edition by Henry G. Bohn, 6 vols. (London, 1888–1892).

Works of Other Authors

CESC .... *Critical Essays of the Seventeenth Century,* ed. Joel E. Spingarn, 3 vols. (Oxford, 1908–1909).

Dennis .... *The Critical Works of John Dennis,* ed. Edward Niles Hooker, 2 vols. (Baltimore, 1939–1943).

Descartes .... *The Philosophical Works of Descartes,* trans. Elizabeth S. Haldane and G. R. T. Ross, 2 vols.

(New York, 1955: reprint of corrected ed. of 1931).

EHU .... John Locke, *Essay concerning Human Understanding,* ed. Alexander Campbell Fraser, 2 vols. (Oxford, 1894).

Hobbes, *Works* ... *The English Works of Thomas Hobbes,* ed. William Molesworth, 11 vols. (London, 1839–1849).

Lev. .... Thomas Hobbes, *Leviathan,* introduction by A. D. Lindsay (New York, 1950).

EDITIONS CITED

Aristotle .... *Works,* The Oxford Translation, ed. J. A. Smith and W. D. Ross, 12 vols. (Oxford, 1910–1952).

Plato .... *The Dialogues of Plato,* trans. Benjamin Jowett, 2 vols. (New York, 1937).

Mr. *Lock's* Essay on Human Understanding would be thought a very odd book for a Man to make himself a Master of, who would get a Reputation by Critical Writings; though at the same Time it is very certain, that an Author who has not learned the Art of distinguishing between Words and Things, and of ranging his Thoughts, and setting them in proper Lights, whatever Notions he may have, will lose himself in Confusion and Obscurity . . .

The Truth of it is, there is nothing more absurd, than for a Man to set up for a Critick, without a good Insight into all the Parts of Learning; whereas many of those who have endeavoured to signalize themselves by Works of this Nature among our *English* Writers, are not only defective in the above-mentioned Particulars, but plainly discover by the Phrases they make use of, and by their confused way of thinking, that they are not acquainted with the most common and ordinary Systems of the Arts and Sciences.

Addison, *Spectator* 291

THE

CULTURAL MILIEU

OF

ADDISON'S

LITERARY CRITICISM

Toward a Method for the

History of Criticism

> We must be content, then, in speaking of such sub-
> jects and with such premisses to indicate the truth
> roughly and in outline, and in speaking about things
> which are only for the most part true and with
> premisses of the same kind to reach conclusions that
> are no better. In the same spirit, therefore, should
> each type of statement be received; for it is the mark
> of an educated man to look for precision in each
> class of things just so far as the nature of the sub-
> ject admits; it is evidently equally foolish to accept
> probable reasoning from a mathematician and to
> demand from a rhetorician scientific proofs.
>
> Aristotle, *Ethica Nicomachea* 1094b
> (Ingram Bywater, trans.)

THE HISTORY of literary criticism is one of the youngest and
least self-conscious of the literary disciplines. The essential
unity of critical theory from the Renaissance through the end
of the eighteenth century and the nature of the romantic revolt
against the earlier critics, each in its own way, discouraged a
systematic and dispassionate study of the history of the premises
of literary judgment. Two early works, Joel E. Spingarn's *History of Literary Criticism in the Renaissance* (1899)[1] and
George Saintsbury's *History of Criticism and Literary Taste in
Europe* (1900–1904), were justly applauded soon after they
were published, but both of them are informed by Saintsbury's

[1] Edition cited is the 1925 reprint of the 2nd ed. (1908), p. v.

explicitly stated principles: "The Criticism which will be dealt with here is that function of the judgment which busies itself with the goodness or badness, success or ill-success, of literature from the *purely literary* point of view."[2] Although the earlier work does not share Saintsbury's acknowledged disdain for aesthetic questions, Spingarn's emphasis is also almost exclusively literary; both books were written on the supposition, explicit or implicit, that the literary critic thinks in terms which, for the most part, exclude other intellectual and social concerns.

The history of criticism must begin, as Austin Warren insists, with the history of literature,[3] but it cannot end there. A study of only the literary backgrounds of neoclassical criticism, primarily Greek and Roman literature, will show how neoclassical criticism came into being, but will not explain its development. A history of criticism based exclusively upon a knowledge of the "literary experience" of the given age may be adequate when the criticism of that age is static, when the fundamental tenets and vocabulary of critical discourse are handed from generation to generation and only the works criticized change. But unless we are prepared to study the revolution in metaphysics, ethics, psychology, natural philosophy, and aesthetics of the seventeenth and eighteenth centuries, we shall never fully understand the revolution in criticism of the nineteenth century and its origins in the criticism of the eighteenth. Whatever our respective beliefs may be concerning the independence of literary criticism as an intellectual discipline in our own time, we cannot impose these views upon the past. The most influential critics from Plato to T. S. Eliot wrote with an urgent concern about the moral, political, and philosophical—as well as literary—issues of their day.

If literary standards and judgments have not been made in a

---

[2] I, 3.

[3] "Literary Criticism," in *Literary Scholarship: Its Aims and Methods,* p. 134. Cf. René Wellek and Austin Warren, Chapter IV: "Literary Theory, Criticism, and History," *Theory of Literature,* 2nd ed.; Northrop Frye, *Anatomy of Criticism,* pp. 5–6.

world emptied of all intellectual concerns other than literary issues, the historian of criticism who aspires to be something more than a curator of antiquated conceptions of literary excellence must see his material in terms of all those circumstances of the culture which gave rise to them. At the same time, in order to preserve the integrity of criticism as an intellectual discipline, he must eliminate the purely fortuitous elements, private feuds, and inconsequential personal tastes, which occasionally wear the mask of "objective" literary criticism. Only then can he concentrate upon those aspects of criticism which most clearly represent the age's dominant critical opinions and the direction in which its less well-established, but no less important, principles are leading it.[4]

The immediate value of such a history of criticism lies in its illumination of the present critical situation, not merely past debates. Thus, the highest aim of the historian of criticism is that proposed by René Wellek in his discussion of the value of investigation of the history of the theoretical assumptions of literary history: "It would not only satisfy the instinctive desires of men to commemorate the achievements of their predecessors, but would serve a practical purpose as well: it would help to show by what ways the present vantage-point, or *impasse,* of literary studies has been reached. It would elucidate the present-day problems and increase a consciousness of the principles basic to our discipline." [5] This is also the underlying principle of his *History of Modern Criticism;* therefore, if I part company with Professor Wellek, I do so only because I do not find the study of early eighteenth-century criticism so "largely an antiquarian task" [6] as he does, but, rather, seek the sources of modern literary criticism in the works of Joseph Addison and his contemporaries, especially in their responses to problems, both literary and nonliterary, central to their culture.

[4] Cf. René Wellek, *A History of Modern Criticism: 1750–1950. Later Eighteenth Century,* pp. 8–10.
[5] *The Rise of English Literary History,* p. v.
[6] *A History of Modern Criticism,* p. v.

The problems raised by many of Addison's essays, especially those on *The Pleasures of the Imagination,* are those of a distinctly "modern" psychological critic whose immediate concern is the effect of literature upon its audience. Insofar as this interest remains unsubordinated to the consideration of art as moral discourse, imitation of nature, or formal structure, Addison's essays extend the boundaries of neoclassical criticism, establishing a new context, with its own questions and problems, for the criticism of art and literature. To be sure, even in his papers on *The Pleasures of the Imagination* Addison does not achieve complete independence. He freely acknowledges the superiority of the ancient critics,[7] and his relation to them and to their heirs of the Renaissance and the seventeenth century is the most important aspect of the cultural milieu of Addison's criticism. I hope that the organization of this study of the criticism of Queen Anne's England will be of some value through its ordering of the relationship between criticism and its milieu in a setting less complex than our own.

I

The most important models for this essay are *The Intellectual Milieu of John Dryden* and *The Great Chain of Being.*[8] Professor Bredvold's explanation of the dramatic changes in Dryden's political and religious thought through an elucidation of its background in the ideas of the period offers an instructive parallel for the less dramatic but no less important changes which the premises of literary criticism underwent in the writings of Joseph Addison. The merits and limitations of Professor Lovejoy's "unit-idea," which reduces literary texts to documents for the historian of ideas, are surely too well known to make extensive commentary necessary; the value of this con-

---

[7] See, for example, S. 253, 291. All quotations from the *Spectator* will be taken from G. Gregory Smith's edition. The text of this edition will be followed except where it deviates from the sense of the original folio sheets (1711–1714) or the first octavo edition (Vols. 1–7, 1712–1713; Nos. 1–555). See Donald F. Bond, "The Text of the *Spectator*," *SB*, V (1952–1953), 109–128.

[8] Louis I. Bredvold, *The Intellectual Milieu of John Dryden;* Arthur O. Lovejoy, *The Great Chain of Being: A Study in the History of an Idea.*

cept for the discussion of such terms as *Nature, taste,* and *imagination* will become apparent as this work develops.

However stimulating the methods of both scholars may have been to literary studies in the 1930's, they fall a little short of explaining the entire complex of events which gave rise to Addison's literary criticism. Professor Bredvold assumes that his readers understand what is meant by *milieu;* consequently, the most important term in his title is left undefined, and large areas of the literary and social aspects of the intellectual milieu are not discussed. More important from the point of view of the present study is the need to understand the milieu of Addison's criticism in terms of such factors as political and national loyalties, literary and theatrical practices, and shifts in taste which do not fall entirely within the domain of intellectual history or are too diffuse to lend themselves to the history-of-ideas approach. For this reason, *cultural milieu,* which takes into account feelings and reactions which are largely nonideological in content, is more accurate than *intellectual milieu* as a designation for the subject matter of this study.

II

The critical milieu of Addison's criticism is largely that inherited from the classical philosophers and rhetoricians. Literary criticism in Western Europe had not been fundamentally altered by the postmedieval followers of Plato, Aristotle, Horace, Cicero, and Quintilian. But only if we neglect several important developments between 1700 and 1750 can we give unqualified support to René Wellek's contention that the history of "modern" criticism does not begin until 1750: [9]

The history of criticism from the beginning of the Renaissance to the middle of the eighteenth century consists in the establishment, elaboration, and spread of a view which is substantially the same in 1750 as it was in 1550. Of course there are shifts in emphasis, changes in terminology; there are differences between individual critics, the main countries of Europe, and the different stages of

[9] *History of Modern Criticism,* p. 5.

development. There were three clearly recognizable stages which could be distinguished as governed by authority, reason, and finally by taste.

Surely, Samuel Johnson, writing well into the period after which Professor Wellek dates the beginning of modern criticism, is closer to Ben Jonson and John Dryden than to the Addison of *The Pleasures of the Imagination* or even to Thomas Purney when he wrote that the first task of the critic is to speculate "on the Nature and Constitution of the human Mind, and what Pleasures it is capable of receiving from Poetry." [10] Although Professor Wellek notes that the philosophies of Descartes, Locke, and Leibniz were responsible for the differences among the critical theories of their respective nations, [11] he does not see, as Walter Jackson Bate does, [12] that the psychological assumptions of Hobbesian and Lockean philosophy are largely responsible for the changes in the structure and assumptions of English criticism. The change is certainly not sudden or complete. As late as 1776 Samuel Johnson dismisses the most important exemplification of Lockean psychology in the literature of his time with " 'Nothing odd will do long. *Tristram Shandy* did not last'." [13] Many questions asked by critics at the beginning of the eighteenth century cannot be explained in the context of Aristotelian-Horatian criticism, however. These new questions, when answered, became the foundation of modern criticism.

The synthesis of the morally centered "mimetic-formal" criticism, whose early history is described in Marvin T. Herrick's *The Fusion of Horatian and Aristotelian Criticism, 1531–1555*, [14] produced a system of critical concepts and a criti-

[10] *The Works of Thomas Purney*, ed. H. O. White, p. 48. The introduction and the editor's "Thomas Purney, a Forgotten Poet and Critic of the Eighteenth Century," *E&S*, XV (1929), 67–97, give Purney credit for being more extraordinary than he was. See below, Note 26.

[11] Wellek, *History of Modern Criticism*, p. 8.

[12] *From Classic to Romantic: Premises of Taste in Eighteenth-Century England*, p. vii. See Jean Hagstrum, *Samuel Johnson's Literary Criticism*; Meyer Abrams, *The Mirror and the Lamp*.

[13] Boswell, *Life of Johnson*, ed. Chauncey Brewster Tinker, I, 660.

[14] Illinois Studies in Language and Literature, Vol. XXXII, No. 1.

cal vocabulary which remained dominant until the early part
of the nineteenth century. An examination of the presuppositions of critics from Minturno to Boileau will reveal systems
whose general structures are identical; that is, they address
themselves to a common set of critical problems with a critical
vocabulary and a method supplied by Aristotle, Horace, and
Quintilian. The specific differences produced by the milieux
of these critics did not give rise to a corresponding change in
their critical frame of reference. Julius Caesar Scaliger's formulation of the dramatic unities represents an addition to
Aristotle, but this addition was made within the framework of
Aristotelian formal criticism. The influence of Cartesian philosophy and French theatrical practices contributed to a more
rigid adherence to these unities in France than in England,
but the difference between Boileau and Dryden is one of degree. Both would have agreed that the problems of the unities
of time and place are of real concern to the critic. If they disagreed about the extent to which the rules were to be followed,
their common commitment to the basic tenets of Aristotelian
criticism would have led them to join against those critics who
completely dismissed these regulations.

The preceding remarks are not offered as a suggestion that
neoclassical criticism, completely patterned after classical
sources, was static through the last half of the seventeenth century. The biological and metaphysical rationale of Aristotle's
Poetics [15] was hardly functional even during the Renaissance.
His literary theory was understood most often in terms of the
rhetorical tradition of Quintilian, which did much to explain
Horace's notion of *utile et dulce* with references to moral precepts and virtues of style, embodied in the ideals of "correctness," "lucidity," and "elegance." Changing conceptions of
taste and imagination, however, mark the beginning of the development of a distinctly new frame of reference. Although
these new conceptions were not to dominate the older criticism

[15] William K. Wimsatt, Jr., and Cleanth Brooks, *Literary Criticism: A Short
History,* p. 23.

until the nineteenth century (they never entirely replaced Aristotelian and Horatian criticism) , the origins of affective literary and aesthetic theory are to be found in the late seventeenth and early eighteenth centuries. Addison's importance to the history of English criticism lies in his simultaneous adherence to the principles of "mimetic-formal" criticism and his formulation of the first coherent statement of affective literary theory in English literary criticism.

III

Addison's education was classical, and his Latin oration on the new philosophy, *Nova Philosophia, veteri Praeferenda Est* (1693) , suggests that its young author would follow the French classical critics. Descartes, not Bacon or Newton, is hailed as the genius who stood against the Aristotelians and "broke the orbs of glass." Addison's early respect for Descartes and the largely neoclassical bent of his literary criticism remained throughout his life, but his active participation in the political and intellectual life of his time stimulated changes in his critical thinking which cannot be accounted for by reference to his critical forebears. The empirical tradition in English philosophy and political thought, together with his contact with Steele and the English theatre, are the most important elements of the milieu of his papers on *The Pleasures of the Imagination,* pastorals, and opera. These papers frequently present unresolved conflicts between his inherited critical principles and those which developed out of his contact with his broader cultural surroundings.

If the relationship between changes in the milieu and changes in the overall pattern of Addison's criticism is to be understood, we must differentiate between "extrinsic" and "intrinsic" relations of the milieu and the critical system.[16] When the rela-

[16] *System* has been used to denote two principal types of structure in literary criticism. As representative of the first type, Addison's critical system is that loosely thought-out and by no means philosophically consistent body of beliefs, explicit and implicit, which underlie his specific literary judgments. This "system," rather than individual judgments, is the principal subject of this work. "Aristotelian-Horatian" or "mimetic-formal" system refers to those critical pre-

tions of the milieu and the critical system are extrinsic, as they are in Addison's opera and pastoral criticism, the influence of the milieu produces no significant changes in Addison's criticism; the principles of neither Addison's criticism nor that of his successors were altered. The warfare of the critical camps subsided when the genres involved ceased to interest the critics of the period. The relationship of the milieu and Addison's papers on *The Pleasures of the Imagination,* taste, and wit was intrinsic insofar as the result was a change in the procedures of literary criticism. Evaluation of a literary work by examination of its effect upon the reader is a critical procedure which had been applied only to tragedy, in Aristotle's discussion of catharsis.[17]

It is hoped that this essay will demonstrate two principles concerning the relationship of Addison's criticism to its milieu. First, an absolute definition of milieu *a priori* for the age is impossible. The effect, for example, of the new science upon Steele's thought was negligible and in Swift it produced an impassioned antagonism. Second, the presence of certain elements in the milieu encourages changes in the significant patterns of a critical system and is a prerequisite for these changes. The Cartesian notion of *bon sens,* most clearly stated in the beginning of the *Discourse on Method,* lent support to the rationalistic phase of neoclassical criticism, but did not challenge or encourage the modification of its basic premises. The psychological emphases of the philosophies of Hobbes and Locke, on the other hand, encouraged the reader to examine the effects of a poem upon the mind of its reader from a psychological point of view, rather than from that of a Christian humanist or a didactic critic committed to the framework of a "mimetic-formal" criticism, as Samuel Johnson was. Although the latter group rather than the former continued to dominate literary

---

suppositions which are the bases of European criticism from the Renaissance through the seventeenth century. See below, Chapter 2.

[17] Aristotle, in his discussion of catharsis, is not concerned about the evocation of emotions, but with the therapeutic means of eliminating or suppressing them. See Paul Goodman, *The Structure of Literature,* p. 2.

criticism for decades after Locke's death, the psychological orientation of English criticism could not have arisen independently.

Operating on the premise that elements of the cultural surroundings do not become part of the milieu of a critical system until the author has made use of them, I shall attempt to show how Addison drew more extensively upon certain elements of his culture, especially English empirical philosophy, than his contemporaries did. Dennis and Pope, for example, who frequently reacted more sensitively to literary texts than Addison did, were much less aware of the potential relationship of Hobbes's and Locke's philosophies to literary criticism than Addison was. Consequently, the criticism of Dennis and Pope, influenced as it was by Longinus and his seventeenth-century commentators, looks backward toward the earlier neoclassical critics, rather than forward toward Edward Young and Edmund Burke.

IV

The three large sections of this essay—The Critical Milieu, Addison and Eighteenth-Century England, and The Empirical Tradition—correspond to the three major aspects of the milieu of Addison's criticism. The first section is centered about the changing conceptions of the role of the critic and Addison's debt to the classical critics and their followers of the sixteenth and seventeenth centuries, with special emphasis upon Addison's criticism of the epic and tragedy. The discussion of the ballad as a form of heroic poetry is a proposed explanation of a new sensibility which found its expression only through the inadequate critical vocabulary of Aristotelian criticism. Unable to devise a new critical framework to express his "unorthodox" taste, Addison failed to defend convincingly these native heroic poems by neoclassical standards.

The second section illustrates primarily what is meant by extrinsic relations of a critical system to its milieu. Addison's writings on the sublime are linked with Longinian criticism, on the one hand, and with a conception of the immensity of the universe as a reflection of divine glory, on the other. When Edmund Burke adapted Addison's theory of the sublime, however, he did so in psychological terms, largely eliminating Addison's theological arguments. The pastoral criticism, which is related to the conflict between "Whig" and "Tory" conceptions of nature, has its roots in cosmological and political, as well as aesthetic issues, with the "Whig" argument for constitutional government providing the pattern for the case against Virgilian pastorals in England. But, whereas Addison's discussion of the sublime was transformed, the "Whig" theory of pastoral lost its audience with the decline of the neoclassical pastoral form in the later eighteenth century.

The third section follows from the discussion of the Whig world-view, but is more centrally concerned with intrinsic relations of Addison's critical system to its milieu. Addison's early interest in Descartes's physiological explanation of mental processes is superseded by an interest in Hobbes's and Locke's psychologically oriented epistemologies. This shift in emphasis was accompanied by a shift from the egocentric predicament of Descartes's *Cogito, ergo sum* to Locke's rejection of faculty psychology, which led him to view the mind as the sum of its processes and ideas, pushing aside the Cartesian notion of *self* as a valid philosophical concept. This change is reflected in Addison's concentration upon the affective workings of literature and art in the papers on *The Pleasures of the Imagination*.[18]

The problems implicit in the preceding analysis of the relationship of Addison's literary criticism to its cultural milieu suggest the conclusion that the most fruitful approach to the history of criticism is through cultural history. There should be no argument with the observation that "Plato has a bearing on Croce and Freud, and vice versa," [19] unless the historian of criticism is publicly disappointed when Plato does not answer the questions asked by Freud and Croce. When Professors Wimsatt

[18] Ernest Tuveson, "Locke and the Dissociation of the Ego," *UTQ*, XXII (1954–1955), 157–174.
[19] Wimsatt and Brooks, *Literary Criticism: A Short History*, p. vii.

and Brooks propose that a history of criticism, insofar as it is a history of ideas, "can scarcely escape being written from a point of view" in defense of their own "argumentative" history of criticism,[20] they are imposing their critical relativism upon the history of criticism. If we cannot re-create all of the conditions under which a given work was written, we can discover what questions the critic was attempting to answer and what problems he was trying to solve. As historians of criticism, we must ask next how well he answered these questions in light of the information available to him. And we must ask, too, why he did not ask other questions. Why, for instance, did Johnson dismiss *Tristram Shandy* as something "odd" rather than explain the novel in terms of Lockean psychology? At the next step the historian of criticism begins to ask questions which are more directly relevant to the contemporary critical situation. Having examined the most important critical problems of a given period in their historical context, we may inquire whether these questions are still useful ones by contemporary standards, whether they must be rephrased in light of what we now know or believe, and whether we now have more adequate answers to these questions.

The last questions are certainly the most important ones the historian of criticism can ask if he sees himself not as one who merely brings light to the museum but as one who brings the museum's treasures to the marketplace. The history of criticism, however, must be kept distinct from the related discipline of literary history. Professor Wellek has made a good case for an aesthetic history of literature centered about a formalist conception of structure and linguistic analysis,[21] but the history of criticism, unlike the history of literature, is an intellectual, not an aesthetic, discipline. And the basic principles in the history of criticism have not always been literary. This is made clear

---

[20] *Ibid.*
[21] René Wellek, "Theory of Literary History," *Travaux du Cercle Linguistique de Prague,* VI (1936), 176–178; see also "Literary History," in *Literary Scholarship: Its Aims and Methods,* pp. 91–130; and Wellek and Warren, *Theory of Literature,* Chapter XIX and its bibliography.

by the following characterization of Samuel Johnson: "Dr. Johnson is, of course, no romanticist or even an unconscious forerunner of romanticism: he is rather one of the first great critics who has almost ceased to understand the nature of art, and who, in central passages, treats art as life. He has lost faith in art as the classicists understood it and has not found the romantic faith. He paves the way for a view which makes art really superfluous, a mere vehicle for the communication of moral or psychological truth." [22]

Unless we ignore the Platonic strain in neoclassical criticism, this statement is misleading. A major premise of Book X of Plato's *Republic* is that art is a mirror of life, and a bad one at that. Johnson, who does not share Plato's cosmology, admits the possibility of art mirroring life well, "ideally"; and his criticism, with its moral center, gives moral values priority over aesthetic ones. The critic who is content to leave the moral evaluation of literature to the pious reviewers for the tabloids and the terribly clever ones for *Time* is not so much at odds with Dr. Johnson's aesthetics, such as it is, as he is with Dr. Johnson's moral conception of life. The critic who dismisses Plato's theory of imitation could not consistently do so unless he rejected Plato's theory of ideas. If the contemporary critic is less candid about his presuppositions—whether they are derived from Husserl's phenomenology or from logical positivism —than Plato was, it is not because he is criticizing from an isolated point in space, but because the foundations of his criticism are less clearly formulated than Plato's or because he prefers to leave them unexpressed.

If the case for the history of criticism as a chapter of cultural history proves to be a sound one, it will present special problems of its own. Only tentative limits may be set here. That which is unique to the experience of the individual critic, such as his personal history and education (insofar as the latter is not relevant to the criticism and sensibility of his peers), may be excluded prior to historical investigation. If literary criti-

---

[22] Wellek, *History of Modern Criticism*, p. 79.

cism is in some sense an intellectual discipline, then speculation about the mental state of the critic is hardly relevant to the history of criticism. Plato's role in the declining aristocracy of Athens is the source of interesting psychological comments upon his cosmology and critique of art, but it is neither desirable nor possible to re-create his mental state at the time of the formulation of his ideas.[23] The same response may be made to the scholar who sees Addison's criticism as the product of a new middle-class mentality. Insofar as this premise is true there is no need to reproduce the conditions of this mentality, except to understand its standards and its relationship to Addison's criticism. To understand, Ludwig Wittgenstein reminds us, means to understand principles and their underlying assumptions and presuppositions, not the mental states which "caused" them.[24]

If the structure of critical thought is as closely related to other forms of thought and human activity as has been claimed here, how does one separate criticism from its milieu? The most direct, if not the most philosophically sophisticated, solution is to define a particular critical situation, a system and its cultural environment, not in absolute terms but in terms of the problems to be solved. The central problems of literary criticism are well defined by René Wellek: "The term 'criticism' I shall interpret broadly to mean not only judgments of individual books and authors, 'judicial' criticism, practical criticism, evidences of literary taste, but mainly what has been thought about the principles and theory of literature, its nature, its creation, its function, its effects, its kinds, its devices, and techniques, its origins and history." [25] If this is not the most exact formulation of the structure and scope of criticism, its heuristic promise is greater than that of any other definition of the problems of the history of criticism offered to date, especially as it

[23] Wellek, "Literary History," in *Literary Scholarship*, pp. 102 ff., on the relationship between biography and literary history.
[24] Ludwig Wittgenstein, *Philosophical Investigations*, with translation by G. E. M. Anscombe, 2nd ed., p. 61.
[25] *History of Modern Criticism*, p. v.

encourages us to clarify and define critical systems and their milieux by concentrating upon the principles and theories of literature, rather than upon personal taste and the judgment of specific works.

The total structure of the history of criticism as a chapter in cultural history is a universe of discourse composed of a number of critical systems, which are concerned with all or some of the questions mentioned by Professor Wellek, and their respective cultural milieux. The immediate concern of this discipline is the relationship of the critic's recorded literary principles and judgments to his cultural surroundings, which are judged to be part of his cultural milieu when there is evidence that he has reacted to them in the formulation of his literary principles. Consequently, the writer whose critical output is small or is composed largely of reviews and close analyses of particular texts, as brilliant as these may be, is less likely to assume an important place in such a history of criticism than a less perceptive critic who has speculated more widely upon literary issues and whose writings provide the historian of criticism with sufficient material to reconstruct a coherent picture of his critical thinking.[26]

Although we cannot reconstruct the precise mental conditions under which a given critical system was formulated, we can and must separate the purely idiosyncratic judgments from the central issues of criticism. Pope's opinion of Addison's writings, insofar as it was determined by his personal animosity toward Addison, is part of the social history of literature and not the history of criticism. More important is the responsibility of the historian of criticism for assuming the burden of proof for the case that a given element is part of the cultural milieu

[26] The major critics from Plato and Aristotle through Coleridge and Matthew Arnold have written in the speculative tradition, even when they were not important theoretical critics. An intriguing problem for the historian of criticism is presented in the remarks of Thomas Purney (see Note 10, above) about the relationship between literature and psychology. This one remark suggests that Purney was well ahead of the other critical theorists of his time, but sufficient evidence is lacking that this remark was more than accidental or that it has the significance which H. O. White assigns to it.

of the critical system, that it did produce the proposed effect upon the author's critical thought. Only now does Aristotle's injunction that we demand no more exactness from a science than its nature allows assume its full import; for, one must prove that the critic found the element of the cultural milieu both psychologically prior (in time) and, in some sense, logically prior to the critical concept which it inspired. To prove the latter without proving the former leaves the historian of criticism open to the argument that the two elements arose independently or that the line of influence has been reversed.

The critic, searching for what is relevant to the contemporary critical situation in the history of literary criticism, may accept the principles or a principle of a critical system without justifying its relevance in terms of its source in its propounder's cultural milieu. Burke and Kant, who modified Addison's concept of the sublime, defended the validity of the concept for aesthetics and criticism in their own terms; as indeed, critics, unaware of the origins of their critical principles in their cultural milieu, justify them in terms only peripherally related or completely unrelated to their origins. This essay, an historical exercise, is an attempt to reconstruct a critical system and its origins, and sets aside the value questions reluctantly, recognizing that understanding is the ancilla to evaluation in criticism.

THE
CRITICAL
MILIEU

2

The Critic as Anti-Pedant

> A true Critick ought to dwell rather upon Excel-
> lencies than Imperfections, to discover concealed
> Beauties of a Writer, and communicate to the World
> such Things as are worth their Observation. The
> most exquisite Words and finest Strokes of an Au-
> thor are those which very often appear the most
> doubtful and exceptionable, to a Man who wants a
> Relish for polite Learning ; and they are these, which
> a soure undistinguishing Critick generally attacks
> with the greatest Violence.
>
> Addison, *Spectator* 291

THE PROFESSED CRITIC was a new figure on the English literary scene in the early eighteenth century. He reached his public
by writing prefaces to plays and poems, by contributing to the
growing numbers of newspapers and periodicals, or, less frequently, by publishing treatises upon criticism and the art of
poetry. He was influenced in his writings by ideals not of his
own making, and he was censured, sometimes quite severely,
if he did not live up to them. No English writer with any pre-
tensions to the title of gentleman would have written either
Wilson's *Art of Rhetorique* or Puttenham's *Arte of English
Poesie*. Both works have the mark of the classroom upon them.
The English gentleman, as satisfied as he was with his Oxford
education, preferred to keep the harsher evidences of learning
and scholarship carefully concealed from public view.

Thus, when Addison writes that a true critic has a relish for
polite learning, he is emphasizing his own role as a gentleman
of learning and polite taste, and setting aside the carping and

sour critic as unworthy of the most important title that he could own, that of gentleman.

By the close of the [seventeenth] century the controversy about style was settled in favour neither of the scholar nor the artisan, but of the gentleman. While both Dryden and Glanvill believed that learning is necessary to the writer, John Hughes in 1698 is more concerned that his learning be polite. The philosopher is now to be saved from the "Rust of the Academy" by "Polite learning." "In a Word," says Hughes, "it adds the Gentleman to the Scholar"; and this was the addition that in contemporary eyes gave Boyle the advantage over Bentley.[1]

Fifty years earlier few men would have bothered to make the distinction between the polite and the pedantic critic. There were not enough of either of them in print to cause a controversy. The rise of science and pedantic scholarship prompted the lovers of humane learning to defend themselves against their worst enemies, not the ignorant, but the possessors of useless and unassimilated knowledge.

If Addison agreed wholeheartedly with Temple and Swift in their attacks upon the pedants in letters and science, there would be little reason for this discussion, but he does not. Although Addison sees himself as a gentleman in terms which have their origin in the courtesy books of the Renaissance, he disagrees with the majority of the men of his time about the extent to which a gentleman should be learned. Neither Temple nor Swift agreed that a gentleman should be learned in all of the arts and sciences. Daniello could argue, in 1536, that "the Poet must practically know all of the arts and sciences, in order that he may properly deal with his universal subject." [2] Only fifty years later, Thomas Wilson wrote that the orator does not

[1] George Williamson, *The Senecan Amble: A Study in Prose Form from Bacon to Collier*, p. 336. The quote from John Hughes is from "Of Style," *Critical Essays of the Eighteenth Century: 1700–1725*, ed. W. H. Durham, p. 79. See Leonard Welsted, ed. *The Works of Dionysius Longinus . . .* , Preface [sig. B 3ᵛ]: *"For my own part, I have endeavour'd to make* Longinus *speak in the free familiar Style of a Gentleman, and to take from him, as far as I was able, the Stiffness of a Critick."*

[2] George Saintsbury, *History of Criticism and Literary Taste in Europe*, II, 44.

need to know astronomy, arithmetic, and geometry in order to be eloquent.[3] Both Daniello and Wilson thought in terms of the Trivium and Quadrivium. Neither would have anticipated the advances in natural philosophy which took place during the seventeenth century. Certainly, it is not likely that either one of them would have sided with Addison, when he wrote in 1712 that the critic should be learned in all of the arts and sciences (S. 291).

Although Addison disagrees with many of his contemporaries about the scope of polite learning, he does not quarrel with the ideal. This ideal is not a new one during the late seventeenth century, but has its roots in the Renaissance concept of the ideal courtier; its modifications may be traced through the character-books, and it emerges, after the Restoration, further influenced by the notions of *bon sens* and taste. The evolution of the ideal is a slow one; the classical authorities in criticism yielded only gradually to contemporary thought.

I

The Renaissance conceptions of the prince and gentleman have histories which extend back through the Middle Ages to the ideal of the Roman orator as citizen and to the Ciceronian view of the relationship between learning and civic virtue. Castiglione, when he looked for models for his "Courtier," held up the learning of Socrates, Scipio Africanus, and Caesar for emulation. For Castiglione, to be learned meant to be familiar with "letters," primarily Greek and Latin orators and historians, and verse and prose, especially in the vulgar tongue. These works are not only the sources of valuable knowledge; they teach the courtier to be graceful, to conceal the diligence upon which both his learning and his art are founded, with the appearance of ease.[4] The courtier must be learned if he is to per-

---

[3] Thomas Wilson, *The Arte of Rhetorique*, ed. G. H. Mair, p. 1.

[4] Baldessare Castiglione, *The Covrtyer of Covnt Baldessar Castilio* . . . , trans. Thomas Hoby, Sigs. Hiii–Hv. See Walter Göricke, *Das Bildungsideal bei Addison und Steele*, Bonner Studien zur englischen Philologie, XIV (1921), 10–29.

The ideal of the gentleman of learning has its origins in classical rhetoric. See

form his public duties, but he must be a gentleman, a man without pride in the pains which he has taken to master difficult subjects.

The influence of these two aspects of the courtier upon the conception of the gentleman is evident in the popularity of Hoby's translation of *The Book of the Courtier* in sixteenth-century England and in the repetition of the same ideas in the works of other men of such diverse interests as Sir Thomas Elyot, Roger Ascham, and Sir Philip Sidney. Elyot, stressing the values of learning to those who will govern, advises that the young gentleman be taught logic, rhetoric, cosmography, history, and moral philosophy. Not so much interested in the social graces of the ruling class as Castiglione was, Elyot emphasized the importance of learning, as well as common experience, for the maintenance of an honorable and wealthy "publike weale." [5]

In Ascham, however, we have one of the first expressions of English concern about the dangers of too much study, especially study of those sciences which are not directly related to man's life in society:

Some wits, moderate enough by nature, be many times marred by over-much study and use of some sciences, namely, music, arithmetic, and geometry. These sciences, as they sharpen men's wits over-much, so they change men's manners over-sore, if they be not moderately mingled, and wisely applied to some good use of life. Mark mathematical heads, which be only and wholly bent to those sciences, how solitary they be themselves, how unfit to live with others, and how unapt to serve in the world. [6]

The insistence upon the relation between learning and civil life may be traced back to the Greeks, but the widespread distrust of the pedant is a growing phenomenon only in sixteenth-century Europe.

Cicero, *De Officiis* I, i–ii; *Brutus* lix, 213–214; *De Oratore* I, iv, 16, and I, vi, 20; and Quintilian, *Institutio Oratoria* IV, ii, 42–43.

[5] Sir Thomas Elyot, *The boke named the Gouernour*, Book I, Chapters iv, xi.

[6] *The Scholemaster*, in *The Whole Works of Roger Ascham*, ed. J. A. Giles, III, 100.

One manifestation of this distrust is to be found in Sidney's preference for poetry rather than philosophy. Sidney amplifies greatly upon Aristotle's argument when he writes that the philosopher "setting downe with thorny argument the bare rule, is so hard of vtterance, and so mistie to be conceiued, that one that hath no other guide but him shall wade in him till hee be olde before he shall finde sufficient cause to be honest . . ." [7] Surely, there is something of this suspicion of abstract philosophy in Isocrates' "common sense" critique of Plato. The preference of the Roman philosophers and orators for concrete analyses of specific vices and virtues is part of the Isocratic tradition which carries through the Middle Ages, and is seen in Chaucer's ballade on "Gentilesse." The older ideal is a social one insofar as it is concerned with man's morals in the Roman and Christian state. The Renaissance and neoclassical ideal centers about manners as well as morals. The philosopher-pedant is condemned not only because he is a poor guide for a man trying to lead a virtuous life, but also because his way of life, his modes of thought, prevent him from communicating with his fellow men.

The categories of pedantry were broadened during the seventeenth century, and the pedant was chiefly represented by the antiquary, the scholar, and the critic in the character-books. For John Earle and his contemporaries the three prototypes had one characteristic in common: all were completely detached from life as it was being lived about them. The antiquary is lost in his old and rotten trinkets, the scholar in his college, and the critic in his syntax. Earle, however, is not completely out of sympathy with his "Downright Scholar":

He has not humbled his meditations to the industry of compliment, not afflicted his brain in an elaborate leg. His body is not set upon

---

[7] Sir Philip Sidney, "An Apology for Poetry," in *Elizabethan Critical Essays,* ed. G. Gregory Smith, I, 164. The English critics of the sixteenth century were generally less concerned with abstract critical questions than their contemporaries on the continent. See Thomas Wilson, *The Arte of Rhetorique,* p. 5; George Puttenham, *The Arte of English Poesie,* ed. Gladys Doidge Willcock and Alice Walker, pp. 8, 24. The classical origin of this rejection of abstract debate is

nice pins, to be turning and flexible for every notion, but his scrape
is homely, and his nod worse. He cannot kiss his hand and cry
"Madame," nor talk idly enough to bear her company. His smack-
ing of a gentleman is somewhat too savoury, and mistakes her nose
for her lips. A very woodcock would puzzle him in carving, and
he wants the logic of a capon. He has not the glib faculty of sliding
over a tale, but his words come squeamishly out of his mouth, and
the laughter commonly before the jest. He names this word "College" too often, and his discourse beats too much on the University.[8]

The virtues which the scholar lacks are not cardinal ones, and
his life is less empty than that of "A Mere Young Gentleman of
the University," who was sent to Oxford to study fencing and
dancing. This virtuoso of tennis and pedigrees is no closer to
the ideal of the gentleman of learning than the cloistered scholar is. The one is all manner without matter; the other has substance without a social function.

Earle's critic presents only one aspect of Addison's "soure and
undistinguishing" practitioner, and that is the core of him: "A
Critick is one that has spelled over a great many of books, and
his observation is the orthography. He is the surgeon of old
authors, and heals the wounds of dust and ignorance. He con-
verses much in fragments and *Desunt multa's* and if he piece it
up with two lines he is more proud of that book than the author.
He runs over all sciences to peruse their syntaxis, and thinks
all learning comprised in writing Latin." All critics are
grammarians and fault-finders. They comprise one group of
stereotypes from which the character writers drew throughout
the seventeenth century and into the eighteenth. For La
Bruyère criticism is a trade, not a science: ". . . it requires
more Health than Understanding, more Labour than Capacity,
and Habit than Genius." [9]

Subtle distinctions between the pedant and the gentleman of

---

probably Isocrates' criticism of Plato; see, especially, Isocrates' *Panegyricus* 47–48,
in *Isocrates,* with English trans. by George Norlin and Larue Van Hook, I, 147.

[8] John Earle, *Microcosmography,* ed. Harold Osborne, pp. 49–50.

[9] Jean de La Bruyère, *Works,* 6th ed., II, 28.

learning are outside the province of the makers of characters. The tradesman-critic, who reads everything and understands nothing, and the fanciful philosopher, who pretends to know everything and discovers nothing but his own mistakes,[10] are better subjects for charcoal sketches than Dryden's and Addison's true critics are. "In the first, I must take leave to tell them, that they wholly mistake the nature of criticism, who think its business is wholly to find fault. Criticism, as it was first instituted by Aristotle, was meant a standard of judging well; the chiefest part of which is, to observe those excellencies which delight a reasonable reader." [11] The ideal critic, who conceals his own art so that he may reveal that of his subject, lacks the sharp outlines of character of men who "with *Scaliger* would sell the Empire of *Germany* (if it were in his Power) for an old Song." [12]

But even the character writers begin to recognize the difference between the true and the false critics as defined by men whose interest in literature extended beyond satire and social reform. The author of *The English Theophrastus* could write that "Criticks are useful, that's most certain, so are Executioners and Informers . . . How can we love the Man, whose Office is to torture and execute other Men's Reputation." [13] He does not do so, however, without acknowledging that this practice is characteristic of modern critics only, men who have departed from the virtue of their classical predecessors. He provides, too, the basis for distinguishing the true from the false critic in his discussion of the reasons for seeking knowledge: "There are two sorts of *Curiosity*, the first proceeds from *Interest*, and is the desire to learn things that can be useful and beneficial to us, the other springs from *Pride*, and is a desire to be wiser than our Neighbours." [14] This is the pride which Pope blames for

[10] Samuel Butler, *Characters and Passages from Notebooks*, ed. A. R. Waller, p. 57.
[11] John Dryden, *Essays*, ed. W. P. Ker, I, 79. See, too, II, 3.
[12] Butler, p. 42.
[13] *The English Theophrastus: or the Manners of the Age*, 3rd ed., p. 6.
[14] *Ibid.*, p. 212.

leading true judgment astray to look for petty faults without
concern for the spirit in which the poet wrote.[15] The last of the
character portraits of the critic marks the culmination of the
feeling that the critic could not fully explain the spirit of a
work of art by reference to grammar, condemned by John
Earle, or to a set of critical rules, accepted either on authority
or from reason. There was something in art, *"le je ne sais quoi,"*
which surpassed the understanding. Only the man of taste, one
born with the ability to distinguish between good and bad art,
could perceive the qualities of true art. Learning could improve his understanding, but it could not give him the faculty
which he did not already possess. European criticism was pass-
ing from an authoritarian criticism through its rationalistic
phase to one dominated by the concept of taste. Each stage
left its mark upon its successor. In Addison's conception of the
critic, we see primarily the tension between the rationalist and
the man of taste.

II

Respect for the authority of the classical critics and poets,
which characterized the first of the three phases of neoclassical
criticism, was by no means servile in the sense of being an un-
questioned acceptance of ancient rules and models. The critic
acknowledged that poetry is a divine gift, but inspiration, he
insisted, is not enough to produce good poetry. For Dubellay,
as for the later neoclassical critics, imitation meant chiefly imitation of the ancients, because they knew nature best. Other
French critics, like Peletier du Mans, warned the writer to
watch nature with greater care than he expends upon the observation of his poetic models. "For Ronsard the key word is
invention, the work of 'an imagination which conceives ideas
and forms of all imaginable things'." [16] The difference in emphasis, however, tends to obscure a basic similarity in their attitudes toward their classical forebears. Vida and Cintio fre-

[15] *Ibid.,* pp. 214, 215. Pope, *Essay on Criticism,* II, 1 ff.
[16] Margaret Gilman, *The Idea of Poetry in France,* p. 3. The Ronsard quotation
is from "L'Art poétique," *Oeuvres complètes,* Bibliotheque de la Pléiade, II, 1001.

quently accepted the authority of Aristotle and Horace, as they interpreted them, on the most minute questions of precept, on the assumption that the ancients were the most astute observers of nature. Dubellay and Ronsard, more concerned with the Pléiade's attempts to enrich the poetic language of France, interpreted this authority in a much less literal way. What is significant here is not the literalness or liberality with which the Renaissance critics read the classics, but their common acceptance of classical principles and practices without trying to rationalize them in any systematic manner.

In fact, the rationalistic critics did more to codify and reduce to precept the principles of classical criticism than did their predecessors, who were much less systematic and less self-conscious in their borrowings. "In the theories of poetry, we find lofty early conceptions of the poet swept away by Malherbe's pronouncement that a good poet is of no more use to the state than a good skittles player. In Malherbe's hands poetic doctrine becomes the rigid regimentation of syntax, vocabulary, and versification. For him poetry is essentially the same as prose, the only difference being that poetry is subject to a few more rules." [17] The dual standards of classical authority and rational deduction which we find in Scaliger's criticism are gradually resolved in favor of the latter when the conception of individual reason is replaced by the idea of *bon sens,* a universal standard which all men of right reason can use to confirm their judgments.[18]

This concept of *bon sens* is Descartes's most specific and important contribution to neoclassical criticism.

Good sense is of all things in the world the most equally distributed, for everybody thinks himself so abundantly provided with it, that even those who are most difficult to please in all other matters do not commonly desire more of it than they already possess. It is unlikely that this is an error on their part; it seems rather to be evidence in support of the view that the power of forming a judgment

[17] Gilman, p. 4.
[18] Spingarn, *History of Literary Criticism in the Renaissance,* p. 149. Aisso Bosker, *Literary Criticism in the Age of Johnson,* 2nd ed., pp. 8, 9.

and of distinguishing the true from the false, which is properly speaking what is called Good Sense or Reason, is by nature equal in all men. Hence too it will show that the diversity of our opinions do not proceed from some men being more rational than others, but solely from the fact that our thoughts pass through diverse channels and the same objects are not considered at all. For to be possessed of good mental powers is not sufficient; the principal matter is to apply them well. The greatest minds are capable of the greatest vices as well as the greatest virtues, and those who proceed very slowly, provided they follow the straight road, really advance much faster than those who, though they run, forsake it.[19]

The conception of good sense could not but lend support to Malherbe's preference for linguistic purity, as opposed to Ronsard's desire to expand the language and its resources.[20] All men have good sense, but only those who use it are likely to discover the truth. Only the poets who use their *bon sens* are likely to write correctly. Therefore, what distinguishes the good poet (or critic) from the bad one is not the state of his natural faculties or the influence of divine inspiration, but his ability to use reason in the production (or judgment) of poetry.

When R. F. Jones writes that seventeenth-century criticism is authoritarian and antiscientific, he sees the scientific revolution as an exclusively empirical and antirationalistic movement. "Here, then, was a critical philosophy which upheld the principle of authority (though many critics tried to equate it with reason or common sense) . . . It would be difficult to find a more exact antithesis to the views characteristic of the scientific movement than is found in this criticism." [21] The authorities were being upheld not on the principle of the sacredness of authority, but on the principle of reason. The principles of the classical critics were explicated, systematized, and expanded deductively according to what the French critics took to be rea-

---

[19] René Descartes, *Discourse on Method,* in *The Philosophical Works of Descartes,* trans. Elizabeth S. Haldane and G. R. T. Ross, I, 81–82.

[20] Spingarn, *History of Literary Criticism in the Renaissance,* pp. 237–238.

[21] R. F. Jones, "Science and Criticism in the Neo-Classical Age of English Literature," *JHI,* I (1940), 383; cited by Emerson Marks, *Relativist and Absolutist: The Early Neo-Classical Debate in England,* p. 134.

sonable in the classical authors. Boileau and Le Bossu, and, in England, Dryden and Addison, rarely accepted the authority of the classical critics as the medieval clerk accepted the authority of the Bible and the Church Fathers. The principles and the practices of the classical authors were often condemned for being contrary to reason. This irrationality was occasionally explained, but this lack of rational order was never excused. To the degree that the seventeenth-century critics attempted to reduce their principles to a rational scheme, they were not being antiscientific, but were following, sometimes quite consciously, the examples of Galileo and Descartes.

Descartes's notion of *bon sens,* and the rationalization process in general, was extrinsic to the entire critical process insofar as the premises of neoclassical criticism were already set and the rationalization was merely a justification for existing procedures. Here Professor Jones is correct in seeing an antithesis between science and criticism. There was no radical revision of literary values in the application of the standard of *bon sens* to literary criticism. On the other hand, the concept of *bon sens* did produce an intrinsic change in literary criticism by giving it a new method for determining literary excellence. The standard for judging a work of art became correctness, and correctness was described in terms of reasonableness and clarity.

Le culte de l'idée claire est incompatible avec le souci de la beauté, étendant sans cesse sa domination, il tarit l'imagination, la fantasie, qui est avec la sensibilité la source la plus abondante de poésie. Saint-Évremond le dit ailleurs, dans son traité *Sur les poèmes des anciens,* où il critique Homère et Sophocle: "La génie de notre siècle est tout opposé à cet esprit des fables et de faux mystères. Nous aimons les vérités déclarées, le sens prévaut aux illusions de la fantaisie; rien ne nous contente aujourd'hui que la solidité et raison." [22]

The fables and mysteries of Homer are those of good sense led astray. The business of good sense in the poet, like that of "judgment" to Hobbes, is to check the inspiration and imagina-

[22] René Bray, *La Formation de la doctrine classique en France,* p. 121.

tion of the poet and to lead him once again in the path of right
reason. The function of good sense in the critic is to help him
show every reader what he would see for himself if he followed
the right path.

Good sense makes men aware of the reasonable by showing
them the way through the peculiarities of national custom and
individual taste. Surely the Greeks and Romans had their own
notion of what is true. "Chaque nation repliqua Philante, a
son goût en esprit de même qu'un beauté, en habits et en toute
le reste. —Comme si la justesse du sens, repartit Eudoxe, n'était
pas de toutes les langues, et que ce qui est mauvais de soi-même
dût passer pour bon en aucun pays parmi les personnes raison-
ables." [23] Each nation has its own beliefs in poetry as in religion, but given the truth all reasonable men will agree immediately. This confidence in the power of good sense led
Bouhours and Boileau (and later Dryden, Rymer, and Addison) to assume that had the Greeks and Romans been aware
of the truth of Christian revelation they, too, would have been
immediately persuaded by the force of these clear and distinct
ideas.

Cartesian rationalism, emphasizing the propositional, structure of truth, tended to impose a literal interpretation upon the
understanding of the truth of poetry. The French critics, especially, accepted the concept of *bon sens* as the guiding principle for the creation and criticism of poetry. Boileau, perhaps
recalling Descartes's warning that great minds often deviate
furthest from the truth, writes of the difficulties which confront
the reason when it attempts to take the path of *bon sens*.[24] Bouhours defines the other key term of rationalistic neoclassicism,
bel esprit, in terms of *bon sens:* "Le vrai bel esprit, repartit
Ariste, est inséparable du bon sens, et c'est se méprendre que
de la le confondre avec je ne sais quelle vivacité qui n'a rien de
solide. Le jugement est comme le fond de la beauté de l'esprit,
ou plutôt le bel esprit est de la nature de ces pierres precieuses

[23] Dominique Bouhours, *La manière de bien penser dans les ouvrages d'esprit,*
p. 54; cited by Bray, p. 128.
[24] Boileau, *Art poétique,* I, 45–48.

qui n'ont pas moins de solidité que d'éclat. Il n'y a rien de plus beau qu'un diamant bien poli et bien net; il éclate de tous côtés et dans tous ses parties." [25] *Bel esprit* is a "happy fertility of spirit" grounded in *bon sens* and *bonnes choses*.[26] The aspect of this quality of the noble soul which is indebted to *bon sens* gives rise to the strength and stability, propriety, and universality of the works of the spirit. The last two qualities are the ones which relate the work to the experience of other rational men. This emphasis upon the common experience of rational men is re-enforced by Bouhours' partial explanation of *bel esprit* in terms of the operation of the animal spirits, which is largely taken from the fifth part of Descartes's *Discourse on Method*.[27] God has created the same spirits and channels for their operation in all men. Good sense is led astray only through abuse of these natural faculties.

Bel esprit has another aspect, however, that of *"bonnes choses,"* the things that the spirit selects for its subject matter, which provide evidence of the fertility, delicacy, and emotive power of the "genius" of *le bel esprit*.[28] Here, Bouhours frankly admits that this "genius" is largely inexplicable. Earlier in the century Jean Balzac had emphasized the importance of natural vigor, delicacy, and greatness of spirit to poetry,[29] but he had not come to this conclusion by Bouhours' path. Balzac's distaste for rationalistic explanation and organization is the distaste of the followers of the Pléiade, which had conceived a higher role for the poet than Malherbe had. Chapelain complained to Balzac in 1640 about the restrictions of authority upon French poetry. Twenty-two years later he wrote to Grentemesnil to the same effect. "But he judged that it was not for him to deliver French poets from their chains 'et ce serait s'opposer en vain au torrent'." [30] Bouhours' recognition

---

[25] Dominique Bouhours, *Entretiens d'Ariste et d'Eugène,* ed. René Radouant, p. 151.

[26] *Ibid.,* pp. 155–156.   [27] *Ibid.,* pp. 165–166.

[28] *Ibid.,* p. 160.

[29] Jean Balzac, *Oeuvres,* ed. L. Moreau, I, 277–280, 283; cited by E. B. O. Borgerhoff, *The Freedom of French Classicism,* pp. 12–13.

[30] Borgerhoff, p. 39. Chapelain, *Lettres,* ed. Tamizey de Larroque, II, 210 n.

of *"le je ne sais quoi"* [31] in art is the result of the rationalist's discovery that the rules do not completely explain the nature of the artist's creation. Chapelain was right in his observation that he could not oppose the flood of rationalism. But it was the virtue of the rationalist's position which enabled it to eventually discover the weaknesses and limitations of his own method.

The discovery of the limitation of rationalistic criticism by no means shattered the critic's faith in the efficacy of reason in criticism, but prompted many critics during the latter part of the seventeenth century to supplement reason with the concept of taste and the "Grace beyond the Reach of Art." Professor Monk traces this notion of artistic grace to its classical sources, noting that the Renaissance critics had little to say about this quality.[32] Indeed, Castiglione wrote more about the importance of grace to the courtier than the critics did about the importance of this quality to the poet. But grace for Castiglione implied an artful means of concealing artifice; for Bouhours it was "a mysterious quality," as Roger de Piles wrote, "that the painter derives from nature alone and that he possesses without understanding." [33]

Conscious of the advances made in the physical sciences, Bouhours recognized that the tools of natural philosophy, especially the telescope and microscope, help to explain the delicacy of nature and that the critic has no such tools for examining the delicacy of the soul and its chief product, thought. Delicacy of thought, therefore, remains something of a mystery, too elusive to be defined.[34] English critics, sometimes more rationalistic than their continental sources, occasionally wrote as if the criticism of literature were a completely rational process. "The truth is, what *Aristotle* writes on this Subject, are not the dictates of his own magisterial will, or dry deductions of

---

[31] Bouhours, *Entretiens d'Ariste* . . . , p. 197.

[32] Samuel H. Monk, " 'Grace beyond the Reach of Art,' " *JHI*, V (1944), 131–150. See Pope, *Essay on Criticism*, I, 155.

[33] Monk, pp. 131–132; Roger de Piles, *L'Idée de Peinture Parfait.*

[34] Bouhours, *The Art of Criticism: or, the Method of making a Right Judgment upon Subjects of Wit and Learning*, pp. 110–111.

his Metaphysicks: But the Poets were his Masters, and what was their practice, he reduced to principles. Nor would the *modern Poets* resign to this practice of the *Ancients,* were not the Reasons convincing and clear as any demonstration in *Mathematicks.* 'Tis only needful that we understand them, for our consent to the truth of them." [35] Even in the eighteenth century Samuel Cobb could write that Roscommon's rules are immutable and will last as long as poetry is written.[36]

The reduction of criticism to rules, even rationally deduced ones, neglects Boileau's condemnation of those *"petits Esprits,"* the modern critics, who in criticizing Homer, *"ce grand Pöete,"* are reproaching one who is greater than they are.[37] These men are scholars whose limited imaginations keep them from the ranks of the *bel esprit.*[38] Boileau's remarks about the pedant *("scavant")* read like lines from a character-book. Nourished in a college, the pedant is full of Latin and Greek and blindly admires and praises all of the ancients. He believes that, after Aristotle and Hippocrates, no new discoveries in nature can be made.[39]

John Dryden and Sir Richard Blackmore assume critical positions which are more consistent with the twin values of *bon sens* and *bel esprit* than Rymer does in his belief that Aristotle is the epitome of right reason in criticism. "Good sense and good nature are never separated, though the ignorant world thought otherwise. Good nature, by which I mean beneficence and candour, is the product of right reason; which will of necessity give allowance to the failings of others, by considering that there is nothing perfect in mankind; and by distinguishing that which comes nearest to excellency, though not absolutely free from faults, will certainly produce a candour in

[35] "Preface to Rapin," *The Critical Works of Thomas Rymer,* ed. Curt Zimansky, pp. 2–3.
[36] Samuel Cobb, *Discourse on Criticism and of Poetry from Poems on Several Occasions,* p. 204.
[37] Boileau, "Réflexion V," *Réflexions Critiques. Sur quelques passages du Rheteur Longin* (1694), p. 77.
[38] C. H. C. Wright, *French Classicism,* p. 105.
[39] Boileau, "Réflexion V," *Réflexions Critiques,* p. 83.

the judge." [40] Good sense preserves the critic from becoming minute and carping. Faults may be found in Homer, but they are insignificant when set beside Homer's greatness. "Good nature," derived from *bel esprit,* sets the limits of criticism by insisting upon the value of providing the reader and poet with objects of imitation, not examples of what is to be avoided. Within these limits good sense, rather than particular rules, explains the virtues of particular poems.

The key position of good sense in English criticism at the end of the seventeenth century and the beginning of the eighteenth is demonstrated in the attitude of a great number of critics toward the authority of Aristotle. Blackmore, admitting Aristotle's greatness, will no more submit to his authority in poetry than in philosophy, but will accept his rules only after giving them a "fair Hearing; and if upon an impartial Tryal they appear to build upon good foundations, to confirm the Authority of the *Greek* Critick by the Force of Reason." [41] Thomas Pope Blount thinks that the ancients are worthy of reverence, but we do them no justice by following them *"Supinely* and *Superstitiously."* The critic reads them "to Examine their Writings, to avoid their mistakes, and to use their Discoveries, in order to the further Improvement of knowledge." [42] Release from Aristotle's philosophical authority led to release from his poetic authority, but the latter was still great enough

---

[40] Dryden, "A Discourse concerning the Original and Progress of Satire" (1693), *Essays,* II, 17. See "The Author's Apology for Heroic Poetry, &c." (1677), *Essays,* I, 179: "In the first place, I must take leave to tell them, that they wholly mistake the nature of criticism, who thinks its business is principally to find fault. Criticism, as it was first instituted by Aristotle, was meant a standard of judging well; the chiefest part of which is, to observe those excellencies which should delight a reasonable reader." This remark prefaces his support of Longinus's preference for a sublime genius who sometimes errs rather than a lesser genius who has no faults.

Addison (G. 110) also recognizes the relevance of man's natural imperfections to critical activity when he writes that "there can be no more perfect Work in the World than a perfect Man. To say of a celebrated Piece that there are Faults in it, is in effect to say no more, than that the Author of it was a Man. For this Reason, I consider every Critick that attacks an Author in high Reputation, as a Slave in the *Roman* Triumph, who was to call out to the Conqueror, *Remember, Sir that you are a Man."*

[41] Sir Richard Blackmore, *Essays upon Several Subjects,* pp. 12, 14.
[42] Sir Thomas Pope Blount, *Essays on Several Subjects,* pp. 78, 79.

for Blount to note that Aristotle was a great censurer of error
and that by censuring error the English critic maintained his
own philosophical liberty.[43]

English critics, as their preference for great rather than correct poetry increased, came to realize that Dryden was correct
in his suggestion that the role of the critic is to show the beauties of a poem rather than to give rules. Bysshe opened his *Art
of English Poetry* with the observation that the poet needs too
many natural and acquired abilities to be able to make his poetical reputation by following rules.[44] George Farquhar was
even more suspicious of theoretical criticism and the learning
of pedantic critics. He had "no *Speculative Curiosities* . . . only
some present Sentiments which Hazard, not Study, brings into
[his] Head, without any preliminary *Method* or *Cogitation.*" [45]
The poet cannot fall back on any divine mysteries, as in the
days of Plato, and he lacks the confounding terminology of
logicians and physicians, leaving him prey to the "Insults of all
Pretenders." Farquhar agrees with Rymer that Aristotle derived his rules from particular poets, but he sees this as Aristotle's weakness rather than his strength. Since Aristotle was
not a poet, he was not familiar with the problems confronting
poets, and, therefore, was "not capable of giving Instructions
in the Art of Poetry." [46]

Farquhar's anti-Aristotelianism is extreme, but its foundation
is, apart from his own practical interests, representative of the
growing antispeculative strain which is characteristic of many
of the rationalistic critics. It grew from the belief that the critic
should serve some social and artistic purpose, and, among more
speculative critics, from the critic's awareness of the limits of reason in criticism. Abbé d'Aubignac refuses to give general max-
ims, because he is more interested in stage practices than in dramatic theory. He will not be troubled by the objections of

[43] *Ibid.*, pp. 79, 84.
[44] Edward Bysshe, *The Art of English Poetry*, "Preface."
[45] George Farquhar, "A Discourse upon Comedy," *Critical Essays of the
Eighteenth Century*, p. 257.
[46] *Ibid.*, p. 271.

grammarians and logicians, because he is certain that "all rational and polite learning will not oppose me." [47] The true critic is not a philosopher, but a guide for the poet.[48] Dennis and Pope, following Rapin, set the tone for one aspect of English criticism of the early eighteenth century when they wrote that "The Rules of *Aristotle* are nothing but Nature and Good Sence reduc'd to a Method," "Nature to advantage dress'd." [49] This, however, is not to be taken as an argument for pedantic rules, or an argument against Sir William Temple's "There is something in the *Genius* of Poetry too libertine to be confined to so many Rules." [50]

Arising from the awareness of the limits of the rule of reason in criticism is the critic's growing concern with the concept of *taste* and his own status as a man of taste.

> In Poets as true Genius is but rare,
> True Taste as seldom is the Critic's share;
> Both must alike from Heav'n derive their light,
> These born to judge, as well as those to write.[51]

Although *taste* appears in continental criticism during the early seventeenth century, it is not an important critical term until the early eighteenth century.[52] Like the concept of the gentleman, taste arose first in the courtesy books, and the French deserve credit for its "aesthetic acclimatization." [53] The *"je ne sais*

---

[47] François Hédelin d'Aubignac, *The Whole Art of the Stage. Containing not only the Rules of the Dramatick Art, but many curious Observations upon it* (1657), Book I, Chapter iii, pp. 17–18. The books and chapters are the same in the French and English editions unless a disparity is noted.

[48] Pope, *Essay on Criticism*, I, 99 ff.

[49] Dennis, *The Impartial Critick* (1693), in *Critical Works* . . . , ed. Edward Niles Hooker, I, 39. Pope, *Essay on Criticism*, II, 97.

[50] Sir William Temple, "Of Poetry," *CESC*, III, 83–84.

[51] Pope, *Essay on Criticism*, I, 11–14.

[52] Wellek, *History of Modern Criticism*, p. 24. For the history of the term "taste" see Andrew C. Smith, "Theories of Nature and Standard of Taste in England, 1700–1790," unpublished dissertation. Addison acknowledges his debt to Balthasar Gracian's *El Hero* (1637) for *gusto* (S. 409). Dr. Smith notes that Balzac's and Chapelain's *goût* probably arose independent of Gracian's work. See Robert Lee Morris, "Joseph Addison's Literary Criticism," unpublished dissertation, pp. 5–8, on Addison's concept of taste.

[53] Andrew C. Smith, p. 24.

quoi" aspect of this aesthetic sense, emphasized by Bouhours, is apparent in Pope's characterization of taste as a divinely given sense found only in the best judges of poetry.

In Hobbes and Sir Robert Howard taste was an individual concern determined by what Aubignac had referred to as "the Customs and Manners, as well as Opinions of the Spectators." [54] The rationalization of criticism elevated taste to the position in which we find it in Pope and Addison, a faculty of the mind which, insofar as it is good taste, is an absolute standard for the judgment of poetry.[55] Taste, innate to the mind of the poet or critic, is characterized by its affinity for grace and beauty. "Even in the Arts, which are merely Imitations of that outward Grace and Beauty, we not only confess a *Taste;* but make it a part of refin'd Breeding, to discover, amidst the many false manners and ill Stiles, the true and natural one, which represents the real *Beauty* and Venus of the kind." [56] Taste becomes rationalized into a distinct faculty which replaces *bon sens* as the most important faculty which the critic possesses, corresponding, as Pope writes, to the genius of the poet. In this Leonard Welsted speaks for his age when he writes that the rules are not enough for making a good poet, as they are for making a good geometrician. "As the common Rules of Logic serve only for disputing, so the common Rules of Poetry serve only for Pedantry." [57] In a sense, the concept of taste, in its implied admission that Aristotelian and Horatian principles and precepts do not completely explain the nature of poetry, marks the end of neoclassical criticism. At the same time, through its vagueness, the concept of taste is used to give authority to those principles whose limitations the concept was designed to supplement. The result is what one would expect; the dynamics of Addison's criticism, which is the product of the neoclassicism of reason and taste, constantly undergoes the

[54] Aubignac, Book II, Chapter i; pp. 69–70.
[55] Bosker, pp. 20–21.
[56] Anthony Ashley Cooper, third Earl of Shaftesbury, *Characteristicks*, I, 336.
[57] Leonard Welsted, "A Dissertation concerning the Perfection of the English Language, the State of Poetry, &c." (1724), *Critical Essays of the Eighteenth Century*, p. 375.

strain produced by its own conflicting, if not contradictory principles.[58]

III

Addison, as noted at the beginning of this chapter, is an unusual figure in the history of neoclassical criticism. He admired Boileau, as most of his contemporaries did, and in a letter to Dr. Hough in 1700 mentioned his meeting with him. The admiration, however, was critical; Boileau was then an old man, and Addison was not certain that Boileau had been correct in his adverse judgment of the young French poets of the 1690's.[59] This admiration had grown by the time Addison wrote for the *Spectator*.

And here give me Leave to mention what Monsieur *Boileau* has so very well enlarged upon in the Preface to his Works, that Wit and fine Writing doth not consist so much in advancing Things that are new, as in giving things that are known an agreeable Turn. It is impossible for us who live in the later Ages of the World, to make Observations in Criticism, Morality, or in any Art or Science, which has not been touched upon by others. We have little else left to us, but to represent the common Sense of Mankind in more strong, more beautiful, or more uncommon Lights. (*S.* 253)

Were this the only surviving specimen of Addison's criticism we could justifiably assume that Addison sided with the ancients rather than the moderns. Indeed, we could find additional support for such a hypothesis in Addison's praise of the classical critics for practicing their precepts in their own writings. "Among the Moderns likewise no Critick has ever pleased, or been looked upon as Authentick, who did not show by his Practice, that he was a Master of the Theory" (*G.* 115).

Less than two months after the appearance of *Spectator* 253, however, Addison wrote in a different vein, to the effect that the critic must be a man of universal learning.

Mr. *Lock's* Essay on Human Understanding would be thought a very odd Book for a Man to make himself Master of, who would get

---

[58] See discussion of "taste" as a function of the imagination in Chapter 8.
[59] Addison, *Letters*, ed. Walter Graham, pp. 25–26.

a Reputation by Critical Writings; though at the same Time it is
very certain, that an Author who has not learned the Art of distinguishing between Words and Things, and of ranging his
Thoughts, and setting them in proper Lights, whatever Notions he
may have, will lose himself in Confusion and Obscurity . . . The
Truth of it is, there is nothing more absurd, than for a Man to set
himself up for a Critick, without a good Insight into all the Parts of
Learning . . . (S. 291)

Undoubtedly, Addison, if pressed, could have reconciled these
two positions if he agreed that there was an essential contradiction in them. What is extraordinary in this statement Addison
himself is aware of, that a critic should want to read *An Essay
concerning Human Understanding* at all.

In the 1690's Peter Motteux, the critic, librettist, and editor,
contributed scientific articles to his own *Gentleman's Journal*,[60]
but natural science was by no means taken to be a necessary
part of a gentleman's learning. René Rapin observes and approves of the learned Ancients who devoted themselves to the
arts and sciences so that they could better serve the public
weal. But when he speaks of "all parts of learning," he refers
to what we now call "letters." "And this may seem no improper
Method of Instruction for Persons of Quality, who shall thus
not be oblig'd to the too mechanical Way of Vulgar Rules, and
that minuteness of Grammatical Construction, which is ever
disagreeable to Men of advanc'd Understandings." [61] The "Universal Study of the Sciences" for Cicero is equated with a
knowledge of Plato and Aristotle, "and all that wrote after
them, that had any thing relating to Eloquence." [62] Modern
philosophers are criticized for their lack of good sense and their
interest in chemistry and geometry. This knowledge neither
relates to the proper study of mankind, man, nor entitles the
modern philosopher to dispute with Plato and Aristotle about
the most important of philosophical subjects, ethics.[63] Boyle is

[60] Robert Newton Cunningham, *Peter Anthony Motteux: 1663–1718*, pp. 48–50.
[61] René Rapin, *The Whole Critical Works of* . . . , trans. Basil Kennet and
others, I, Sig. B 3ʳ.
[62] "A Comparison of Demosthenes and Cicero," *ibid.*, I, 22.
[63] "A Comparison between Plato and Aristotle," *ibid.*, I, 320–321.

praised for his observations and experiments; Hobbes is learned, but too capricious; Descartes is too skeptical; Bacon is widely learned, but not accurate. Galileo, the Platonist, is the great genius of modern philosophy.[64] In fact, most of the valid observations of modern philosophers in natural philosophy had been made previously by Aristotle.[65] The history of philosophy after Plato and Aristotle is seen as one of steady decline. Rapin does not ask for servile imitation of the ancients, but he disapproves of the reduction of philosophy to natural philosophy. Philosophy so conceived has nothing to say about man's life in society and tells him nothing about the proper conduct of his affairs. In this respect, the poorest ancient philosopher is better than the best modern one, and Rapin writes of the best philosophers: "To write with any Agreeableness, on a Matter so dry and barren as *Philosophy,* may be another Difficulty, considering the delicate Tastes the Men of this Age have, even to excess." [66]

Addison would have agreed with much of what Rapin had to say. He would have supported his assertion that men in the later ages of the world have no new observations to make by agreeing with Rapin that the really important sciences are those which relate to man's conduct. And the modern philosophers, from the humanist's point of view, had added little to what Plato and Aristotle had written in this area. Addison, however, refused to stop here. He read Descartes, Hobbes, Locke, Newton, Malebranche, and Boyle with great interest. The *Spectator* papers are filled with his references to physics, biology, astronomy, and psychology. He conducted his own experiments. In short, he compensated for his lack of genius by applying his intelligence to a wide range of interests; interests which, C. S. Lewis notes, are beyond those of the Renaissance humanists.

Whatever is not immediately intelligible to a man versed in the Latin and French classics appears to them to be charlatanism or

[64] "Reflexions upon Philosophy in General," *ibid.,* II, 380–381.
[65] *Ibid.,* II, 414–415.
[66] "A Comparison between Plato and Aristotle," *ibid.,* I, 327.

barbarity. The number of things they do not want to hear about is enormous.

But Addison wants to hear about everything. He is quite as good a classical scholar as the Tories, but he does not live in a Humanist prison. He notes with satisfaction "that curiosity is one of the strongest and most lasting appetites implanted in us, and that admiration is one of our most pleasing passions.". . . He lived habitually in a world of horizons and possibilities which Pope touched, I think, only in the *Essay on Man,* and Swift hardly touches at all.[67]

Too much may be made of these horizons; for Addison periodically cuts himself off from them, as he does when he writes that there is little new to be written in his own age. Throughout his life he remained a product of his age and of his classical education. Most of his early writings, those published before 1700, were orations or poems in Latin or translations from the classics. The trip from Lichfield grammar school to Charterhouse to Oxford offered no sideroads to divert Addison from the humanist and neoclassical tastes which almost every Englishman took away from the University. Richard Steele, far less successful at Oxford than Addison was, had remarked that a classical education does not suit everyone for his life in society (*T.* 173; *S.* 157).[68] Had the Queen's and King's ministers insisted upon dispatch in the conduct of their business, Addison's Oxford training in classical correctness would have left him poorly prepared for his role in the world. He was constantly revising and correcting what he had written. "Mr. Addison could not give out a common order in writing, from his endeavouring always to write it too finely. He had too beautiful an imagination to be a man of business." [69] In a very real sense, his world was still a classical world, more precisely the world of the Latin poets from Lucretius to Prudentius,

[67] C. S. Lewis, "Addison," *Essays on the Eighteenth Century Presented to David Nichol Smith in Honour of his Seventieth Birthday*, pp. 10–11.

[68] Alice Stayert Brandenburg, "English Education and Neo-Classical Taste in the Eighteenth Century," *MLQ*, VIII (1947) , 176.

[69] Joseph Spence, *Anecdotes, Observations and Characters of Books and Men*, ed. S. W. Singer, p. 132. See pp. 37–38.

poets whom he imitated as well as any of his contemporaries did.[70]

Unfortunately, we know very little about Addison's early readings other than that which we can glean from the poems, essays, and letters of this period. Bishop Hurd's remarks on "An Account of the Greatest English Poets" (1694) adequately sum up Addison's stature as a critic at this time: "The introductory and concluding lines of this poem are a bad imitation of Horace's manner—*Sermoni propiora.* In the rest, the poetry is better than the *criticism,* which is right or wrong, as it chances; being echoed from the common voice."[71] The *Dissertatio de Insignioribus Romanorum Poetis* (1692) is much the same. The Romans excelled all other nations in the art of poetry, and Virgil is the first of them. To see the *"virtutes et vitia"* of other heroic poets, one must compare them with Virgil.[72]

Addison's early commonplace views on poetry are paralleled by his unexceptionable disdain for pedantic scholarship, a feeling which remained with him throughout his life. "This distrust of abstruse detail extended even to the Royal Society, whose Fellows he classified with 'all contemplative tradesmen, titular physicians . . . templars that are not given to be contentious, and statesmen that are out of business'" (*S.* 10).[73] He is no less harsh toward the critics who, unlike Dacier and Boileau, write without elegance, propriety, and knowledge of Greek and Latin. "In short, the Writings of these Criticks compared with those of the Ancients, are like the Works of the Sophists compared with those of the old Philosophers" (*S.* 592). The parallel between the mechanical critic and the mechanical philosopher immediately suggests itself. Both deal in those aspects of learning which are of no use to the gentleman, because the two "mechanics" have neither the faculties

[70] Thomas Babington Macaulay, *Essay on Addison,* ed. Herbert Augustine Smith, p. 70.

[71] Addison, *Works,* I, 22 n.

[72] *Ibid.,* VI, 587–588, with translation by Christopher Hayes.

[73] Peter Smithers, *The Life of Joseph Addison,* p. 17. Smithers notes that Addison's books were sparsely annotated (Sotheby Sale Catalogue 27/5 1799) .

nor the training to pursue those forms of learning which are of real value to mankind.

The criterion of usefulness is the most important one for the separation of pedantry from true science and criticism.[74] Arguing that poetry is as useful as medicine and more useful than abstract philosophy, Addison's protegé Leonard Welsted wrote, five years after Addison's death, "With respect to Metaphysical Knowledge, no Body, I am perswaded, will contend much for the Usefulness of it: Mr. *Cowley,* I think, has said, that he could never determine whether there is any truth or no in that Science; but he was either too hasty in that Judgment, or he had not entered into the finest Parts of it; but however that be, let us add to it Natural Philosophy, and what do they both together serve for, further than Curiosity and Amusement?" [75] His argument is supported by the Renaissance adaptation of the Aristotelian and Horatian principles, that poetry teaches and delights by being more specific than philosophy, and by making the reader not only commend and admire virtue, but enchanted with and enamoured of it.[76]

Addison, certainly, would have sided with Cowley rather than with Welsted on the question of the value of natural philosophy. Among men of letters, however, the opinions of Cowley and Addison concerning science were minority views. "To Mr. Hobs," "To the Royal Society," and *A Proposition for the Advancement of Experimental Philosophy* are Cowley's testaments to the reformed state of philosophy which replaced the tyranny of scholasticism.

> Philosophy the great and only Heir
> Of all that Human Knowledge which has bin
> Unforfeited by Mans rebellious Sin,
> ("To the Royal Society," 1–3)

[74] Wilhelm Papenheim, *Die Charakterschilderungen im Tatler, Spectator, und Guardian, ihr Verhältnis zu Theophrast, La Bruyère und den Englischen Character-Writers des 17. Jahrhunderts,* pp. 88–93, for sources and analogues of Addison's characters.

[75] Welsted, in *Critical Essays of the Eighteenth Century,* p. 381. Professor Durham conjectures that Welsted is referring to Cowley's *Proposition for the Advancement of Experimental Philosophy.*

[76] *Ibid.,* p. 382.

The reformation of scholastic philosophy by the followers of
Bacon, the "Moses" of the new philosophy, is seen as the
analogue to the reformation of the Catholic Church by the
Protestants. This conception of the new philosophy had been
building up outside literary circles as early as the 1640's.
"Though the character of the age was predominantly religious,
two spirits, both springing from Bacon and the new science,
and closely related, soon became conspicuous. One may be
described as public-spirited and humanitarian: and the other
as materialistic, utilitarian, scientific." [77]

The religious and scientific impulses cannot be separated
easily in Addison, or in Cowley. Addison's treatise *Nova Philosophia veteri Praeferenda Est* (1693) shows that he is the
product of a generation which is convinced of the truths of the
new philosophy.[78] Addison, however, opposes pedantry in
science as he does in letters.[79] The study of atoms and ani-
malcules for its own sake is the task of the virtuoso, not the
gentleman (*T.* 216). But the study of experimental philosophy
for the purpose of understanding the marvelous aspects of
God's creation is for Addison, as for Newton, the proper business of the Christian gentleman.[80]

Addison is not unique in his belief that natural science is the
proper study of a gentleman; Cowley and Shaftesbury agreed.
But few men of the time believed that the new science was a
relevant part of the learning of a critic. E. N. Hooker cites John
Dennis's interest in the new philosophy and the influence of

[77] R. F. Jones, *Ancients and Moderns: A Study of the Background of the
Battle of the Books*, p. 92.

[78] The *Dissertation on Ancient and Modern Learning* (1735), if it is Addison's,
cannot be dated with any certainty. There are no references to this essay in any
of his other writings.

[79] Beverly Sprague Allen, *Tides in English Taste (1619–1800)*, I, 48. See Addison against the use of architectural terms in *Paradise Lost*, I, 713–716 (*S.* 297).
See *T.* 158 and Marjorie Hope Nicolson, "The Microscope and English Imagination," *Smith College Studies in Modern Languages*, Vol. XVI, No. 4, pp.
25–26, 31.

[80] See especially, *S.* 543, 569; R. L. Brett, *The Third Earl of Shaftesbury: A
Study in Eighteenth Century Literary Theory*, p. 61, for suggestion that Shaftesbury's interest in bringing philosophy to the common reader influenced Addison.

Descartes and Newton upon his thinking.[81] What one detects are elements of the old microcosm-macrocosm analogy working in his thought.[82] More important is Dennis's insistence that the poet, like the scientist and philosopher, is the best judge of his own profession.[83] Fontenelle had defended natural philosophy against its detractors, but he, too, made no attempt to show its relevance to criticism.[84]

The common Restoration-eighteenth century opinion was that of Sir Thomas Pope Blount, who phrased the problem in terms of wisdom and learning. "Learning does but serve to fill us full of Artificial Errors . . . A Learned Man may not improperly be compared to a *Crow*, deckt with Feathers that he hath stolen from other Birds." The learned man is a pedant; he invents "Subtilties, artificial cunning Devices, and whatsoever is an Enemy to Virtue and Innocence." Finally, in an obvious reference to the new philosophy, he cites the Church Fathers and Cornelius Agrippa against the vanity of philosophizing.[85]

Thomas Sprat was aware of the possible objections to experimental philosophy when he wrote that experiments would not interfere with the classical education of boys, because these experiments would be performed only by men.[86] But even as liberal a critic as Saint-Evremond, who admires Gassendi, refuses to admit that philosophy and mathematics are proper studies for gentlemen.[87] Swift, the most ardent defender of humane learning during the eighteenth century, confesses without apology that he knows nothing about mathematics.[88]

[81] *Dennis,* II, xcix.
[82] *Ibid.,* I, 335.
[83] *Ibid.,* II, 208.
[84] See Leonard M. Marsak, "Bernard de Fontenelle: In Defense of Science," *JHI,* XX (1959), 111–122.
[85] Sir Thomas Pope Blount, pp. 33, 36, 38. See *HWL,* I (1699), March, p. 157; a review, of Bentley's *Dissertation upon the Epistles of Phalaris,* which condemns controversy and contentiousness.
[86] Thomas Sprat, *The History of the Royal Society,* III, ii, p. 323.
[87] *The Works of Monsieur De St. Évremond made English from the French Original . . . by Mr. Des Maizeaux,* I, 56–57.
[88] Jonathan Swift, *Correspondence,* ed. F. Elrington Ball and J. H. Bernard, I, 324–325.

To describe Addison's contribution to this revised conception of the scope of genteel learning in terms of the growing influence of the middle-class virtues embodied in the doctrine of "calling" and the value of socially useful work is to give only part of a more complex cultural situation. Certainly, the *Spectator* of Addison and Steele did much "to make the merchant class acceptable to the landed gentry." [89] Steele, like Addison, objected to absurd projects of members of the Royal Society, but he, too, defended the value of natural philosophy for rational creatures (*T*. 236). The issue must be seen in the context of the growing battle concerning the value of a classical education, with Addison and Steele suggesting that perhaps the classical values are not the only important ones. Swift's defense of the older humanism in *An Essay on Modern Education* (1728) reflects the degree to which the traditional values had lost the power to exclusively determine curricula in the eighteenth-century English schools. These values were by no means rejected, but the opinion we see represented in Thomas Maidwell's *Essay upon the Necessity and Excellency of Education* (1705), that the old education does not prepare men for the world of affairs, is gaining strength. The Whig Addison, who was his party's most eloquent apologist for English mercantile success and the Exchange, was keenly aware of these new values, which he presented within the framework of Christian humanism.[90] The framework is hardly altered, but the result is a revised notion of the critic as a gentleman of taste.

[89] Lewis Maidwell, *An Essay upon the Necessity and Excellency of Education* (1705), p. v.
[90] See appendix on "Opera and the Decline of English Virtue."

3

The Narrative Genres

> There is Nothing in Nature so irksome as general
> Discourses, especially when they turn chiefly upon
> Words. For this Reason I shall wave the Discus-
> sion of that Point which was started some Years
> since, Whether *Milton's Paradise Lost* may be called
> an Heroick Poem? Those who will not give it that
> Title, may call it (if they please) a *Divine Poem*.
>
> Addison, *Spectator* 267.

THE BEST EVIDENCE of Addison's commitment to the principles of those critics who preceded him may be found in his
analyses of the epic and tragedy. Aristotle, as interpreted by Le
Bossu and Rapin, is Addison's chief guide to the understanding
of *Paradise Lost,* especially in the preliminary general papers
on that poem.[1] The most important additions to Le Bossu's
categories for the discussion of heroic poetry (fable, character,
sentiment, and expression) were made by the French writers
and critics of the Christian epic of the seventeenth century and
John Dennis, who most solidly associated the idea of sublimity
with Milton's epic.

Similarly, the rules for tragedy are sought in classical sources,
especially Aristotle and Seneca (*S.* 39–41). Addison prefers the
modern fable and classical morals. His common sense and a
changing conception of tragic emotion lead him to condemn
English tragedians who insist upon maintaining the doctrine
of poetic justice, on the grounds that the doctrine is contrary to

---

[1] See *S.* 267 (January 5, 1712) and the papers for the following seventeen
Saturdays, through *S.* 369.

nature; the guilty are not always punished and the good re-
warded. Indeed, rigorously preserved poetic justice and tragic
pleasure are incompatible, because, Addison tells us, we will
not participate in the sorrows of the afflicted if we know that he
will come to a happy end.

Neoclassical criticism provided Addison with ideal tools for
the interpretation of heroic and tragic poetry, which were
written with its principles in mind. But Addison was less successful when he attempted to analyze ballads as heroic forms
(S. 70, 74, 85). If Wagstaffe's *Comment upon the History of
Tom Thumb*[2] is brutal in its attack upon the dignity with
which Addison invested "Chevy Chase," it successfully exposed the disparity between the stature of the poem and the
critical apparatus being used to analyze it. But Wagstaffe did
not recognize any merit in the ballads, and he would not have
been at all concerned with the fact that, given a new sensibility,
the critic had to either create a new critical vocabulary or use
the old one as best he could. Addison, who was to publish his
papers on *The Pleasures of the Imagination* less than thirteen
months after the appearance of the first essay on "Chevy
Chase," chose the latter alternative in this instance. The re-
sulting papers, failures insofar as they do not explain the underlying reasons for the growing interest in ballads, are examples
of that type of criticism which treats James Joyce's *Ulysses* as if
it were constructed like *Tom Jones.*

Addison's approach to his texts is more likely to absorb our
attention than are his specific comments and observations
about the poems, because his critiques of "Chevy Chase" and
Paradise Lost, teach us more about the structure and scope of
Addison's critical thought than they do about either of these
poems. In this respect Addison resembles every critic who at
one time in his career finds himself at the mercy of his critical
tools rather than in control of them. As much as he tells us
about the work of art, he tells us more about the conflict be-

[2] In *Parodies of Ballad Criticism* (*1711–1787*) .

tween what he sees and feels and what he is capable of expressing.

I

> Whate'er his pen describes I more than see,
> Whilst every verse arrayed in majesty,
> Bold, and sublime, my whole attention draws,
> And seems above the Critic's nicer laws.[3]

At twenty-two Addison thought of Milton as a sublime genius, not in rebellion against the laws, but above them. "An Account of the Greatest English Poets" is not a critique, but an effusive appreciation. Indeed, it does not offer evidence that Addison had read *Paradise Lost* carefully, or even completely. What is more likely is that he drew upon Roscommon's "Essay on Blank Verse," with its lines patched together from the sixth book of *Paradise Lost*.[4] His opinions about Milton's neglect of the rules resemble those of Dryden and Dennis,[5] especially in their mutual admiration of the transcendent sublimity of the sixth book of the poem. Addison finds nothing to condemn but Milton's politics; he is a great poet who should never have soiled his reputation by writing in defense of the "faithless" enemies of the King and Church.

The praise of Milton in the "Account" is no more representative of Addison's mature opinion of Milton than his "Milton's Style Imitated In a Translation out of the Story of the Third Aeneid" (1694) [6] is a miniature of *Paradise Lost*. Addison is uncomfortable outside of the confines of the "nicer laws" of rhyme. Compound adjectives, inverted word order, and nouns converted into adjectives help to create a Miltonic atmosphere without reproducing the level of either Milton's thought or

[3] Addison, "Account of the Greatest English Poets," *Works,* I, 23.

[4] G. Blakemore Evans, "Addison's Early Knowledge of Milton," *JEGP,* XLIX (1950), 205–206. The "Essay on Blank Verse" was appended to Roscommon's *Essay on Translated Verse* (1685).

[5] Dryden, *Essays,* II, 29, 109. *Dennis,* I, 3–4. See, too, Charles Gildon, in *CESC,* III, 198.

[6] Addison, *Works,* I, 38–41.

feeling. Between 1694 and the time Addison defended the classical correctness of *Paradise Lost* in the *Spectator,* Milton had become solidly entrenched as an English classic. Dryden's objections to his blank verse and his failure to imitate the classical fable did not seem to be such impressive charges as the imitations of Milton's style and subject matter became more frequent.[7] Dennis's *Grounds of Criticism in Poetry* (1704),[8] with its elaborate discussion of the sublimity of *Paradise Lost,* left little for Addison or any other critic to do but establish, in Aristotelian terms, the poet's claim as a worthy successor to the *Iliad* and the *Aeneid.*

When Addison's papers on *Paradise Lost* appear in the *Spectator,* his former unexplained praise of the sublimity and boldness of the poem is subordinated to his proof of its classical correctness, though he can still write that "I have seen in the Works of a Modern Philosopher, a Map of the Spots in the Sun. My last Paper of the Faults and Blemishes in *Milton's Paradise Lost,* may be considered a Piece of the same Nature" (*S.* 303). Without denying the faults of the poem, he can see them in perspective, infinitesimal beside the greatness and harmony of the entire work. Moreover, during the seventeen years which had passed between the publication of the "Account" and the *Spectator* papers on *Paradise Lost,* Addison had gained sufficient confidence in his critical powers and his conception of the function of criticism to stand against the less favorable comments in Dryden's criticism of Milton's epic.

The opening of the first paper could not have been written by a critic who was uncertain about the validity of his principles.

There is Nothing in Nature so irksome as general Discourses, especially when they turn chiefly upon Words. For this Reason I

[7] Raymond D. Havens, *The Influence of Milton on English Poetry,* pp. 89–102. See Blackmore, *Prince Arthur* (1695), with the flight of Satan through Chaos, and his *Eliza* (1705), with a battle in heaven. Both are rhymed. Dennis, *Court of Death* (1695); John Philips, *Imitation of Milton* and *Splendid Shilling* (1705), praised by Addison in *T.* 249; Defoe, *Hymn to Truth* (1706); Isaac Watts, eight poems in *Horae Lyricae* (1706).

[8] *Dennis,* I, 329–379.

shall wave the Discussion of that Point which was started many Years since, Whether *Milton's Paradise Lost* may be called an Heroick Poem? Those who will not give it that Title, may call it (if they please) a *Divine Poem*. It will be sufficient to its Perfection, if it has in it all the Beauties of the highest Kind of Poetry; and as for those who alledge it is not an Heroick Poem, they advance no more to the Diminution of it, than if they say *Adam* is not *Aeneas*, nor *Eve Helen*. (*S.* 267)

The most unequivocal doubts about the heroic qualities of *Paradise Lost* had been voiced by Dryden, before the publication of Addison's "Account." "As for Mr. Milton, whom we all admire with so much justice, his subject is not that of an Heroick Poem, properly so called. His design is the losing of our happiness, his event is not prosperous, like that of other epic works; his heavenly machines are many, and his human persons are but two." [9] Nothing could be less equivocal than Addison's response to this type of criticism; general discourses upon genre are futile. The end of criticism is not to catalogue a poem, but to discover its beauties and, to a lesser degree, its faults.

Addison persists in his efforts to describe *Paradise Lost* in epic terms because the heroic poem is the "highest Kind of Poetry." The Christian theme and personages do not make the poem less heroic, but rather increase its stature. "I think we may say without derogating from those wonderful Performances [the *Iliad* and the *Aeneid*], that there is an unquestionable Magnificence in every Part of *Paradise Lost,* and indeed a much greater than could have been formed on any Pagan System" (*S.* 267). Addison's categorical refusal to discuss the epic in general terms is the result not only of his objections to abstract criticism, but, also, of the vagueness of the neoclassical definition of epic poetry due to the introduction of Christian materials into the French epics of the seventeenth century.[10]

Le Bossu had offered a general definition of epic poetry

[9] Dryden, *Essays,* II, 29.
[10] Archimede Marni, *Allegory in the French Heroic Poem of the Seventeenth Century,* pp. 91–92.

which would admit any type of fable, either Christian or pagan, so long as it forms "the Manners by such Instructions as are disguis'd under the Allegories of some one important Action, which is related in Verse, after a probable, diverting, and surprising Manner." [11] Le Bossu's analysis of the epic in terms of the exordium, proposition, and peroration of an oration, and the categories of fable, character, thought, and expression derived from Aristotle [12] became the critical standard during the last years of the seventeenth century. But there was no unanimity about the essential properties of epic poetry or about the proper method of criticizing the epic. Sir Richard Blackmore could declare that allegory is not a necessary element of the epic and that a heroine will serve as well here as she does in tragedy. What is reasonable in *Antigone* and *Medea* is reasonable in an heroic poem. [13] Pope objected to the entire "recipe" approach to heroic poetry which he found embodied in Le Bossu's *Traité du Poéme épique* (G. 78).

To these animadversions upon Le Bossu's definition and methods, Addison added his own: "I question not but *Bossu* and the two *Daciers,* who are for vindicating every thing that is censured in *Homer,* by something that is parallel in Holy Writ, would have been very well pleased had they thought of confronting *Vulcan's Tripodes* with *Ezekiel's Wheels*" (S. 327). Addison may quarrel with Le Bossu also about the proper dating of the action of the *Aeneid,* but the scheme for the analysis of the epic and the emphasis upon the need for a great moral are derived from Le Bossu's *Treatise* (S. 267, 369). [14]

In basing his discussion of the epic upon Aristotle and Horace, Le Bossu joins his Renaissance predecessors in defining

[11] René Le Bossu, *Monsieur Bossu's Treatise of the Epick Poem . . . Made English from the French, with a Preface upon the same Subject, by W. J. To which is added, An Essay upon Satyr, by Mons. D'Acier; with a Treatise upon Pastoral, by Mons. Fontenelle. The Second Edition . . . ,* I, 11.

[12] *Ibid.,* II, 3.

[13] Sir Richard Blackmore, *Essays upon Several Subjects,* I, 88–89; cited by H. T. Swedenberg, *The Theory of the Epic in England, 1650–1800,* pp. 155, 158.

[14] A. F. B. Clark, *Boileau and the French Classical Critics in England (1660–1800)* , p. 246.

the epic in dramatic terms,[15] though not as explicitly as Davenant does when he writes that he used tragedy as the model for the organization of *Gondibert,* with five books corresponding to the five acts, cantos to the scenes, and descriptions to the sets and costumes.[16] Of the six parts of the tragedy listed in Aristotle's *Poetics* (1450a 8–10), Le Bossu has eliminated only spectacle and melody in his consideration of epic poetry, following Minturno and the sixteenth-century tendency to see plot as the soul not only of tragedy but of all poetry, subordinating the other elements to this scheme.[17]

Published in 1675, Le Bossu's *Treatise* was influential in England before its translation in 1695. Blackmore's *Prince Arthur* (1695), however, was the "earliest practical application" of Le Bossu's principles.[18] Both the preface and the poem followed Le Bossu so carefully that the 1695 translation was dedicated to Blackmore, who is praised for following the rules of Aristotle, Horace, and Le Bossu.[19] The same principles were conveyed to the English reader by Rapin's *Comparison of Homer and Virgil* and *Reflexions on Aristotle's Treatise of Poesie, in general,* translated by Thomas Rymer.[20]

By the time Addison wrote his papers on *Paradise Lost,* the pattern of criticism after the manner of Le Bossu was common. Dryden uses Le Bossu's schema in his "Dedication of the *Aeneis*" (1697), though he occasionally disagrees with Le Bossu's judgment of Virgil. Dennis uses Le Bossu's criteria, sometimes literally translating him, to damn the work written after his principles, Blackmore's *Prince Arthur.*[21] The *Treatise* was so highly regarded in early eighteenth-century England

[15] Le Bossu, I, 3.

[16] William Davenant, "Preface to *Gondibert*," *CESC,* II, 17.

[17] Herrick, *Fusion of Horatian and Aristotelian Criticism,* pp. 69–70. See Alexander Pope, *Prose Works,* ed. Norman Ault, I, 226, on fable as the *"Soul of Poetry."*

[18] A. F. B. Clark, pp. 243–244.

[19] Le Bossu, I, 42.

[20] See René Rapin, *The Whole Critical Works of . . . in Two Volumes,* trans. Basil Kennet, et al.

[21] *Dennis,* I, 46–144.

that the editors of *Memoirs of Literature* summarized a large part of Mme. Dacier's analysis of the *Iliad*, which is heavily indebted to Le Bossu.[22]

At the center of Le Bossu's Aristotelian view of the epic is the idea that the fable is the soul of the poem. For Addison, this opinion pointed in two not entirely independent directions, one Christian and the other didactic.[23] In *Spectator* 523, Addison praises the use of pagan mythology in mock-heroic poetry, especially in the first version of *The Rape of the Lock*. But pagan machinery is not to be tolerated in serious Christian poetry. It does not command belief, and it debases Christian themes through its violation of decorum. The sources of this view are to be sought not simply in a Christian aversion to falsehood in religion, but also in an artistic tradition originating in late sixteenth-century France, which presented the world with engravings of Old Testament figures in Roman dress, a form of presentation which became popular even in illustrations for the Bible.[24] The followers of Du Bartas, however, became increasingly didactic in their interpretation of Scripture. Jacque du Coras, dissatisfied with Achan's confession to Joshua before he is condemned to die, makes Achan too depraved to confess, in an attempt to make his execution more praiseworthy.[25]

Chapelain, in his *Préface à l'Adonis* (1623), had condemned the mixture of profane poetry and sacred themes, but the issue was still very much alive when Jean Balzac and Daniel Heinsius argued about the Latin tragedy *Herodes infanticida* (1636), with Balzac charging that the mixture of themes is contrary to both decorum and piety, and Heinsius defending the pagan devices as proper allegorical personifications of the virtues.[26]

[22] Anne Lefèvre Dacier, trans. *L'Iliade D'Homère*, I, vi–vii; *Memoirs of Literature*, III (1713), 322–333.

[23] "The theory of Le Bossu is the ultimate in the conception of the didactic purpose of the epic, a principle that was almost universally accepted in seventeenth-century France." Swedenberg, *Theory of the Epic . . .* , p. 17.

[24] R. A. Sayce, *The French Biblical Epic in the Seventeenth Century*, pp. 32, 33.

[25] *Ibid.*, p. 155; Joshua 7:18 ff.; Jacque du Coras, *Josué* (1665), p. 66.

[26] René Bray, *La Formation de la doctrine classique . . .* , pp. 297–298.

The vogue of the Christian epic was not without its effect in England. Davenant, maintaining the superiority of the Christian religion, insisted that the epic hero should be Christian.[27] Cowley, writing in praise of *Gondibert,* highly approved of Davenant's replacement of the heathen "monsters" with probable human actors, thereby playing more upon the passions of admiration and love than upon delight in the marvelous.[28] Boileau's objection to the mixture of Christian poetry and pagan devices[29] makes it easy to understand why Tasso's *Gerusalemme liberata* could not have been written in late seventeenth-century France. The English, emulating the French poetical and critical followers of Du Bartas, applauded, as the translator of Le Bossu's *Treatise* did, when evidence was offered that the Christian religion provided as good epic machinery as the pagan did.[30]

Because the exclusion of pagan machinery from serious Christian poetry had become an almost universally accepted literary principle before 1675, it was a less important issue than the question of the relation between the fable and its moral. Le Bossu interpreted Aristotle's remark that poetry is more serious and philosophical than history to mean that the epic is by nature a moral work which teaches by example.[31] The chief business of tragedy is with the passions. "The *End* of the *Epick Poem* is to lay down *Moral Instructions* for all sorts of People both in *general* and in *particular.*"[32] This theory of the end of the epic led Le Bossu to the conclusion that the poet must have the moral in mind before he sets out to exemplify it in the epic fable.[33]

[27] "Preface to *Gondibert*," *CESC*, II, 9.
[28] Abraham Cowley, "To Sir William Davenant upon his Two First Books of Gondibert," in "Preface to *Gondibert*," (1650).
[29] Boileau, *Art poétique*, II, 217–226.
[30] Le Bossu, I, Sig. [A10].
[31] *Ibid.*, I, 9.
[32] *Ibid.*, I, 14.
[33] A. F. B. Clark, pp. 243–244. The "great *Truth*" upon which the *Iliad* is founded is "*That a Misunderstanding between Princes is the Ruin of their own States*" (Le Bossu, I, 35–36).

The logical priority of the moral to the epic fable, in Dryden, illustrates the strictness with which Le Bossu's schema had been followed.

For the moral (as Bossu observes) is the first business of the poet, as being the groundwork of his instruction. This being formed, he contrives such a design, or fable as may be most suitable to the moral; after this he begins to think of the persons whom he is to employ in carrying out his design; and he gives them the manners which are most proper to the several characters. The thoughts and words are the last parts, which give beauty and colouring to the piece.[34]

John Dennis insisted throughout his career that the epic action exists only for instruction and that which is extraneous to this goal should be eliminated from the action.[35] Four years after the publication of Addison's last paper on *Paradise Lost,* and perhaps in response to it, Dennis reminded his readers that the moral is too important a part of the epic to be left to chance. There is no reason to believe, Dennis wrote, that the moral will arise naturally from the action, rather it must be in the poet's mind from the beginning.[36]

Addison refused to participate in the tradition which, from the sixteenth century, had imposed an external moral end upon epic poetry.[37] "Some writers discounted Le Bossu's theory. Addison refused to believe that the moral is first laid down by the poet, and sagely observed that a moral can be deduced from any epic; still in order to accede to popular opinion, he drew a moral from *Paradise Lost*" (S. 369) .[38] In this Addison proved himself to be more consistent in his Aristotelianism than did Le Bossu. Addison does not place himself in the uncomfortable position of having to reconcile the belief that the moral of the epic exists before the epic itself does, determining the structure

[34] *Essays,* II, 127–128.
[35] *Dennis,* I, 57–58. See, too, I, 198–199.
[36] *Ibid.,* II, 110. See Samuel Wesley, *Essay on Heroic Poetry* in *Series Two: Essays on Poetry, No. 2,* pp. 1, 3.
[37] Marni, pp. 193–194.
[38] Swedenberg, pp. 193–194.

of the epic fable, and the belief that imitation of an action is the essence (formal cause) of poetry.[39] Dryden remains consistent with his and Le Bossu's moral position by maintaining that epic style and moral concern make that genre superior to tragedy.[40] This position is true to the Platonic argument of Minturno which elevated epic poetry above tragedy on moral grounds,[41] and Boileau and Rapin supported the claims of the epic for much the same reason. Le Bossu, however, remained Aristotelian in his claims of superiority for tragedy.[42] He did so because he believed that imitation is the essence of poetry and that tragic imitation is more coherent than that of epic poetry. Addison, who also supported the claims of tragedy, refused to accept Le Bossu's psychology of art when Le Bossu insisted that the moral must exist in the mind of the author before the fable does. His objection to this form of literary Platonism is implicitly Mme. Dacier's objection to Plato's reduction of the art of poetry to the art of politics: "Le but de la poësie est d'imiter, & son [Homer's] imitation pourroit estre vicieuse en bonne politique, qu'elle seroit excellente en bonne poësie." [43] The poet is first an imitator of action. Any action which is unified, great, and entire will certainly provide a moral (S. 369), but the action, and not the moral, is the end and essence of the poem.

In his examination of the fable of *Paradise Lost,* as well as other parts of the poem, Addison proceeds as Le Bossu had, by examining the work as a successor to the *Iliad* and the *Aeneid.* "There are four Qualifications in the *Epick Action:* the first is its *Unity;* the second its *Integrity;* the third its *Importance;* the fourth its *Duration.*" [44] Addison reduces these to three, subsuming greatness and duration of action under a single head-

---

[39] Le Bossu, I, 7–8.
[40] *Essays,* II, 165.
[41] M. T. Herrick, p. 58.
[42] Rapin, *Whole Critical Works,* I, 116–117; Sayce, p. 6.
[43] Anne Lefèvre Dacier, *L'Iliade D'Homère,* I, xxii–xxiii.
[44] Le Bossu, I, 92, 96, 136. Addison does not offer an historical explanation of the difference between ancient and modern allegories and fables, such as one finds in Mme. Dacier's *Iliade,* but compares them on absolute terms. See *Iliade,* I, vii ff.

ing (S. 267). Addison, on two occasions, condemns the episodes
of *Paradise Lost* because they do not arise naturally from the
action of the poem (S. 297, 315), but praises the poem as a
whole for exceeding both Homer and Virgil in the integrity
and greatness of the action (S. 267).

Stressing the value of the fable as a means of relating action
rather than of conveying a moral,[45] Addison differentiates between simple and implex fables, after the manner of the French
critics, favoring the implex plot for the epic as Aristotle had
done for tragedy (*Poetics* 1452a). Addison, however, takes
notice of Dryden's objection to *Paradise Lost*[46] when he remarks that the change from good to bad fortune is proper to
tragedy, but not to epic poetry. Milton, Addison writes, avoids
this fault through the vision of the future greater paradise in
the twelfth book (S. 297). Therefore, the total effect of the
action of the poem is not seen in terms of the expulsion of
Adam and Eve from paradise, but in the context of the paradox
of the fortunate fall, of which the expulsion from Eden is but
the first part.

As Addison's discussion of *Paradise Lost* progresses, the nature of his argument becomes more clear. Although he denies
that a moral is to be imposed upon epic action from without,
his argument does not preclude an allegorical interpretation
of the action of the poem. Indeed, only by reading *Paradise
Lost* as a Christian allegory can we see its end as anything but
disaster. Addison's argument is parallel to Le Bossu's more
moderate statement of his own position: "The Action . . . has
four Qualifications: It is *Universal,* it is *Imitated,* it is *Feign'd,*
and it contains *Allegorically, a Moral Truth.*"[47] It is not in
this sense that Sir Richard Blackmore has said that allegory is
unnecessary, but in the sense in which Addison claimed that
Sin and Death are unnecessary to *Paradise Lost* (S. 297).[48] In
the former sense, allegory raises the poem above its literal

[45] Swedenberg, p. 167.
[46] Dryden, *Essays*, II, 229.
[47] Le Bossu, I, 29.
[48] Blackmore, *Essays on Several Subjects*, I, 88–89.

meaning and "vulgar Expression" through the use of metaphor. In the latter sense, the virtues and vices are personified. For Blackmore, a poem cannot be too morally allegorical, but the latter form of allegory, which reminds Addison of what is worst in Tasso and Spenser, is not necessary, at all.[49]

The general papers on *Paradise Lost* follow Le Bossu in good order after the one on fable. Homer excelled in multitude and variety of character. All of his protagonists' actions and speeches fit them, but Virgil's are not so clearly delineated. *Paradise Lost* poses special problems for the critic, because there were only two people in the world, Adam and Eve, who present four selves in their pre- and postlapsarian states. Therefore, supernatural characters and allegorical figures had to be introduced to fill out the action. The remaining problem of character arises from the status of Adam and Eve as perfect individuals, who would not excite either pity or terror were it not for our own participation in their fall (S. 273).

Whereas Le Bossu notes that the epic combines the passions of both comedy and tragedy,[50] Addison concentrates his attention upon the tragic passions and the sentiments which arouse them. He expends less energy upon theory than upon the problems of representing probable sentiments of characters outside nature, especially Shakespeare's Caliban and Milton's infernal council (S. 279). As he becomes more engrossed in the poem, Addison leans less upon Le Bossu and his moral precepts.[51] Instead his thoughts follow the more fashionable Longinian tendency to seek the foundation of appropriate heroic thought and expression in the realm of the sublime. Here Addison finds Milton exceeded only by Homer, though both Homer and Milton abound more than Virgil in both appropriate and low expressions, which for Milton usually take the form of puns (S. 279, 285).

Sublimity has no part in Le Bossu's critique of the epic. Although Boileau was largely responsible for the vogue of Longinian criticism in seventeenth-century Europe, John Den-

---

[49] *Ibid.*, I, 41–42.   [50] Le Bossu, II, 56.   [51] *Ibid.*, II, 259, 262.

nis was immediately responsible for citing and explaining the
sublime passages which Addison refers to so frequently in his
papers on *Paradise Lost*.[52] Dennis had represented Milton as
"one of the greatest and most daring Genius's that has ever
appear'd in the World, and who has made his Country a glorious present of the most lofty, but most irregular Poem, that has
ever been produc'd by the Mind of Man." [53] Milton knew
Aristotle's rules, writes Dennis, but he realized that they apply
only to relationships between man and man, not man and God.
Addison, without acknowledging his debt to Dennis, accepted
his judgment of Milton's genius (*S.* 333), adopted his view of
Milton's sublimity, used his illustrative passages, but refused to
admit, as we have seen, that *Paradise Lost* is as irregular as
Dennis had maintained.[54]

Significantly, Addison uses the term *sublime* in its aesthetic
sense more often in the papers on *Paradise Lost* than in all of
his other writings combined. In the papers on *The Pleasures of
the Imagination, sublimity* becomes *greatness.* Here, however,
the influence of Dennis and those who followed him [55] determined the vocabulary with which Milton's genius was to be
described.[56] Addison used the notion of sublimity to explain the
great originality of Milton's invention and, especially in the
cosmic parts of the poem, to justify the irregularity of the poem.
The sublimity, with its own irregularity, becomes one of the
central values of the epic.[57]

Longinus has observed, that there may be a Loftiness in Sentiments, where there is no Passion . . . The Pathetick, as that great

[52] Robert Lee Morris, "Joseph Addison's Literary Criticism," unpublished
dissertation, p. 99.

[53] *Dennis,* I, 333. See I, 3, 222.

[54] Dennis, disturbed by Addison's failure to acknowledge his debt to Dennis's
Milton criticism and by Addison's criticism of Milton by the rules, replied to
Addison's critique more than two years after Addison's death. "Letter II,"
Letters on Milton and Wycherley, ibid., II, 223–227.

[55] See, for example, Samuel Cobb, *Discourse on Criticism and of Poetry from
Poems on Several Occasions* (1707) .

[56] For the critical and theological origins of Addison's concept of the sublime,
or greatness, see Chapter 7.

[57] Arthur Barker, "And on his Crest Sat Horror: Eighteenth Century Interpretations of Milton's Sublimity and his Satan," *UTQ,* XI (1942) , 423.

Critick observes, may animate and inflame the Sublime, but is not essential to it. Accordingly, as he further remarks, we very often find that those who excel in stirring up the Passions very often want the Talent of writing in the great and sublime Manner . . . *Milton* has shown himself a Master in both Ways of Writing. The seventh Book . . . is an Instance of that Sublime which is not mixt and work'd up with Passion. The Author appears in a kind of composed and sedate Majesty; and tho' the Sentiments do not give so great an Emotion as those in the former Book, they abound with magnificent Ideas. The sixth Book, like a troubled Ocean, represents Greatness in Confusion; the seventh Book affects the Mind of the Reader, without producing in it any Thing like Tumult or Agitation. (*S.* 339)

The impulse to praise the irregularity of the sublime, in Shakespeare and Milton particularly, is a new one for neoclassical critics. In this, Dennis, whose conception of the "enthusiastic passions" colors his understanding of sublimity, seems to be more advanced than Addison. But Addison, not Dennis, follows this trend in contemporary sensibility to its logical conclusion in his praise of the ballads. There, as in his criticism of *Paradise Lost,* Addison attempts to justify the new sensibility by showing that the object of his admiration shares, to some degree, the qualities of a genre whose regularity is universally admired.

II

Addison's papers on "Chevy Chase" and "Two Children in the Wood" are extraordinary products from the hands of an Oxonian and neoclassicist. "Not that he invents anything, but he catches every current whisper and swells it to journalistic audibility." [58] The *Pepys Ballads* [59] collection is evidence enough that the taste for ballads had never been extinguished in England in the lower and middle classes, and the members of the upper classes, even if they did not sing these songs, sometimes collected them. Cowley's "The Chronicle" and Matthew Prior's

---

[58] Wagstaffe, p. ii.
[59] Hyder Edward Rollins, ed. *The Pepys Ballads.*

"Down Hall" represent the neoclassical strain in light and amorous ballads, which is closer to the cavalier song and broadside than it is to either "Sir Patrick Spens" or "Chevy Chase." Even the version of "Chevy Chase" which Addison read and applauded is a more modern version than the one which moved Sir Philip Sidney.[60]

The extraordinary nature of Addison's ballad criticism is recognized by the author himself when he acknowledges that it is strange that he should write seriously about these popular poems. The critic brought up to admire poetry adorned with the "Advantages of Art" can hardly be expected to approve those poems which possess only the "Beauties of Nature" (S. 85). The influence of this criticism was, in the long run, to encourage the publication and appreciation of popular poetry,[61] but, more immediately, Addison's ballad criticism drew only condemnation and satirical jibes. Men who agreed with the critical principles which Addison used to support his defense of "Chevy Chase" and "Two Children in the Wood" refused to accept or take seriously his application of these principles.

Although Addison never suggests that "Chevy Chase" is a conscious imitation of classical models,[62] he uses the parallel between the ballad and the epic as one of the chief supports for his argument that this ballad is worthy of the attention of a gentleman of taste.[63] To strengthen his case, he opens this argument by proving that "Chevy Chase" obeys the precept that "an Heroic Poem should be founded upon some important Precept of Morality, adapted to the Constitution of the Country in which the Poet writes" (S. 70). The precept is from Le

[60] "Apology for Poetry," *Elizabethan Critical Essays*, I, 178.

[61] Sigurd Bernhard Hustvedt, *Ballad Criticism in Scandinavia and Great Britain during the Eighteenth Century*, p. 65. See Edmund K. Broadus, "Addison's Influence on the Development of Interest in Folk-Poetry in the Eighteenth Century," *MP*, VIII (1910–1911), 123–134; Keith Stewart, "The Ballad and the Genres," *ELH*, XXIV (1957), 120–137; Albert B. Friedman, "Addison's Ballad Papers and the Reactions to Metaphysical Wit," *CL*, XII (1960), 1–13; Albert B. Friedman, *The Ballad Revival* (Chicago, 1961), pp. 84–113.

[62] Hustvedt, p. 77.

[63] A. F. B. Clark, p. 246; Karl Kabelman, *Joseph Addisons literarische Kritik*, p. 20.

Bossu: "La première chose . . . est de choisir l'instruction et le
point de Morale" and ". . . il emploie moins la force du raison-
nement que l'insinuation et le plaisir, s'accomodant aux
coûtumes et aux inclinations particulières de ses auditeurs." [64]
Certainly, Addison does not take this argument very seriously.
A year later, as has been noted, he rejects Le Bossu's contention
that an epic poem is *founded* upon a preconceived moral (*S.*
369). Yet, to give his argument the greatest possible chance for
success, Addison applies the prevailing conception of the relationship between the epic moral and fable to "Chevy Chase" in
the hope that proof of the poem's high moral purpose would
win the approval of readers of more refined and regular heroic
works.

The argument from neoclassical principles was a failure. Few
readers took the high moral purpose of stopping "unnatural
contentions" between the rival barons seriously enough to
agree that the moral raised the poem above the commonplace.
The hero, though he should have appealed to the reader's
patriotic sentiments, was no more satisfactory. Addison's elaborate comparisons between the sentiments of "Chevy Chase" and
the *Aeneid,* his praise of the heroism of both the English and
the Scots, and the comments on the generosity of Earl Percy
(*S.* 70, 74) were lost because his defense of the "majesty" of the
diction was unconvincing. To the claim that the diction had the
heroic simplicity of the *Iliad,* Dr. Wagstaffe had the most appropriate reply. He "found" a poem in the library of a school-
boy which was worthy of the Bodley or Vatican.

> *His Father was a Plowman plain,*
> His Mother milk'd the Cow.
> And yet a Way to get a Son
> This Couple knew not how . . .[65]

The poem is *The History of Tom Thumb;* the subject is
puerile, but yet it may be criticized by the rules of Le Bossu
and Aristotle. This satirical critique by Wagstaffe is the most

[64] Le Bossu, *Traité du Poème épique* (Paris, 1675), pp. 37, 44; cited by G. G.
Smith, *Spectator,* II, 356–357.
[65] Wagstaffe, p. 8.

telling attack upon the part of Addison's analysis of "Chevy Chase" which depends upon neoclassical rules. Addison had used neoclassical formal criteria, even those which he did not accept, to buttress his argument, because these criteria were the surest guides to the discovery of literary excellence. This argument failed to convince his contemporaries, because they could not take his argument seriously; they could not believe that these criteria were in any way relevant to the poem to which they were applied.

Addison's more telling argument in favor of the ballads, one which answered more directly contemporary objections to "medieval" poetry, was that "Chevy Chase" and "Two Children in the Wood" were not "Gothick" in their style and that their virtues were upheld by the *consensus gentium*. Addison, by adapting the argument of Sir William Temple, rejects the belief that the ballad is without form and is, therefore, fit to be read only by the vulgar.

The common vein of the *Gothick Runes* . . . was of a raving or rambling sort of Wit or Invention, loose and flowing, with little Art or Confinement to any certain Measures or Rules; yet some of it wanted not the true Spirit of Poetry in some Degree, or that natural Inspiration which has been said to arise from some Spark of Poetical Fire wherewith particular Men are born. And such as it was, it served the turn, not only to please, but even to charm the Ignorant and Barbarous Vulgar, where it was in use . . .

The subjects of them are various, but commonly the same with those already observed in the true antient Poetry. Yet this Vein was chiefly imployed upon the Records of Bold and Martial Actions, and the Praises of Valiant Men that had Fought Successfully or Dyed Bravely; and these Songs or Ballads were usually sung at Feasts, or in Circles of Young and Idle Persons, and served to inflame the Humour of War, of Slaughter, and of Spoils among them. More refined Honour or Love had little part in the Writings, because it had little in the Lives or Actions of those fierce People and bloody Times. Honour among them consisted in Victory, and Love in Rape and in Lust.[66]

[66] Sir William Temple, "Of Poetry," *CESC*, III, 95. See Hustvedt, p. 48.

Although Temple would hardly have thought a sixteenth-century English balladeer as barbaric as a Goth, he would have considered him "Gothick" by late seventeenth-century standards, as we see in his opinion of Spenser.[67] The English neo-classicists were, after all, the heirs of Augustan Rome. Their virtues, "wisdom, discipline, and liberal arts," are superior to the warlike ones of the Numidians. The Romans are the civilizers of mankind, and their values, based upon intelligent choice rather than barbaric ignorance are the ones which distinguish the hero from the barbaric savage.[68]

Addison writes, in defense of "Chevy Chase," that this ballad combines height of thought with "majestick" simplicity and nobility of expression (S. 70, 74). The thought, as Temple admits of "Gothick" heroic poetry in general, is appropriate to the speakers, and the expression is free of the "Gothick" manner of the modern poets, with its epigrams and pointed wit. "Two Children in the Wood," which cannot be defended as an heroic poem, is praised as a plain, simple copy of nature, "destitute of all the Helps and Ornaments of Art. There is even a despicable Simplicity in the Verse; and yet, because the Sentiments seem genuine and unaffected, they are able to move the Mind of the most polite Reader with inward Meltings of Humanity and Compassion" (S. 85). Even this "despicable Simplicity" contains a naturalness of thought which will please the best judges of language, "but only those who are endowed with a true Greatness of Soul and Genius, can divest themselves of the little Images of Ridicule, and admire Nature in her Simplicity and Nakedness."

The simplicity of thought and expression praised here is not that mentioned in Temple's account of the "formless" Gothick ballads and songs, but the classical simplicity and ease of Homer, which is opposed to the overelaborate poetry of the seventeenth-century wits. Bouhours, who finds simple and common expressions more agreeable than complex and esoteric ones, defines one of the reasons for the superiority of the

[67] Ibid., III, 99.   [68] Addison, Cato, I, iv.

French language in terms of its "naïveté," its freedom from the "bizarre" qualities which he finds characteristic of Italian and Spanish elegance.[69]

> Words are like leaves; and where they most abound,
> Much fruit of sense beneath is rarely found.[70]

This simplicity has two aspects; one is plainness of diction, and the other is appropriateness of the language to the thoughts expressed, its decorum. Both of these figure in Addison's comparison of the diction of "Chevy Chase" and the *Aeneid*, a comparison used to show that the language of each of these poems is appropriate to the level of its thought, intimating that some of the lines of the ballad would be proper in the works of Homer and Virgil (*S.* 74).

Whereas Bouhours defines decorous simplicity entirely in terms of the relationship between thought and expression, Addison adds the criterion of appropriateness to the taste of the age, explicitly appealing to the *consensus gentium,* much as Farquhar does in his definition of dramatic decorum: "The Rules of English Comedy don't lie in the Compass of *Aristotle,* or his Followers, but in the Pit, Box, and Galleries. And to examine into the Humour of an English Audience, let us see by what means our own English Poets have succeeded in this point." Shakespeare, Jonson, and Fletcher have "fairly dispenc'd with the greatest part of Critical Formalities; the Decorum of Time and Place . . . have no force of Decorum with them . . ." [71] The underlying argument here is clearly stated in *Spectator* 70 and in Mme. Dacier's *Causes de la corruption du goust.*[72] The authority of universal reason, not particular rules, is the source of universal popularity through the ages and the basis of common consent.

[69] Bouhours, *Entretiens d'Ariste et d'Eugène,* pp. 54–55, 57, 58.

[70] Pope, *Essay on Criticism,* II, 109–110.

[71] George Farquhar, *A Discourse upon Comedy, in Reference to the English Stage, Critical Essays of the Eighteenth Century: 1700–1725,* p. 277.

[72] (Paris, 1714), pp. 53–55; cited by Andrew C. Smith, unpublished dissertation, pp. 124–125. Broadus, *MP,* VIII (1910–1911), p. 129, cites *On the Sublime,* Chapter 8, which states that long approbation by diverse people is a sign of merit.

The rationale of the argument is to be found in the Cartesian notion of *bon sens,* which all men possess to some degree.

When I travelled, I took a particular Delight in hearing the Songs and Fables that are come from Father to Son, and are most in vogue among the common People of the Countries through which I passed; for it is impossible that any thing should be universally tasted and approved by a Multitude, tho' they are only the Rabble of a Nation, which hath not in it some peculiar Aptness to please and gratify the Mind of Man. Human Nature is the same in all reasonable Creatures; and whatever falls in with it, will meet with Admirers amongst Readers of all Qualities and Conditions. (*S.* 70)

Bouhours and the great majority of his contemporaries were inclined to deduce the laws of their arts, especially decorum, from the principles of the arts themselves, but Addison specifically rejects this approach in favor of deducing these principles "from the general Sense and Taste of Mankind . . . in other words, the Taste is not to conform to the Art, but the Art to the Taste" (*S.* 29). Since all men possess good sense, universal approbation or taste is taken as a sign of value in the thing approved. The critic, then, does not look first to the rules of poetry, but for the concealed beauties which have excited the taste. The critic's function here is not a prescriptive one; his duty is to describe the affective workings of the poem upon a reader of sensitivity.

This approach is at the heart of the papers on *The Pleasures of the Imagination* and offers the best internal evidence for Addison's authorship of the *Discourse on Antient and Modern Learning.* Addison is aware of the singularity of his judgment of "Chevy Chase"; therefore, he supports his argument with parallel quotations from the *Aeneid* (*S.* 74). In the *Discourse* his justification for such a parallel takes shape, as it does not in his earlier works. Addison writes that the object of the *Discourse* is to discover what beauties of the ancient writers were admired by their contemporaries, but are no longer appreciated by the moderns. The latter can see only the wit and good sense

of the ancient poems, but they pass over the accidental circumstances which provided the ancient reader with a variety of
pleasures.[73] The modern misses the jests, idioms, and *mores*
of the ancients; consequently, their language sounds more
dignified and solemn than it had sounded to contemporary
readers.[74]

Earlier neoclassicists had not seen the *Iliad* or *Aeneid* as the
product of a particular cultural situation, but had thought of
them as models for contemporary emulation.[75] Only in the latter part of the seventeenth century did historical criticism and
historical justifications of *consensus gentium* appear with any
regularity upon the literary scene. St. Évremond had complained of the barbarism of Homer's heroes, and he explained
this failing in Homer in terms of the Greek national character.[76]
Summarizing Mme. Dacier's reasons for finding the translation
of the *Iliad* a difficult task, the reviewer for *The History of the
Works of the Learned* writes, "The third is owing to the Manners and Customs of those Heroick Times, which are too plain
and simple to be valued by the present Age. Can *Achilles,
Patroclus, Agamemnon,* and *Ulysses* (says Madam Dacier) Men
of Functions, which we account Servile, can such be endured
by those of the present times, who are taken with our Roman-
tick Heroes and Town Fops, that are all so Fine, Delicate and
Handsome." [77]

This is not an argument for the noble savage or the heroic
Goth; it is a defense, like Addison's, of the neoclassical values
of plainness and simplicity, values which "the little conceited
Wits of the Age" can neither understand nor appreciate (*S.*
85) . Addison does not argue against the Shaftesburian concept
of taste as an individual response which may be either culti-

[73] *Discourse on Antient and Modern Learning,* pp. 3–4.

[74] *Ibid.,* p. 28.

[75] Donald M. Foerster, *Homer in English Criticism: The Historical Approach
in the Eighteenth Century,* p. 1.

[76] *Miscellanea: or Various Discourses,* pp. 11–20, 33; cited by Emerson Marks,
Relativist and Absolutist, p. 72. For the influence of theories of race and climate,
see F. H. Hadley, "The Theories of Milieu in English Criticism from 1660–
1801 (unpublished dissertation, University of Chicago, 1926) .

[77] *HWL,* XII (August, 1711) , 232.

vated or vulgar, right or wrong.[78] But he does reject the idea
that the judgment of the millions cannot be trusted, though he
hesitates to argue that popular taste for a poem at any given
time is a reliable sign of real value.[79] His claim for the judgment of the multitude is principally that their unaided and
unencumbered good sense appreciates "Nature in her Simplicity and Nakedness," which a learned man will admire only
if he possesses "a true Greatness of Soul" (S. 85).

I know not which more shews the essential and inherent Perfection of Simplicity of Thought, above that which I call the Gothick
Manner in Writing, than this, that the first pleases all Kinds of Pal-
ates, and the latter only such as have formed to themselves a wrong
artificial Taste upon little fanciful Authors and Writers of Epigram. *Homer, Virgil,* or *Milton,* so far as the Language of their Poems is understood, will please a Reader of plain common Sense,
who would neither relish nor comprehend an Epigram of *Martial,*
or a Poem of *Cowley:* So, on the contrary an ordinary Song or Ballad that is the delight of the common People, cannot fail to please
all such Readers as are not unqualified for the Entertainment by
their Affectation or Ignorance; and the Reason is plain, because the
same Paintings of Nature which recommend it to the ordinary
Reader, will appear Beautiful to the most refined. (S. 70)

Learning, when affected, can lead the mind from the path of
natural beauty, because a "Gothick" wit has refined his understanding to a point at which he is capable of reading only with
his head and not with his heart. René Rapin noted this danger
when he remarked that the vulgar are better judges of eloquence than the learned are, because they are not moved by the
"Sentiments and Notions" of the learned world, but "judge . . .
according to the Heart." [80] The heart, the seat of the animal
spirits and emotions, cannot be mistaken, as the understanding
can be.[81] True rhetoric is not simple instruction, which operates
only upon the intellect, a faculty which may be led astray by its

[78] *Characteristicks,* III, 167–168.
[79] *Cato Examin'd; or Animadversions on . . . the New Tragedy of Cato . . .
Dedicated to Joseph Addison, Esq.,* Sig. A2, pp. 1–2.
[80] *Whole Critical Works,* I, 101.
[81] See Descartes, above, p. 33, on animal spirits and *bon sens.*

affections. Rhetoric must move the heart, which directs the animal spirits in the proper functioning of *bon sens,* as well as produce "more glorious Effects" than that which convinces only the mind.[82]

The crux of Addison's defense of simplicity by the argument from *consensus gentium* is that the multitude, when directly moved by a poem, is not likely to be led astray by irrelevant or affected learning. This argument is analogous to Descartes's on *bon sens,* a faculty which provides the average understanding with a better guide to the truth than a genius has when he strays from the path of the truth. This argument was never met by Addison's critics. John Dennis, who certainly had the better of the duel as far as their contemporaries were concerned, countered Addison's defense of "Chevy Chase" with a discussion of real and ideal human nature, pre- and postlapsarian nature.[83] Education is designed to help recover the state of perfection lost through man's fall. True simplicity of thought, Dennis wrote, is "not imbecility, Affectation and Extravagance," but propriety of thought to the subject, which the rabble are incapable of judging.[84] Dennis is as prepared as Addison to admit that historical conditions prohibit exact imitation of Greek and Latin poetry by modern poets,[85] but he refuses to acknowledge the value of any taste other than educated taste, re-enforced by "a warm and strong imagination," and "a solid and piercing judgment." [86] The end of any work of art is not to please the multitude, but to please the best judges. If they are pleased, the rest will be. If they are not, the others will soon be "cloy'd." [87]

In a sense Dennis's argument is beside the point. Addison

---

[82] Rapin, *Whole Critical Works,* I, 101–102; II, 25. See *Descartes,* I, 115, 335 sq.

[83] *Dennis,* II, 30.

[84] *Ibid.,* II, 32, 33.

[85] *Ibid.,* I, 11–12.

[86] *Ibid.,* I, 290.

[87] *Ibid.,* I, 71. Hooker notes (II, 458) that Dennis approves of Boileau's seventh "Reflection on Longinus" (I, 400), where the criterion of long and constant approval of a work is offered as a reason for continued admiration. See, too, I, 398; II, 318. Dennis, however, does not give the majority of men credit for good taste: I, 49–50, 197, 287; II, 174, 277.

never contends that one should not aim to please the best judges. Instead, he claims that critics with the greatest souls will approve the best popular poetry. Only men with middling souls and classical learning are likely to condemn these ballads. Uninterested in learned men of little imagination and uneducated men with a taste for natural beauty only, Dennis makes short work of Addison's contention that "Chevy Chase" is an example of true simplicity in poetry by admitting that the subject is noble, but denying that the poem has anything that will pass for figurative language. The ballad has "No Magnificence, No Vehemence, No Painting, No Poetry." In short, to compare "Chevy Chase" to the *Aeneid* is ridiculous.[88] Dennis reverts to Sir William Temple's epithet in calling this ballad a *"Gothick* Tune,"[89] whose martial strains had attracted Sir Philip Sidney. But Addison should have censured Sidney, rather than exceed his praise.

In calling "Chevy Chase" *Gothick,* Dennis states his age's principal objection to the ballad, that its thought and expression are of so primitive a nature as to be beneath serious consideration. This defense of the classical genre supported the absolute authority of Aristotelian and Horatian standards by denying the relevance of particular historical conditions and individual tastes to the determination of objective standards of taste. In effect, Dennis rejects the belief that there is any connection between critical inquiry and the affective workings of literary art by defining simplicity objectively in terms of the relationship between thought and its mode of expression, without reference to its effects upon the mind of its reader or auditor. This is one of the many paradoxes of eighteenth-century English criticism. For Dennis was the critic who did most to stimulate interest in the sublimity of *Paradise Lost* and had condemned Addison for his formalistic criticism of what Dennis had called a great and irregular poem.

[88] *Ibid.*, II, 37.   [89] *Ibid.*, II, 33.

4

The Most Valued Genre

My Friend Sir *Roger de Coverly,* when we last
met together at the Club, told me, that he had a
great Mind to see the new Tragedy with me, assur-
ing me at the same Time, that he had not been at a
Play these twenty Years. The last I saw, says Sir
Roger, was the *Committee,* which I should not have
gone to neither, had I not been told before-hand
that it was a good Church of *England* Comedy.

Addison, *Spectator* 335.

NEOCLASSICAL CRITICISM of tragedy in late seventeenth-
century England was more responsive to the claims of popular
taste than criticism of the epic had been. Dryden, indebted as
he was to Aristotle's definition of tragedy and Le Bossu's ex-
plication of this definition,[1] objected on occasion to Rymer's
exclusively rationalistic criticism of this genre, especially Shake-
spearean tragedy, and argued from the point of view of the effect of the play upon the spectator or reader.[2] The early growth
of the periodicals and newspapers did little to influence the
criticism of the drama, because the editors confined themselves
to announcing and reporting theatrical performances, or, as in
the case of Defoe's *Weekly Review,* demanding moral reform.[3]

[1] *Essays,* I, 207, 213.
[2] Wellek, *History of Modern Criticism,* pp. 28–29. At the same time Dryden
could write that Rymer's *Tragedies of the Last Age* is the best piece of English
criticism and, perhaps, the best modern one. *Letters of John Dryden,* ed.
Charles E. Ward, pp. 13–14. See Fred G. Walcott, "Dryden's Answer to Rymer's
The Tragedies of the Last Age," PQ, XV (1936), 194–214.
[3] Charles Harold Gray, *Theatrical Criticism in London to 1795,* pp. 31–33, 37.

It was only with Richard Steele, whose criticism was hardly free of didactic and moral elements, that we find a consistent interest in stage presentation, actors' performances, and the difference between a good play and a good production.[4] His knowledge and admiration of Shakespeare are indicative of Steele's lack of subservience to the rules, and his demand for theatrical reform is not founded in the religious zeal of a Jeremy Collier, but in a demand for good taste.[5]

The nature and extent of Steele's influence upon Addison's theatre criticism cannot be determined with precision. We know that Steele's essays on the theatre in the *Tatler* antedate any of Addison's surviving writings on the subject, with the exception of some comments on Italian opera and comedy in *Remarks on Several Parts of Italy*.[6] Addison, who rarely went to the theatre, reviewed no contemporary plays or recent performances, though he did comment on *The Distrest Mother* in an essay which reveals more about Sir Roger de Coverley's provincialism than it does about the play (*S.* 335).[7] In the absence of an informative Addison-Steele correspondence, we must base our conjectures about the relationship between their thoughts on the theatre upon those writings which have survived, noting that Steele, with his great respect for the theatre, had probably contributed to the tempering of Addison's neoclassical principles and to his interest in the conditions of the performance of tragedy upon the stage.

Tempered as his criticism is by some appreciation of the problems of the theatre, Addison's principles are still basically Aristotelian, religious, and didactic.

As a perfect Tragedy is the noblest Production of human Nature, so it is capable of giving the Mind one of the most delightful and improving Entertainments. A virtuous Man (says *Seneca*) strugling

[4] Herbert Spencer Robinson, *English Shakespeare Criticism in the Eighteenth Century*, p. 35; Gray, pp. 42–45.
[5] George Winchester Stone, Jr., "Shakespeare in the Periodicals, 1700–1740," *SQ*, II (1951), 225. See *T.* 35, 42, 47, 53, 68, 111.
[6] Addison, *Works*, I, 392–395. His opera *Rosamund* was produced in 1707.
[7] Richard Steele, "Preface to *The Drummer*," in Addison, *Works*, V, 156; cited by Smithers, p. 261. See Gray, pp. 48, 50.

with Misfortunes, is such a Spectacle as Gods might look upon with Pleasure: and such a Pleasure it is which one meets with in the Representation of a well-written Tragedy. Diversions of this kind wear out of our Thoughts every thing that is mean and little. They cherish and cultivate that Humanity which is the Ornament of our Nature. They soften Insolence, sooth Affliction, and subdue the Mind to the Dispensations of Providence. (*S.* 39)

Without ascribing the superiority of tragedy to epic poetry to the superiority of the former's moral, Addison maintains the prevalent belief that the moral is the most significant part of the tragic fable in terms which are reminiscent of Collier's *Short View of the Immorality and Profaneness of the English Stage.*[8] *Venice Preserv'd* is condemned because the heroes are "rebels and traitors." No pity and fear are to be expended upon men who died in the defense of an immoral cause (*S.* 39) .

The critical emphasis upon a moral plot, as well as the presentation of such a plot in *Cato,* is part of the religious and didactic reaction against the "unreal" heroic values of valor, beauty, and love in Restoration tragedy.[9] For a French audience, who delighted in heroic romance, or for English theatregoers, who sought a dramatic substitute for the absent real heroes in the age of Charles II, Jaffeir of *Venice Preserv'd* was an ideal dramatic protagonist, because he evoked admiration for his heroic love and valor.[10] The heroic drama, however, did not satisfy the demands of a more settled age which had its hero in the Duke of Marlborough and was content to return to the tragic form prescribed by Aristotle's *Poetics,* as they understood it.

St. Évremond defended the place of heroic love in tragedy,

[8] "The business of *Plays* is to recommend Virtue, and discountenance Vice; To shew the Uncertainties of Humane Greatness, the sudain Turns of Fate, and the Unhappy Conclusion of Violence and Injustice: 'Tis to expose the Singularities of Pride and Fancy, to Make Folly and Falshood contemptible, and to bring every Thing that is Ill under Infamy and Neglect" (Collier, *Short View* . . . , p. 1) .

[9] Bonamy Dobrée, *Restoration Tragedy, 1660–1720,* pp. 13–14. See Davenant, *CESC,* II, 50, 51; Hobbes, *CESC,* II, 61.

[10] Henry Carrington Lancaster, *A History of French Dramatic Literature in the Seventeenth Century, Part II,* I, 14; Dobrée, p. 15.

seriously and facetiously, by citing its universal appeal as a passion and its special appeal to the nature of women.[11] But for Addison the chief heroic virtues, success and fortune, are the virtues of Caesar; the true Roman virtues of "watching, abstinence, and toil," the virtues of Cato, are more prosaic and middle-class than romantic and aristocratic in their morality.[12]

Cato was a reaction against this tendency to write Racine in English, and is interesting because it is at once the last flicker of Restoration tragedy, and a breaking away from it. To us it seems much of its period; but to Addison's contemporaries, indeed we know it did seem strikingly original. For what had happened to love? It takes a most insignificant place; one feels that it is only dragged in because no play can be altogether without it. With *Cato,* in fact, we may say that we come to the end of heroic drama, for heroism has become a formula, and was no longer a need of the age.[13]

Before Jeremy Collier incited the demand for reform of the stage, John Dennis had defended the presence of the already established theme of love in tragedy by citing the features in Greek "Climate, Religion and Customs" which discouraged the classical use of this theme, noting that the modern tragedian should imitate the Greeks no more in this regard than he would in copying their choruses.[14] Charles Gildon is more explicit in his justification for the defense of this theme; he will follow the ancients only insofar as they are "nothing but *good sense and Nature reduc'd to Method.*" He refuses to join Rapin and Rymer in equating love with the genre of romance, which only effeminates tragedy. Love, after all, is one of the dominant themes of the classical epic and is given a pre-eminent place among the passions by Horace, Descartes, and Henry More.[15] The interest in love in tragedy, even after the turn of the century, had not completely disappeared. But Bonamy Dobrée's judgment that the love plot of *Cato* is merely a concession to

---

[11] *Miscellaneous Essays,* I, 279.

[12] *Cato,* II, iv.

[13] Dobrée, p. 45.

[14] *Dennis,* I, 12–13, 30.

[15] Charles Gildon, *Miscellaneous Letters and Essays on Several Subjects,* pp. 146, 149, 153–155, 158–159.

popular taste is substantiated by a remark Alexander Pope made to Joseph Spence.[16] And there can be little doubt that the central interest of Addison's audience, at least that part of it which publicly commented upon *Cato,* was Addison's own concern with the moral dilemma and stoic virtues of the tragedy's hero.[17]

More direct evidence of Addison's dissatisfaction with the morality of contemporary tragedy is provided in his claim that the modern tragedian, superior in the "intricacy and disposition" of the tragic fable, is inferior to the ancient tragedians in the provision of the moral part of the fable. Deploring the use of rhyme in tragedy except to close the act, Addison praises the blank verse tragedians, especially Nathaniel Lee, noting that the modern tragedians, except Corneille and Racine, had succeeded better with the style of their productions than with the sentiments. Consonant with his praise of the simply phrased "Two Children in the Wood," he prefers a tragedy with noble sentiments clothed in humble language to one whose diction is bombastic and whose thought is mean *(S.* 39). The predilection for nobility of thought leads Addison to advise the dramatist to write the outline of his argument in "plain *English"* before setting the play to verse, which may conceal the poverty of his thought. Only then will the poet know whether his thought is worthy of eloquent tragic expression.

This exalted conception of the place of morality and thought in tragedy is the focus of Addison's discussion of the decorum of tragedy. He objects to tragicomedy and all other plays with double plots on the assumption, founded upon Aristotle's conception of the tragic plot, that the comic elements of the play will divert the auditor with a subsidiary action which, in the case of tragicomedy, is necessarily an inferior one. He finds tragicomedy "one of the most monstrous Inventions that ever entered into a Poet's Thoughts." Of the other double plots, he

[16] Pope told Spence that *Cato* was complete when he (Pope) accidentally met Addison in Rotterdam. "The love-part (in Cato) was flung in after, to comply with the popular taste . . ." Joseph Spence, *Anecdotes, Observations and Characters of Books and Men,* ed. S. W. Singer, p. 35.

[17] See especially, *Cato Examin'd,* pp. 14–19; and *Dennis,* II, 53.

is more solicitous so long as the less important plots are clearly subordinated to the major one (*S.* 40).

The influence of Horatian criticism had tended to encourage a definition of decorum in terms of character, either of the speakers of the poem or the *dramatis personae* of a tragedy or comedy.[18] Addison, following the majority of the French critics of tragedy, retained his Aristotelian bias, defining this decorum primarily in terms of plot, but he did not see the action of tragedy as the organic working out of an action which led to the catharsis of pity and fear. Instead, he thought of the plot as a vehicle for moral and sententious expression. Therefore, decorum, which Professor Bate has so aptly and succinctly characterized as the "preservation and ennobling of the type," [19] becomes the adherence to probability of action, thought, and language as defined by the moral and sententious level of the genre involved. Only after the propriety of character is defined in terms of the nature of the tragic plot are the actions, thoughts, and language of the individual protagonists assayed in terms of their suitability to their individual natures.

Decorum, the most important rule of poetry in general and tragedy in particular,[20] was applied to the structure of the tragedy primarily through the unities of time, place, and action.[21] Because the neoclassical critics did not associate these rules with the Aristotelian notion of the tragic plot as "coming into being" and because they found the emotions of pity and fear beyond their own "tragic" experiences, their concept of tragic decorum centered more about their own ideals of heroic thought and action. *"Modern Tragedy* turns on other Principles; the *Genius* of our (the *French*) Nation is not strong enough to sustain an *Action* on the *Theatre,* by moving only *Terror* and *Pity.* These are *Machines* that will not play as

18 Rosamund Tuve, *Elizabethan and Metaphysical Imagery,* pp. 192, 231–232.

19 W. J. Bate, *From Classic to Romantic,* p. 14.

20 See Aubignac, *Whole Art of the Stage,* II, ii, p. 75. Rapin, *Oeuvres,* ed. Pierre Gosse, II, 135–136; cited by Borgerhoff, p. 183.

21 Aubignac, II, ii, pp. 78–79, 80, states that the unities of time and place are rules of propriety. Rapin lists the unity of time as a rule of decorum: *Whole Critical Works,* II, 209–210.

they ought, but by great *Thoughts* and noble *Expressions,* of which we are not indeed altogether so capable as the *Greeks.*" [22] Taking this historical view of tragedy, Rapin explains the propriety of French tragedy in terms of his nation's "natural" gallantry, humanity, and tenderness. Neither Rapin nor Thomas Rymer, who translated Rapin's treatise on Aristotle's *Poetics,* is satisfied with what he thought to be inferior modern tragedy. To the charge that the theme of love is not proper in tragedy, Rymer added a complaint that could be more immediately and universally appreciated by his contemporaries when he spoke of the difference between a pleasing performance and a moving tragedy. One may be moved by the accidental pleasures evoked by acting, scenery, and machines while the tragedy itself is bad.[23]

Aristotle tells us of *Two Senses* that must be pleas'd, our *Sight,* and our *Ears:* and it is in vain for a *Poet* (with *Bays* in the Rehearsal) to complain of Injustice, and the wrong judgment in his *Audience,* unless these *Two senses* be gratified . . .

The *Eye* is a quick sense, will be in with our Fancy, and prepossesses the Head strangely. Another means whereby the *Eye* misleads our Judgment is the *Action:* We go to see a Play *Acted;* in Tragedy is represented a Memorable *Action,* so the Spectators are always pleas'd to see *Action,* and are not often so ill-natured to pry into, and examine whether it be Proper, Just, Natural, in season, or out of season.[24]

Addison, still seeing pity and fear as the central emotions elicited by tragic action, agreed that the captivation of the eye was the chief means of concealing an indecorous plot, but he was not as convinced as Rymer was that the ear is not as easily deceived.

The twin deceptions of bombastic language and gorgeous spectacle were the two principal means of concealing a lack of decorum in thought. "Aristotle has observed, that ordinary

---

[22] Rapin, *Whole Critical Works,* II, 209–210.
[23] Rymer, *Critical Works,* p. 19.
[24] *A Short View of Tragedy* (1692) , *ibid.,* p. 85.

Writers in Tragedy endeavour to raise Terror and Pity in their Audience, not by proper Sentiments and Expressions, but by the Dresses and Decorations of the Stage. There is something of this kind very ridiculous in the *English* Theatre. When the Author has a Mind to terrifie us, it thunders; when he would make us melancholy, the Stage is darkened" (*S.* 42). Addison, in his infrequent visits to the theatre, managed to notice all of the most flagrant examples of uses of scenery, costumes, and spectacle to divert the attention from the poverty of thought and poetic expression. Justified as most of his observations must have been, these observations cannot be allowed to divert the reader's attention from the limitations of Addison's conception of the primary function of tragedy. "Our Minds should be opened to great Conceptions, and inflamed with glorious Sentiments, by what the Actor speaks, more than by what he appears. Can all the Trappings or Equipage of a King or Hero, give *Brutus* half that Pomp and Majesty which he receives from a few lines in *Shakespear?*" (*S.* 42). The decorum of tragic action, seen in terms of the thoughts and sentiments which this action communicates, is determined not by the total effect of the tragedy, but by the successive and isolated expressions of thoughts and sentiments.

Within the limits of this idea of tragic decorum, Addison refuses to accept the further restrictions placed upon tragic action by the rules, particularly that of poetic justice. No critic, in England or France, consistently accepted or rejected all of these rules.[25]

Corneille could reject Hardy and other predecessors and work, albeit uncomfortably, in conformity to the critical standards then developing. Dryden could not reject Shakespeare and Fletcher, whose plays were still acted regularly and whose dramatic techniques could still furnish guidance. In France the greatest drama arose with or after the criticism; in England it preceded. Restoration playwrights in general accepted the premises of the critics (although there might be quarrels about specific application, in

[25] C. H. Gray, p. 12.

England as in France) and combined these with admiration for the drama of the giant age before the flood. Rymer showed that they could not have both.[26]

Yet Dryden, Addison, and many of their contemporaries felt that because of Shakespeare they had to have both. The concept of *bon sens* was sufficiently flexible to admit that beauty existed outside the area prescribed by the critical rules, and Shakespeare's merits, though his irregularities were frequently condemned, were too obvious to be easily ignored. Shakespeare's plays did more than anything or anyone else to make the English neoclassical critics examine, but not reject, the principles by which they judged the tragic art.

Dennis, analyzing Shakespeare's beauties and faults, was keenly aware of Shakespeare's limitations by neoclassical standards. Yet he had to admit that Shakespeare was "one of the greatest genius's of the *Tragick* Stage," one who had "great Qualities by Nature, what would he not have been, if he had join'd to so happy a Genius Learning and Poetical Art." [27] Charles Gildon, embarrassed by Shakespeare's irregularity, could only marvel at this miracle which he could not explain by the rules.[28] Addison's good friend and collaborator on the *Spectator* and *Guardian*, John Hughes, made his appreciation of Shakespeare more concrete than that of any other critic of his age. In an essay clearly aimed at Rymer's judgment of *Othello,* Hughes praises that play as a work of genius (G. 37). He is moved by the sufferings of Othello, even as he murders Desdemona. His appreciation of the theatrical effectiveness of the tragedy, even its handkerchief scene, sharply clashes with the jibes offered by Rymer.[29] Addison himself saw the futility of criticizing Shakespeare by the rules, and left his readers the most delightful reply to those who insisted upon doing so: "They are . . . provided with above a Dozen Showers of Snow, which as I am informed, are the Plays of many unsuccessful

[26] Rymer, *Critical Works,* pp. xxi–xxii.
[27] *Dennis,* II, 4, 5.
[28] See Robinson, pp. 24–25.
[29] *Ibid.,* pp. 45–47.

Poets artificially cut up and shreaded for that use. Mr. *Rimer's Edgar* is to fall in Snow at the next acting of *King Lear,* in order to heighten, or rather alleviate, the Distress of that unfortunate Prince; and to serve by way of Decoration to a Piece which that great Critick has written against" (S. 592).

The enemies of the rules were in the minority,[30] but the English advocates of the rules were frequently sufficiently liberal in their application of them to admit that the rules, especially the unities of time and place, were not the most significant tests of the quality of a tragedy. Thus, when Dryden wished to challenge French supremacy in the drama and dramatic criticism, he defined the nature of drama in the broadest possible terms: "For the lively imitation of Nature being in the definition of a play, those which best fulfill that law ought to be esteemed superior to the others." [31] Finding justification in nature for multiple plots in the contrary motions of the spheres, Dryden can also argue that "Eugenius has already shown us, from the confession of the French poets, that the Unity of Action is sufficiently preserved, if all the imperfect actions of the play are conducing to the main design." [32] Corneille's first concern was not with the rules, but with attracting and satisfying audiences. The success of his tragedies written according to the rules only strengthened the position of the rules in drama and criticism, a position which had been well established in France before the middle of the century.[33]

At the same time, Corneille's tragedies were not so unexceptionable by neoclassical standards that English critics could not find justifications for circumventing the rules in his plays. St. Évremond remarks that there is a plethora of rules for writing tragedies and yet there are few good ones written in modern times. As excellent as it is, Aristotle's *Poetics* is not perfect; Corneille discovered new truths in tragedy just as Gassendi

[30] See George Farquhar, *Discourse on Comedy*. Allardyce Nicoll writes that Rowe's *Jane Shore* "silently, but none the less deliberately violated" the rules (*History of Early Eighteenth Century Drama: 1700–1750,* p. 51) .

[31] *Essays*, I, 68.

[32] *Ibid.,* I, 71.

[33] H. C. Lancaster, Pt. II, Vol. 1, pp. 11–12; Pt. V, p. 42.

and Descartes discovered new truths in philosophy.[34] Farquhar, writing from his own experiences in the theatre, is no more inclined to participate in the "Superstitious Veneration for Antiquity," which held Aristotle's rules to be fixed and immutable. Looking to his audience rather than to the critics, he sees the unity of time as a restriction upon variety of incident, and the unity of action as an unreasonable prohibition against delightful songs and dances in comedy. Worst of all, he thought, these rules were imposed by a philosopher with no more experience in poetry than a layman has in theology.[35]

The reaction against the strict application of the rules was symptomatic of a more general dissatisfaction with ancient authority and the growing predisposition to examine the works of the moderns in the light of contemporary literary experience, even while doing so within the context of Aristotelian and Horatian criticism. Abbé d'Aubignac could argue that the rules are rational principles based upon the observation of nature and that the irregular parts of any tragedy have invariably displeased.[36] The unity of place, he claimed, is so obvious that the classical critics did not need to explain it, but "Dryden found comfort in Corneille's explicit refusal to accept the Unity of Place as one of the ancient rules." [37] To some degree the conflict over the unity of place can be explained in terms of the difference between the Elizabethan stage, which was relatively bare, and the stage of the Hôtel de Bourgogne, which inherited the more elaborate tableaux of the medieval stage.[38] Even Corneille's plays are more regular in their observance of the rules than his *Discourse* would lead us to believe. But the English critics, although they were inclined to agree with Abbé d'Aubignac that the rules are nature methodized, were more pragmatic in their application of them than the French critics were. Dennis claimed that the unity of place

[34] St. Évremond, *Miscellaneous Essays*, II, 12.
[35] Farquhar, *A Discourse upon Comedy, Critical Essays of the Eighteenth Century*, pp. 261, 263, 264, 265–266.
[36] *The Whole Art of the Stage*, I, iv, pp. 22, 24–25. See II, vi, pp. 98–103.
[37] Dryden, *Essays*, I, xliv.
[38] *Ibid.*, I, xliv–xlvi.

should be kept if the decorum of the action is not destroyed by doing so, but there is no compulsion to keep it "since there are no express Rules about it" in the classical critics.[39]

The pattern of criticism which emerges, particularly in England, reveals that the authority of Aristotle is invoked whenever it lends support to the critic's argument. Dennis, who argues rationalistically, historically, and, occasionally, psychologically, finds the unity of place neither rational nor irrational; it is conducive to proper writing, but cannot be insisted upon because there is no authority for it in Aristotle. Far from indicating an authoritarian strain in Dennis's criticism, this appeal to Aristotle is more indicative of Dennis's lack of interest in this particular issue, which he sums up and dismisses in terms which his readers will recognize and, to some degree, approve. There is no impetus for elaborate argument or reasoning in this matter.

Though neither critic denied the value of the unities of time and place in ordering the action of a tragedy, Addison shared Dennis's lack of interest in these dramatic rules. For one thing, the growing concern about the poverty of thought and expression on the English stage, re-enforced by demands for moral reform of the theatre, diverted attention from the more technical rules. Jeremy Collier's attack upon the immorality of the stage forced both the friends and the enemies of the theatre to think about the value of the dramatic arts more carefully than they had.

In the midst of this discussion of the relationship between the theatre and morality was the rule concerning poetic justice. "Addison's, as far as can be ascertained, was the first formal expression of the revolt in England against this doctrine." [40] "This Error they [the English tragedians] have been led into by a ridiculous Doctrine in Modern Criticism, that they are obliged to an equal Distribution of Rewards and Punishments, and an impartial Execution of Poetical Justice" (S. 40). Ad-

[39] *Dennis*, II, 75–76.
[40] Michael A. Quinlan, *Poetic Justice in the Drama: History of an Ethical Principle in Literary Criticism*, p. 2.

dison opens his argument with a reason which his readers will both understand and approve, even if they do not take it to be conclusive; there is no ancient authority for the doctrine of poetic justice.

The appeal to the authority of Aristotle would immediately attract the most conservative readers of the *Spectator,* but it is not the heart of the argument. Nor does Addison attempt to meet the Platonic view that poetry is moral discourse. "In former times *Poetry* was another thing than *History,* or than the Law of the Land. *Poetry* discover'd crimes, the *Law* could never find out; and punish'd those the Law had acquitted. The *Areopagus* clear'd *Orestes,* but with what *Furies* did the *Poets* haunt and torment him? and what a wretch made they of *Oedipus,* when the *Casuist* excus'd his *invincible* ignorance." [41] One of Collier's many complaints against the theatre was that *"The Stage-Poets make their Principal Persons Vitious, and reward them at the end of the Play."* [42] The theory of drama, particularly tragedy, which centers itself about the doctrine of poetic justice supposes that the play instructs by providing examples of exemplary conduct and justice. This theory of moral effects assumes that the proper object of poetic imitation is ideal Nature. Therefore, any violation of the rule of poetic justice was taken as evidence of religious or philosophical scepticism. "The Good and the Bad perish promiscuously in the best of *Shakespear's* Tragedies, there can be either none or very weak Instruction in them; for such promiscuous Events call the Government of Providence into Question, and by Scepticks and Libertines are resolv'd into Chance." [43]

Had Addison based his argument against the doctrine of

[41] Rymer, *Critical Works,* p. 27.

[42] *Short View* . . . , Chapter 4, heading.

[43] *Dennis,* II, 7, " 'Tis certainly the Duty of every Tragick Poet, by an exact Distribution of Poetical Justice, to imitate the Divine Dispensation, and to inculcate a particular Providence. 'Tis true indeed upon the Stage of the World the Wicked sometimes prosper, and the Guiltless suffer. But that is permitted by the Governour of the World, to shew from the Attribute of his infinite Justice that there is a Compensation in Futurity, to prove the Immortality of the Human Soul, and the Certainty of future Rewards and Punishments" *(Remarks upon Cato* [1713], II, 49) .

poetic justice upon a view of Nature as an ideal-type, he would have had a weak case, indeed. Instead, he argues that the poet should look at the world about him. The doctrine of poetic justice is not confirmed by the world in which we live (*S.* 40). Dennis refuses to look at empirical nature, because he does not believe that it is the work of the poet to reproduce this reality, but to improve upon it. Addison agrees that tragedy is a moral vehicle, but the regular operation of poetic justice is not the most effective means of inculcating moral truth.[44] Nor does Addison deny that the proper distribution of rewards and punishments is pleasing to a Christian audience. There is neither moral ambiguity nor scepticism in his argument.[45] Addison's principal objection to this form of literary didacticism is that it is psychologically ineffective. In an affective argument similar to that offered in defense of the taste for ballads, he states that we will not participate in the sorrows of the afflicted if we know that they will come to a happy end; "and as the principal Design of Tragedy is to raise Commiseration and Terror in the Minds of the Audience, we shall defeat this great End, if we always make Virtue and Innocence happy and successful. Whatever Crosses and Disappointments a good Man suffers in the Body of the Tragedy, they will make but small Impression on our Minds when we know that in the last Act he is to arrive at the End of his Wishes and Desires" (*S.* 40).

Dennis's reply to this condemnation of poetic justice as a dramatic principle is largely beside the point and, in one instance, is sophistical. He makes no direct reply to the claim that lack of dramatic surprise caused by the knowledge that all will end well would prevent the audience from sympathizing with the hero. To the claim that poetic justice is contrary to our knowledge of the affairs of this world, Dennis answers that we

[44] See *Dennis,* II, 436.
[45] Dennis, comparing Shakespeare's *Julius Caesar* with *Oedipus Rex,* proclaims the former irregular and unjust on moral grounds. Either Caesar is innocent and murdered, or Caesar is guilty and Brutus is murdered. In this moral world of ideal Nature, there is no room for moral ambiguity or an ethics of motives. Moral guilt and innocence are determined entirely by the nature of the act.

do not know the true characters of men or what they suffer. Men offend more often by their passions than by their crimes, and we cannot know the passions of the wicked, who dissemble.[46] To this Addison could very well have replied that even the unpunished villain of tragedy may suffer, just as his counterpart in life does. But even this remark would have been beside the point, because nothing can be clearer to the common sense of mankind than the fact that there are vicious men who do not suffer from either external punishment or internal passions in their life on earth.

Addison and Dennis never meet each other's arguments in their debate over poetic justice, not because they disagree about the function of tragedy as a moral vehicle, but because they disagree about the nature of the pleasures of tragedy though they discuss the matter in the same terms. Professor Wasserman has divided the eighteenth-century theories of tragedy into two basic types, founded upon Cartesian and Hobbesian psychology. Those following Descartes derive these pleasures from emotional agitation; the followers of Hobbes find these pleasures in the principle of self-love.[47] Dennis, though he writes that the basis of pleasure is self-love, considers the tragic pleasures as rationally approved responses of the passions.[48] All poetry, indeed, instructs and delights by exciting the passions.[49] He condemns *Cato* because the stoic hero, while not passionless, makes the reason tyrant over the passions.[50] Although Dennis speaks of "terror and compassion" as the distinguishing passions of tragedy,[51] he does not think of them primarily in terms of tragic catharsis or as the passions superior to admiration. With his high regard for Aristotle, he could not reject the no-

[46] *Dennis*, II, 20. See above, Note 43, where Dennis admits that there is evidence of injustice and triumph of the wicked on earth. See Note 45, on *Julius Caesar*, which Dennis judges by overt acts and crimes, not by passions or motives.

[47] Earl R. Wasserman, "The Pleasures of Tragedy," *ELH*, XIV (1947), 288. Professor Wasserman notes that the followers of either theory did not necessarily accept either Descartes's or Hobbes's theory of the passions (p. 288, n. 15).

[48] *Dennis*, I, 148–150.

[49] *Ibid.*, I, 336–337.

[50] *Ibid.*, II, 49–50.

[51] *Ibid.*, I, 224.

tion of catharsis, but he is clearly influenced by Corneille, who thought of catharsis primarily as a moral force, as did Rapin, Dryden, and Dacier.[52] Corneille differed from his predecessors and contemporaries, however, in that he doubted that tragedy purged the audience of pity and fear.[53] St. Évremond, in an appreciation of Corneille, broadened the criticism of the theory of catharsis by rejecting the tragedy of terror and compassion as a product of the superstitious age of Greek religion, which the moderns had replaced with the more appropriate theme of love.[54] Elsewhere he seeks the pleasures of tragedy in a more general understanding of the operation of human passion. "Tho we may be satisfied with *knowing* persons by their *Actions,* yet *Corneille* did beleive [*sic*], it is *not enough* to make them *Act,* he went to the very *bottom* of their *Souls,* to find out the *Principle* of their *actions,* he descended into their hearts, to see the *passions* form'd, and to *discover* what was most hidden in their *Motions.*"[55] The implicit presupposition of this view of tragic pleasure, made explicit by René Rapin, is that all passions are delightful and are capable of producing pleasure, because the soul enjoys change.[56]

Dennis accepts this view of the pleasures of the passions; he thinks that tragedy tends to the happiness of mankind by producing pleasure through the agitation of passion. What distinguishes tragic passions from less noble ones is the former's rational status: "If Reason is quite overcome, the Pleasure is neither long, nor sincere, nor safe."[57] Though passion is the source of pleasure, the will cannot fully consent to irrational

[52] Spingarn, *History of Literary Criticism in the Renaissance,* p. 75. The moral view of catharsis was the predominant one during the Renaissance, as represented in the opinions of Cintio and Scaliger. Robertello and Minturno offered more emotive theories of catharsis.

[53] H. C. Lancaster, Pt. III, Vol. 1, p. 12.

[54] St. Évremond, *Miscellaneous Essays,* II, 16–17, 19. See Edward Filmer, *A Defence of Dramatick Poetry: Being a Review of Mr. Collier's View of the Immorality and Profaneness of the Stage,* pp. 71–72.

[55] St. Évremond, *Miscellanea,* p. 6.

[56] Rapin, *Whole Critical Works,* II, 141. See, too, Charles Gildon, *The Laws of Poetry,* p. 183; *The Complete Art of Poetry* (1718), p. 189. Cited by Wasserman, *ELH,* XIV (1947), 288, 289.

[57] *Dennis,* I, 150.

passions. Within the context of this view of tragic pleasure, Dennis's view of poetic justice is perfectly understandable. The triumph of vice and the defeat of virtue do not arouse rational (moral) passions and, consequently, are unfit themes for the tragic fable. The effect of the passion is not homeopathic, but moral. The stoic view of tragedy is rejected because such a view leads the auditor to abjure passions, rather than to refine them.[58] Dennis, on the other hand, sees catharsis as the transcendence of passion which comes when the passions are relieved by the ultimate triumph of justice at the close of the play. The auditor enjoys the passions, even those of pity and fear, presented in the body of the tragedy, because they are made "pleasing and safe" by the rational and just conclusion.[59]

Addison's theory of tragic pleasure is grounded in Hobbes's definition of pity, taken from Aristotle's *Rhetoric*. "*Pity* is *imagination,* or *fiction* of *future* calamity to *ourselves,*" proceeding from the sense of another man's calamity." [60] The role of the reason in this interpretation of tragic pleasure is not to select suitable passions for tragic presentations, but to establish a relationship between the auditor and the object of his pity. "It is only when we supplement the emotional response with a rational comparison with our own circumstances, that pleasure arises; for then the recognition of our own comparative safety satisfies our self-love; 'when we read of Torments, Wounds, Deaths, and the like dismal Accidents, our Pleasure does not flow so properly from the Grief which such melancholy descriptions give us as from the secret comparison between our selves and the Person who suffers' " (*S.* 418).[61] The nature of this pleasure had been clarified earlier by Addison in his explanation of the pleasure we derive from terrible objects: "We con-

[58] André Dacier, *Remarks on Aristotle's Poetics,* pp. 78–80. Baxter Levering Hathaway, "John Dryden and the Function of Tragedy," *PMLA,* LVIII (1943), 665–666.

[59] *Dennis,* I, 150–151.

[60] Hobbes, *Works,* IV, 44. See, too, *Lev.* I, vi; and A. O. Aldridge, "The Pleasures of Pity," *ELH,* XVI (1949), 76–87.

[61] Wasserman, *ELH,* XIV (1947), 294.

sider them at the same time, as Dreadful and Harmless, so that
the more frightful Appearance they make, the greater is the
Pleasure we receive from the Sense of our own Safety. In short,
we look upon the Terrors of a Description, with the same
Curiosity and Satisfaction that we survey a dead Monster"
(*S.* 418).

In Dennis's view of tragic pleasure, the "dead Monster" is
killed by the rational and just ending which relieves the tension
of the passions. For Addison, foreknowledge of a just ending
deprives the auditor of his tragic pleasure, because he knows
in advance that the terror and pity which he would lavish on
the tragic protagonist is unnecessary; ultimately, the protagonist's position will be as safe as his own. The "monster" of the
tragedies of invariable poetic justice becomes no monster, at all.

The theory of tragic pleasure as rationally approved passion
is more conducive to a theory of Nature as Platonic Idea or essence than Addison's Hobbesian theory. Charles Gildon, defending the doctrine of poetic justice, largely against Addison,
by quoting Dennis, condemns Addison's advice that a protagonist of consummate virtue should not be introduced into a
tragedy, because he will not arouse pity and fear.[62] In Dennis's
and Gildon's view, the most exalted tragic hero will arouse the
greatest response from the passions, just as the most satisfactory
moral conclusion will. The Hobbesian theory of self-love requires that the spectator be confronted with "a man like himself" in a viable plot situation so that a comparison between
the protagonist and his viewer will be possible. The viewer can
derive satisfaction from the safety of his position only if he can
possibly believe that the predicament of the protagonist could
be his own. There is no challenge of the concept of ideal Nature
by the proponents of empirical natural science in this theory of
tragedy. Addison conceives of Nature as both essence and empirical reality without any question of contradiction.[63] Addi-

[62] Charles Gildon, *The Complete Art of Poetry,* pp. 192–196.
[63] A. O. Lovejoy, " 'Nature' as Aesthetic Norm," *Essays in the History of Ideas,*
pp. 70–71.

son's recourse to the conception of nature as empirical reality, as opposed to Dennis's use of ideal Nature, in the discussion of tragedy is only indirectly related to his response to natural philosophy, and is essentially the product of his conception of the nature of the pleasures provided by the tragic art.

ADDISON
AND
EIGHTEENTH-CENTURY
ENGLAND

5

The Nature of the Sublime

> *Milton,* by the abovementioned Helps, and by the
> Choice of the noblest Words and Phrases which our
> Tongue would afford him, has carried our Language
> to a greater Height than any of the *English* Poets
> have ever done before or after him, and made the
> Sublimity of his Stile equal to that of his Sentiments.
>
> Addison, *Spectator* 285.

ADDISON'S DISCUSSION of the "sublime" under the name of "greatness" in his papers on *The Pleasures of the Imagination* is one of the most curious parts of his literary criticism. In his papers on *Paradise Lost,* Addison clearly distinguishes the "greatness" of Milton's work, characterized by the stature of its theme and its length, from its "sublimity" of thought (*S.* 267, 279), suggesting that the latter is a justification for the irregularity of the epic.[1] On occasion, *greatness* is used to indicate sublimity of thought in these essays (*S.* 279, 333). In the papers on *The Pleasures of the Imagination,* however, *sublime* does not appear, at all, but *greatness* carries the meaning that both terms have in the earlier issues of the *Spectator.*

It has been suggested that Addison did not use *sublime* because the rhetorical overtones of "Longinus's" term tended to obscure the emotive connotations of the usage of Addison and his contemporaries.[2] In fact, it is more likely that Addison pre-

---

[1] Arthur Barker, *UTQ,* XII (1942), 423.
[2] Samuel Holt Monk, *The Sublime: A Study of Critical Theories in XVIII-Century England,* pp. 56–57.

ferred *greatness* to *sublime,* because he wished not only to avoid
the rhetorical overtones of French Longinian criticism, but,
also, the emotional overtones associated with the sublime as
"ravisher" and producer of "enthusiastic passions."

Longinus had cited five sources of the sublime: " (1) the
power of forming great conceptions *(noēseis)* , (2) inspired
and vehement passion *(sphodron kai enthousiastikon pathos)* ,
(3) formation of figures *(schēmata)* , (4) noble diction
(phrasis) , (5) dignified and elevated 'composition' *(sun-
thesis)* ."[3] The first two sources, which are given the least attention in Longinus's treatise, were the most important
sources of the sublime for the English critics of the early eighteenth century. Of the two, great thoughts and vehement passions, the latter was emphasized in making the distinction between the moving powers of rhetoric and sublimity. "For, to
speak properly, the Sublime rather ravishes than persuades; it
creates in us a certain transport and admiration, mixed with
astonishment and surprize, which is altogether distinct from
barely pleasing or perswading. We may say of the Art of Per-
swasion, that in general it has no more power over us than we
please; but not so of the Sublime; It gives Writing a peculiar
nobleness and vigour, an irresistable force which elevates the
Soul of every one that hears it."[4] By accepting the moving
power of the sublime as its distinguishing characteristic, Leonard Welsted, in his translation of Longinus, moved toward an
"emotive" theory of the nature of the sublime which placed
heavy emphasis upon its pathetic element.[5]

Welsted followed the example of Joseph Addison, his political and literary mentor, however, when he admitted that it is
possible to have sublimity without pathos.[6]

[3] Wimsatt and Brooks, *Literary Criticism: A Short History,* p. 99.
[4] *The Works of Dionysius Longinus . . . with some remarks on the English
poets. By Mr. Welsted,* p. 3.
[5] The second source of the sublime is "the Pathetick, that Rapture and that
natural Vehemence which affects and moves . . ." *(ibid.,* p. 20) .
[6] Welsted, "Remarks on Longinus," *ibid.,* p. 147. See Welsted's comments on
the sublimity of Milton's genius (p. 156) and Addison's comment on the subject
(S. 157) . Welsted's remarks on the sublimity of "Chevy Chase" lend support to
the hypothesis that the "friend" addressed in the "Remarks" is Addison.

Longinus has observed, that there may be a Loftiness in Senti-ments, where there is no Passion, and brings Instances out of an-cient Authors to support this his Opinion. The Pathetick, as that great Critick observes, may animate and inflame the Sublime, but is not essential to it. Accordingly, as he further remarks, we very often find that those who excel most in stirring up the Passions very often want the Talent of writing in the great and sublime Manner . . . (S. 339)

Addison's reading of Longinus leads him to the conclusion that the pathetic is not one of the principal sources of the sublime, which consists of great thoughts aptly expressed. Milton's sub-limity does not derive from his ability to work upon the pas-sions, but from his ability to arouse noble thoughts in the minds of his readers (S. 315). In the following year Addison approved of Boileau's note on Longinus which located the sources of the sublime in "the Nobleness of the Thought, the Magnificence of the Words, or the harmonious and lively Turn of the Phrase, and . . . the perfect Sublime arises from all these three in con-junction together" (G. 115).[7] Nothing is said of "vehement passions" as a possible source for what Addison was to call a pleasure of the imagination.

Longinus, writing in the classical rhetorical tradition, con-centrated almost exclusively upon those qualities of style which give rise to the sublime, whereas Addison is more concerned with the effect of the sublime upon the reader or observer.[8] Following Boileau and Rapin, Addison located the most im-portant aspect of the sublime in great thoughts which often move the mind even in the absence of sublimity of style.[9] " 'Tis impossible for any Man to succeed in the true Sublimity of Style, unless he is intirely persuaded, that he must owe this Sublimity rather to the Things of which he treats, to the noble

[7] See Boileau, twelfth *Réflexion sur Longin;* cited by A. F. B. Clark, p. 377 n.

[8] Mitchell Marcus, "Joseph Addison as Literary Critic," unpublished disserta-tion, p. 144.

[9] See S. H. Monk, *The Sublime,* pp. 30–36. Addison, though he does not use "sublime" in connection with "Chevy Chase," was probably influenced in his appreciation of this poem by the idea that great thoughts could move without the aid of a correspondingly great style. Confirmation for this view may be found in Welsted's remarks on "Chevy Chase." See above, Note 6.

Ideas which he forms of them, and to the Elevation of his Genius, than to the Boldness of Expression, or the Pomp and Splendour of Words, or the Equipage of far-fetched Circumlocutions." [10] This dissociation of the sublime from the rhetorical tradition in which it arose is not a romantic or preromantic reaction against neoclassicism, but is rather the result of late seventeenth-century efforts to give poetry a rational foundation in a revised concept of Nature and in philosophically acceptable ideas. Although Longinus's treatise gives priority to the sublime in art, the revival of interest in the sublime in seventeenth-century England was by no means restricted to its origins in the artistic sublime; the interest in "natural grandeur," the source of the artist's sublime ideas, developed before Boileau's interpretation of Longinus had reached English soil. [11] If the natural sublime is subordinate to the artistic sublime in Longinus and Boileau, such is not the case with Addison, whose religious views influenced both his conception of the sublime and his designation of this pleasure of the imagination by the word *greatness*.

I

In John Dennis's discussion of the sublime we find what are probably Addison's chief reasons for his redesignation of the sublime. The first is Dennis's derivation of the sublime from

[10] Rapin, "Reflexions upon the Eloquence of the Times, in General, XV," *Whole Critical Works*, II, 19.

[11] See S. H. Monk, *The Sublime*, p. 17; C. A. Moore, "The Return to Nature in English Poetry of the Eighteenth Century," *Backgrounds of English Literature, 1700–1760*, pp. 59–74.

Marjorie Hope Nicolson's *Mountain Gloom and Mountain Glory: The Development of the Aesthetics of the Infinite* appeared after the first draft of this chapter had been written. Her book provides evidence for the priority of the natural sublime in England, which has been omitted here. In general, the present work is in accord with that of Professor Nicolson. I wish to take issue only with her extreme opposition to the Longinian hypothesis (p. 143) proposed by S. H. Monk and others. Although English interest in the natural sublime preceded Boileau's translation of Longinus, English literary criticism did not assimilate these ideas until after this translation and Boileau's commentary were well known in England. Both Dennis and Addison, influenced as they were by the idea of natural sublimity, expressed their conceptions of the sublime in Longinian terms, especially in their location of the sources of the sublime in thought and strong passions.

the greatness of God and his creation, both the macrocosm and the immense objects of the geocosm, a view which Addison heartily approved. The second is Dennis's equation of the sublime in art with "enthusiastick passion," contrary to Addison's more Lockean view of the sublime as a pleasure of the imagination. Addison, in order to avoid the more emotive overtones which the sublime had taken on in Dennis's *The Grounds of Criticism in Poetry* (1704), may have selected "greatness" as a more appropriate term to convey the impression of sublimity in both nature and art.[12]

Dennis, in his conception of the relationship between natural and artistic sublimity, drew upon a background designed in the Renaissance, which depicted the artist as a creator who imitates God in his act of creation. Time and again he lamented the fallen state of poetry, which he thought could easily be restored to its high state as an instructor of mankind if only poets would submit to the rule and order of reason.[13] The order which dominates this phase of Dennis's thought is not that of the world as God's machine, but that of the macrocosm-microcosm analogy. Just as man becomes more perfect as he comes closer to resembling his creator, so man's works become more perfect as they approach the perfection of God's, which, though infinite, are regular and harmonious works. Man, who once lived in harmony with his universe, has fallen, as the rest of nature has. The purpose of man's work is to restore the perfection of ideal Nature lost through his fall.[14]

That this conception of the relationship between the macrocosm and microcosm played a significant role in Dennis's theory of the sublime is clear enough when we consider that he ascribed the source of the greatest sublime ideas to the realm of the divine: ". . . the Eternal Power, and the Infinite Knowledge

[12] MS. Eng. 772 in Harvard's Houghton Library contains part of the papers on *The Pleasures of the Imagination*. If Marjorie Nicolson is correct in her conjecture that Addison had written part of these papers as early as 1704, then the theory that the papers on the sublime were written to answer Dennis's work is an even more likely one. See *Mountain Gloom and Mountain Glory*, pp. 301 n., 307–308.

[13] *Dennis*, I, 203, 328–329, 375.

[14] *Ibid.*, I, 335–336.

of God, the Wonders of the Creation, and the beautiful Bright-
ness of Virtue, make a powerful Impression on all." [15] Religion
is the inspiration of all of man's greatest poetry. Milton's advantage over the ancients is that his theology provides sounder
and greater ideas than theirs had.[16] Dennis does not praise the
irregularity of God's universe, revealed by investigations of the
world beyond the moon, as Addison did. Rather, he praises
only the immensity of the universe, especially in his paraphrase
of the *Te Deum* and in his admiration of Milton's description
of heaven in the eighth book of *Paradise Lost*.[17]

Dennis is inclined to overlook those aspects of the new philosophy which had moved John Donne to see all that he had believed called in doubt. Instead, he concentrates upon those
phases of natural science which give support to his view of the
world as a mirror of divine greatness. If the highest poetry and
religion are dependent upon each other,[18] both depend upon
the findings of the natural philosopher for an understanding of
the immensity of the universe. *"First,* That the wonders of the
Universe afford the more admirable Ideas, and a more admirable Spirit, the more they shew the Attributes of the Creator,
or relate to his Worship. *Secondly,* That Natural Philosophy is
absolutely necessary to a Poet, not only that he may adorn his
Poem with the useful Knowledge that it affords, but because
the more he knows the immense Phaenomena of the Universe,
the more he will be sure to admire them." [19] Although Dennis
is dismayed that "so great a man as *Longinus"* should miss the
significance of the divine element of sublimity of thought, his
location of the source of the sublime in great thoughts is basically Longinian. The distinctive quality of Dennis's treatment
of the sublime is not in his discussion of sublime thought, but,

[15] *Ibid.,* I, 361.

[16] *Ibid.,* I, 368–369.

[17] *Ibid.,* I, 349. E. N. Hooker notes that this paraphrase of the *Te Deum* first
appeared in *The Advancement and Reformation of Modern Poetry* (1701) and
was later sent to the *Spectator* (*To the Spectator, on Criticism and Plagiarism*)
as an example of his best work (*ibid.,* I, 517) .

Dennis quotes *Paradise Lost,* VIII, 100–106, 15–22, on pp. 349–350.

[18] *Ibid.,* I, 331.

[19] *Ibid.,* I, 350.

as he noted himself, in his discussion of sublimity as passion.

Dennis's chief objection to Longinus is that the Greek rhetorician had mistaken the nature of the operation of sublime ideas upon the human mind.

. . . tho *Longinus* did by long Study and Habitude know the Sublime when he saw it, as well as any Man, yet he had not so clear a Knowledge of the nature of it, as to explain it clearly to others . . . For he tells us in that Chapter which treats of the Fountain of Sublimity, that Loftiness is often without any Passion at all; which is contrary to the true nature of it. The Sublime is often without common Passion, as ordinary Passion is often without that. But then it is never without Enthusiastick Passion: For the Sublime is nothing but a great Thought, or great Thoughts moving the Soul from its ordinary Situation by the Enthusiasm which naturally attends them.[20]

Finding Longinus's relegation of "enthusiastic passion" to a secondary role in the operation of the sublime contrary to Longinus's statement that the distinguishing characteristic of the sublime is that it ravishes rather than persuades, Dennis makes his own interpretation of Longinus's *"enthousiastikon pathos"* the center of his discussion of the operation of the sublime upon the mind.

Early in his career Dennis had used a poem's ability to move the passions as one of the tests of its value. Before setting out to translate a tale from Ovid's *Metamorphoses,* he had circulated the tale among his friends to see whether they were as moved by the story as he had been. When he discovered that "some men of sense" were moved by *The Passions of Byblis,* Dennis proceeded to translate the work.[21] "Passion," he wrote nine years later, "is the Characteristical Mark of Poetry, and therefore it must be every where, for without Passion there can be no Poetry . . ."[22] In characterizing the sublime, however, he distinguished between the ordinary passions of common life and enthusiasms, those higher, inexplicable passions arising from "the Meditation of things that belong not to common

[20] *Ibid.,* I, 359.   [21] *Ibid.,* I, 1.   [22] *Ibid.,* I. 9 г

Life." [23] Enthusiastic passions differ from ordinary ones both in their intensity and in the objects which give rise to them. The lower passions, which are less intense, arise from the contemplation of natural objects, but enthusiastic passions arise only from the action of the mind upon its own ideas. Thunder itself is not impressive, but the contemplation of the idea of thunder may produce enthusiastic terror in us.[24]

Although Dennis does not specifically equate beauty with ordinary passions, as he does the sublime with enthusiastic passions, he certainly thinks of these two sources of aesthetic pleasure as distinct, preceding Addison as the first to distinguish between the sublime and the beautiful.[25] In calling enthusiastic passions "mysterious" and extravagant in their origins, however, he did not mean to suggest that the sublime correctly presented in art is any less reasonable than the beautiful.[26] If the sublime, unlike beauty, cannot be harmonious in its parts, this state of affairs is due to the fact that the objects of the sublime are immense and are not easily harmonized by the human mind. "Poetical Enthusiasm is a Passion guided by Judgment whose Cause is not comprehended by us. . . . That it ought to be guided by Judgment, is indubitable. For otherwise it would be Madness and not Poetical Passion." [27] Dennis is not a religious enthusiast defending fanatical inspiration and dis-

[23] *Ibid.*, I, 216, 338.

[24] *Ibid.*, I, 339.

[25] E. N. Hooker (*ibid.*, I, 516; II, xcv–xcvi) sees this distinction primarily as a difference of intensity of the passions and does not mention the different sources of the two reactions. In 1717 Dennis specifically equated ordinary passions with *dulce*. "These two categories Dennis drew from Horace (*Ars Poetica*, lines 99–100) , but he changed their meaning. The *dulce* arouses—as the word indicates—the softer, tenderer emotions (the vulgar passions) , and corresponds to the Beautiful; whereas the *pulchrum* arouses the vaster, more mysterious emotions (the enthusiastic passions) , and corresponds to the Sublime" (*ibid.*, I, 516) . S. H. Monk (*The Sublime*, p. 543) states that Dennis's failure to talk about the beautiful shows a lack of interest in the distinction between the sublime and the beautiful, maintaining that Dennis believed that the sublime is the highest form of the beautiful. See Marjorie Nicolson, *Mountain Gloom and Mountain Glory*, p. 288 n.

[26] "To Dennis the Sublime was not a 'higher Beauty'; it was completely antithetic to Beauty and could be expressed only in 'Extravagancies . . .' " (Nicolson, *Mountain Gloom and Mountain Glory*, p. 288) .

[27] *Dennis*, I, 217.

order in matters of faith or art. Rather, he is speaking of the inspiration which is produced by the contemplation of the greatest parts of the divine order, such immense objects as mountains, oceans, and deserts. He is not moved by the irregularity of these objects, which reflects the fall of man from grace, but by the immensity of these objects, which is evidence of the greatness of God.[28]

If Dennis found the origins of enthusiastic passions in legitimate religious inspiration, we may wonder why Addison objected to his interpretation of the sublime. The first reason is that Dennis had made passion "The Characteristical Mark of Poetry" [29] and enthusiastic passion the distinguishing feature of the sublime. Although Dennis fully appreciated the need for poetry to instruct as well as delight, by elevating the status of passion in poetry he tended to emphasize the sensuous aspects of poetry in a manner contrary to the belief that poetry is a rational means of providing both pleasure and instruction.[30] Addison, by designating *greatness* as a pleasure of the imagination, placed the sublime above the pleasures of the senses though below those of the understanding (S. 411). Accepting the premise that the aim of poetry is to increase man's physical and moral knowledge, as Addison did, he was bound to find passions and the pleasures of the senses the least informative and the most misleading of human pleasures.[31]

Addison does follow Dennis, however, in his assertion that we cannot know the necessary causes of the pleasures of *greatness*, but, then, he adds that we cannot know the necessary causes of the other pleasures of the imagination either. Both the primary and the secondary pleasures of the imagination, those derived from the operation of the mind upon ideas from both nature and art, are largely inexplicable because we do not

[28] For similar distinctions between these two types of enthusiasm in Shaftesbury and Roger De Piles, see *ibid.*, I, 515–516.

[29] *Ibid.*, I, 215.

[30] "Poetry then is an Art, by which a Poet excites Passion (and for that very Cause entertains Sense) in order to satisfy and improve, to delight and reform the Mind, and so to make Mankind happier and better . . ." (*ibid.*, I, 336) .

[31] See below, Chapter 9.

know the nature of our ideas or souls (*S.* 413). Addison gives
the limitations of our knowledge of the causes of greatness an
explanation from Hobbesian and Lockean psychology, showing
his own greater involvement in contemporary philosophical
developments, though he and Dennis agreed that sublimity
arose from the same sources.

Addison's view of greatness is closest to Dennis's view of the
sublime when the former ascribes the final cause of this pleasure of the imagination to God's creation of the human mind in
such a manner that it can find true happiness in the contemplation of God's Nature. More specifically, in the case of the pleasure of greatness, man moves toward a knowledge of the greatness of God through the contemplation of the greatness of the
natural world. Addison's description of this pleasure as a largely perceptive process, rather than an emotional response, is in
keeping with his philosophical interests and his neoclassical
moderation. John Locke had noted that evidence provided by
the microscope supports the hypothesis that there are no gaps
in nature. Addison expands this hypothesis by analogy to offer
proof of the plurality of habitable worlds, showing his greater
interest in telescopic discoveries, which reveal the greatness of
the divine creation as well as the infinitude of God's creatures
(*S.* 579).[32]

Although Addison's discussion of greatness is centered about
the "bulk" of great objects, he is impressed, also, by the grandeur and expansiveness of view which free the mind from its
usual restraints.[33] "Such wide and undetermined Prospects are
as pleasing to the Fancy, as the Speculations of Eternity or In-

[32] *EHU,* III, vi, 12; Marjorie Hope Nicolson, "The Microscope and English
Imagination," *Smith College Studies in Modern Languages,* Vol. XVI, No. 4
(1935), 72–73, 76; Edward A. Bloom and Lillian D. Bloom, "Addison's 'Enquiry
after Truth': The Moral Assumptions of His Proof for Divine Existence," *PMLA,*
LXX (1950), 198–220.

[33] Ernest Lee Tuveson, *The Imagination as a Means of Grace,* p. 119. Professor
Tuveson writes that "greatness" means only "bigness" to Addison: "Magnificence
in the true sense of the word has no real place in his discussion. 'Stupendousness'
is all, for it is a spiritual quality." See pp. 58–61 of this work for a brief resumé
of the idea of the unlimitedness of God and his works.

finitude are to the Understanding" (*S.* 412). This freedom of imaginative response, though the response feeds upon perceptions of the immense, is not itself a soaring pleasure which operates beyond the bounds of reason. Here Addison's aesthetic views cannot be separated from his religious ones. In matters of faith, as in matters of art, he had pledged himself to moderation. "The terms High Church and Low Church do not so much denote a Principle, as they distinguish a party. They are like words of battle, that have nothing to do with their original significations, but are only given out to keep a body of men together, and to let them know friends from enemies" (*T.* 220). For Addison, principles rather than parties were important, and one of the most important of these principles was toleration based upon the premise that Englishmen cannot be certain that the Establishment teaches the only true Christian doctrine.[34]

Refusing to accept the royalism and divine-right theory of his father, a High Church clergyman,[35] Addison found his theology in the area between zeal and moderation, abjuring the extremes of infidelity and persecution (*T.* 220). Addison joined the Low Churchmen and Dissenters in their suspicion of the pomp and superstition of the Roman church, but he was not pleased by the "enthusiastic" dissenting sects (*T.* 257).[36] In large part, his thought was guided by the "latitudinarian" principles of the Cambridge Platonists and John Locke, with their emphasis upon natural religion and reason as natural revelation given by direct communication from God.[37] This view of religion severely restricted the legitimate occasions for powerful expressions of religious emotion and thoroughly con-

[34] See John Locke, *Posthumous Works,* p. 262; E. A. & L. D. Bloom, *PMLA,* LXX (1950), 198–220; Sterling P. Lamprecht, "Locke's Attack upon Innate Ideas," *Philosophical Review,* XXXVI (1927), 150–156.

[35] W. J. Courthope, *Addison,* p. 23; Peter Smithers, pp. 4–5. On Addison's failure to become a clergyman, see Richard Steele, in Addison, *Works,* V, 150; Spence, *Anecdotes,* p. 145; Smithers, pp. 27–29.

[36] Addison, *Works,* I, 369, 424, 425, 524–525.

[37] *EHU,* IV, xix, 4 ff.; G. R. Cragg, *From Puritanism to the Age of Reason: A Study of Changes in Religious Thought within the Church of England, 1660–1700,* pp. 62–67, 122.

demned all forms of "enthusiastic" display of religious zeal.

This imposition of limits upon socially acceptable display of feeling in religion was bound to have its effects in other areas, as it did in Addison's thought. "Mirth is short and transient, Chearfulness fix't and permanent. Those are often raised into the greatest Transports of Mirth, who are subject to the greatest Depressions of Melancholy: On the contrary, Chearfulness, tho it does not give the such an exquisite Gladness, prevents us from falling into any Depths of Sorrow" (S. 381). The value of the moderation of the passions was held by the Whigs and Tories, High and Low Churchmen. The Low Churchman called his opponent a man of "Imperious and Contentious Temper." [38] In return, it was said, that his *"Actions* are all *Passions,* and his Words *Interjections."* [39] Shaftesbury, who was generally less alarmed by the dangers of religious enthusiasm than were his contemporaries, suggested that enthusiasm was to be overcome only by "a sober kind of Chearfulness." [40] The ideal condition of the soul for the good poet is that of "much serenity and chearfulness of *Spirit . . .* The *Soul* must be fill'd with bright and delightful *Idea's,* when it undertakes to communicate delight to others . . ." [41]

The warmth which Addison recommends as proper to a Christian layman and poet is a tranquil emotion. "A State of Temperance, Sobriety and Justice without Devotion is a cold, lifeless, insipid Condition of Virtue; and is rather to be stiled Philosophy than Religion. Devotion opens the Mind to great Conceptions, and fills it with more sublime Ideas than any that are to be met with in the most exalted Science; and at the same time warms and agitates the Soul more than sensual Pleasure" (S. 201). This devotion does not interfere with the operation of the reason, because, unlike the heated passions of

[38] *The Observator,* I, No. 39 (September 5, 1702).

[39] *The Character of a Whig under several denominations; to which is added the reverse, or the character of a true Englishman, in opposition to the former,* p. 8.

[40] Anthony Ashley Cooper, Earl of Shaftesbury, *Letter concerning Enthusiasm,* p. 21. See St. Évremond, *Miscellaneous Essays,* I, 6.

[41] Thomas Pope Blount, *De Re Poetica,* Pt. I, p. 15.

the religious enthusiast, this emotion is moderate enough to "keep our Reason as cool as possible and to guard our selves in all Parts of Life against the Influence of Passion, Imagination, and Constitution" (S. 201). These three dangers to reason, which are, after all, natural constituents of the human soul, are not condemned outright, but only insofar as they are allowed to dominate the reason. Because Addison sees greatness, or the sublime, as a quality which works upon both the senses and the understanding, rather than the senses and its passions alone, he tends to minimize the ravishing qualities of the sublime and the role of the lower faculties, the senses, in its perception, in order that he may maintain the philosophical respectability of his pleasures of the imagination.

II

The most cursory reading of *Spectator* 412 reveals that Addison's view of greatness as the source of a primary pleasure of the imagination owes more to contemporary developments in natural philosophy and theology than to *On the Sublime* and the French commentators upon Longinus.

By *Greatness*, I do not mean only the Bulk of any single Object, but the Largeness of the whole View, considered as one entire Piece. Such are the Prospects of an open Champaign Country, a vast uncultivated Desart, of huge Heaps of Mountains, high Rocks and Precipices, or a wide Expanse of Waters, where we are not struck by the Novelty or Beauty of the Sight, but with the rude kind of Magnificence which appears in many of those stupendous Works of Nature. Our Imagination loves to be filled with an Object, or to grasp at any thing that is too big for its capacity. (S. 412)

The universe described here is not that of the confined and harmonious macrocosm-microcosm analogy. When Addison writes, in "The Spacious Firmament on High," that the orbs sing " 'The Hand that made us is Divine'," he self-consciously notes, in the interest of scientific truth, that this image from the old astronomy is only a metaphor; there is no "real Voice or Sound" emanating from the spheres, but only a voice in "Reason's Ear."

Admiration of the great in nature is the result of the resolution of the battle about the decay of nature in favor of those who shared the Newtonian world-view that nature is the best evidence of God's handiwork and omnipotence, rather than a sign of man's corruption.[42] During the age of Pope and Addison, the battle of the ancients and the moderns was no longer the important literary issue it had once been in England and on the continent.

> Some foreign writers, some our own despise;
> The ancients only, or the moderns prize.
> Thus Wit, like Faith, by each man is applied
> To one small sect, and all damn'd beside.
> Meanly they seek the blessing to confine,
> And force the sun but on the part to shine . . .[43]

But the conflict between ancient and modern learning left eighteenth-century Englishmen with two prominent and distinct concepts of Nature. The first, the more prominent in literary and theological discussions, identified Nature, as a "Platonic" essence, with *bon sens,* limitedness, and regularity, defining primarily the microcosm and man.[44] Although it was assumed in this view that Nature should evoke man's "Joy and Admiration" because God made it for man's pleasure and profit, there is still sufficient awareness of the limitedness of empirical nature implicit in this view to discourage the aesthetic of "greatness." [45] The second view of Nature, more characteristic of scientific discourse, was identified with immense, em-

[42] R. F. Jones, *Ancients and Moderns: A Study of the Background of the "Battle of the Books,"* pp. 279 ff.; Victor Harris, *All Coherence Gone,* pp. 175 ff.

[43] *Essay on Criticism,* II, 194–199. Clara Marburg, *Sir William Temple: A Seventeenth Century "Libertin",* pp. xvii–xviii, presents a good case for the hypothesis that the battle of the ancients and the moderns was not an important focus of literary debate. In the case of Temple, his scientific statements are unreliable because of his general ignorance of the subject. His position on matters of morals and literature by no means places him unambiguously in the "ancient" camp, as R. F. Jones claims in *The Background of "The Battle of the Books."*

[44] Austin Warren, *Alexander Pope as Critic and Humanist,* pp. 19, 28.

[45] *Theologica Ruris sive Schola et Scala Naturae* (1686), pp. 3, 196, 197; Nathanael Culverwel, *An Elegant and Learned Discourse of the Light of Nature, With Several other Treatises,* pp. 19, 21, 42.

pirical nature, especially the geocosm and macrocosm, rather than the microcosm.

The first, the "Platonic" view of Nature, presupposes that the reason cannot comprehend the order of Nature in its entirety. The light of Nature is the *"Candle of the Lord,"* "a Candle, not a Comet, it is a quiet and peaceable light." [46] Writers with more scientific inclinations were more confident about their ability to discover the order of Nature as it reflects the glory of God. Evaluations of the works of these men of science by moralists and men of letters tended to emphasize the religious significance of the scientific view of Nature, as does Jeremy Collier's short biography of Robert Boyle: "He was constant in his secret Addresses to his [God's] Throne, and in all his Enquiries into Nature, his chief Design was to raise higher thoughts in himself and others, of the Greatness, Glory, Wisdom and Goodness of God, and in that article of his Will relating to the Royal Society, he recommends it to them, and other Searchers into Physical Truths, to referr their Attainments to the Glory of the Great Author of Nature, and the Comfort of Man." [47] The first edition of Newton's *Principia* had no statement about the nature and goodness of God, an omission which caused so many religious objections to the work that the editor of the 1713 edition advised the author to answer his theological detractors. [48]

Among the issues which caused theological debate is Newton's idea of absolute space. [49] The defenders of the view that the universe is finite agreed that only God, and not his creation, is infinite, frequently resorting to the Aristotelian argument that "if the infinite exists as an attribute, it would not be, *qua*

[46] Culverwel, pp. 3, 166.
[47] See "Robert Boyle" in Jeremy Collier, *The Great Historical, Geographical, Genealogical, and Poetical Dictionary* [1688] . . . *mostly out of Lewis Morery* . . .
[48] Sir Isaac Newton, *Mathematical Principles of Natural Philosophy and his System of the World,* Andrew Motte, trans., rev. by Florian Cajori, pp. 668–669.
[49] *Ibid.,* p. 6. Cajori notes that the reviewer for *Memoirs of Literature* (May 5, 1712) finds that George Berkeley (in *Principles of Human Knowledge*) argued that Newton's notion of absolute space and time is atheistical (*ibid.,* p. 669) .

infinite, an element in substances, any more than the invisible would be an element of speech, though the voice is invisible" (*Physics* 204a) .[50] Addison, on the other hand, used Newton's idea of infinite space to support his own contention that Nature is greater than art. "If we consider the Works of *Nature* and *Art,* as they are qualified to entertain the Imagination, we shall find the last very defective, in Comparison of the former; for though they may sometimes appear as Beautiful or Strange, they can have nothing of that Vastness and Immensity, which afford so great an Entertainment to the Mind of the Beholder" (*S.* 414) .[51] The telescope is Addison's symbol of the new science, because the greatness of the universe is evidence of God's omnipotence and omnipresence.

Several Moralists have considered the Creation as the Temple of God, which he has built with his own Hands, and which is filled with his Presence. Others have considered infinite Space as the Receptacle, or rather as the Habitation of the Almighty: but the noblest and most exalted way of considering this infinite Space is that of Sir *Isaac Newton,* who calls it the Sensorium of the Godhead. (*S.* 565) [52]

The telescope gives man an awareness of the boundlessness of space though only God can have a "representation of infinity in his mind." [53]

[50] See Aristotle, *Metaphysics* 1066a; Sir Kenelm Digby, *Observations upon Religio Medici,* 3rd ed., corrected and enlarged, in Sir Thomas Browne, *Religio Medici,* 5th ed., corrected and amended (London, 1659) , pp. 10–11; Sir Matthew Hale, *The Primitive Origination of Mankind, Considered and Examined according to the Light of Nature,* pp. 70–110, 117–118; *Memoirs for the Ingenious,* I (January, 1693) , 18 (February, 1693) , 57 ff.

[51] See, too, *S.* 15 and *G.* 24.

[52] A. D. Atkinson, " 'The Spectator' No. 543," *N&Q,* CXCV (1950) , 275.

[53] *EHU,* II, xvii, 7–8. This view that space and time, which are not composed of matter, are infinite does not contradict Aristotle's theory that substance cannot be infinite. See *EHU,* II, xvii, 4–6.

Henry More, in *Psychodea Platonica* (1642) , wrote that only God is infinite, but four years later, in *Democritus Platonissans,* he admitted that the infinity of space is a manifestation of an unlimited God. Cited by Ernest Tuveson, "Space, Deity, and the 'Natural Sublime'," *MLQ,* XII (1951) , 23–24.

The neo-Platonic phase of the delight in the infinite continues in the work of the third Earl of Shaftesbury, who celebrates the infinity of beings which make up the great chain of being and delights in losing himself in imaginations of the

Only in the turning away from the finite universe of the macrocosm-microcosm analogy could the poet or critic begin to replace the concept of art as representation of ideal Nature and improvement upon empirical nature with a more favorable view of the physical world.[54] The immense Nature of the new science had a great aspect which art could not reproduce. The triumph of the new science did not spell the end of the controversy about the decay of nature. but moved the debate from the center of seventeenth-century thought to the periphery of eighteenth-century thought. The God of Galilean astronomy is the God of plenitude and vastness, and the imperfections of his creation are insignificant beside these qualities.[55]

The sublimity of the theme of *Paradise Lost* for Dennis and Addison consisted largely in the poem's celebration of the vastness of the heavens. But the cosmos, though it is God's greatest creation, was not the most immediate source of the sublime, as were mountains and oceans. Thomas Burnet, very much aware that mountains are evidence of the fall of Nature, admires them just as he would a great ruin. Without defining the pleasure which the sight of the Alps had given him, he clearly sees that these mountains are not beautiful, because they are irregular.[56] But he is enchanted by what he sees, and he explains his pleasure in terms which Addison was to use almost thirty years later (*S.* 412).

The greatest objects of Nature are, methinks the most pleasing to behold; and next to the great Concave of the Heavens, and those

---

vastness of God's being. See *The Moralists, A Rhapsody*, Pt. 3, Section I; cited by R. L. Brett, *The Third Earl of Shaftesbury*, pp. 149–150; see, also, pp. 21, 73–74.

54 Marjorie Nicolson, *The Breaking of the Circle*, pp. 169, 171.

55 A. O. Lovejoy, *The Great Chain of Being*, pp. 99 ff., 144 ff.

56 Thomas Burnet, *The Theory of the Earth*, pp. 140–141. Professor Nicolson writes that Henry More "was the first of our English poets who attempted to put into language man's feeling for what was not yet called *The Sublime*—a Sublime which came from the 'new philosophy' that no longer called all in doubt, but rather released human imagination to a spaciousness of thought man had not known before. The *idea of infinity* had utterly demolished the Circle of Perfection" (*The Breaking of the Circle*, p. 145). In *An Antidote against Atheism* (1652), More defended mountains as God's work. See Nicolson, *Mountain Gloom and Mountain Glory*, pp. 155 ff. But as Professor Nicolson notes (*ibid.*, p. 19ᵗ⁾ "emotionally he was unmoved by them."

boundless Regions where the Stars inhabit, there is nothing that I look upon with more pleasure than the wide Sea and the Mountains of the Earth. There is something august and stately in the Air of these things that inspires the mind with great thoughts and passions; We do naturally upon such occasions think of God and his greatness, and whatsoever hath but the shadow and appearance of *infinite*, as all things have that are too big for our comprehension, they fill and over bear the mind with their Excess, and cast it into a pleasing kind of stupor and admiration.[57]

The theological cast of Burnet's comments upon what he had observed is largely retained by Addison, whose explanation of the appeal of the immense and irregular scenes is Burnet's; such scenes allow the mind to escape its natural limits and approach, though not reach, the Infinite.[58] When Addison crossed the Alps, he described his feelings much as Burnet had described his own. This is understandable; it was Burnet's *Sacred Theory of the Earth* that Addison had praised earlier in a Latin ode written at Oxford.

It is in his affinity with Burnet on the question of the greatness of mountains that Addison proves to be more a man of his time than Dennis does. Both Burnet and, to a lesser degree, Addison are at a loss to explain the pleasure which they derive from the sight of mountains. Dennis accepts his experience of pleasure at the sight of the Alps just as he accepts the irregularity of *Paradise Lost*, without attempting to explain it. Addison, however, seeks a justification for his reaction to the

---

[57] Thomas Burnet, pp. 139–140. Robert Boyle had noticed earlier that the eye cannot take in the prospect of the sea (*A Discourse of Things above Reason*, in *Works*, IV, 421–422; cited by Tuveson, *MLQ*, XII [1951], 34) .

[58] Cf. Tuveson, *Imagination as a Means of Grace*, p. 70. It is difficult to support the view that "For Burnet, two new absolute values have emerged: infinity and irregularity have become desirable in themselves, and have begun to supersede order, symmetry, and other classical components of beauty as primary aesthetic values." For Addison, as well as for Burnet, the "immense" is not valued in absolute terms, as beauty was, but for its effect upon the mind of the perceiver. What we find here is the beginning of an affective approach to aesthetic questions. "Immensity" is not an end in itself, a value which exists regardless of whether there are men to observe the greatness of nature. Burnet and Addison emphasize the effects of immense objects upon men. Burnet, though he finds the irregularity of the world pleasing, sees this feature as his predecessors did, as a sign of the decay of man and the world (*Theory of the Earth*, p. 149) .

mountains, and here he is not so successful as in explaining
Milton's epic according to the rules of Le Bossu. Dennis, accepting the view that beauty is harmony of form, does not think
of the mountains as beautiful, but he responds to the mountains in a way in which Addison does not. It is not only Addison's cooler temper which prevents him from feeling Dennis's
"terrible Joy." [59] Although he sees mountains as Nature's hy-
perboles, something extravagant and contrary to reason, the
principal impression we receive from Dennis's account is the
one made upon his emotions, not upon his understanding. "In
the mean time we walk'd upon the very brink, in a literal sense,
of Destruction; one Stumble, and both Life and Carcass had
been at once destroy'd. The sense of all this produc'd different
motions in me, *viz.* a delightful Horrour, a terrible Joy, and at
the same time, that I was infinitely pleas'd, I trembled." [60] That
Dennis gave his assent to Burnet's view in writing that mountains are "vast, but horrid, hideous, ghastly ruins," [61] while
true, is almost irrelevant. This is not his dominant impression.
For Dennis, "these Ruines of the old World [are] the great
Wonders of the New."

Addison is more immediately concerned with the paradox
which confronted Thomas Burnet: why are these irregular,
nonbeautiful things objects of pleasure? Like Burnet, he has
no explanation for the efficient cause of this pleasure, only one
for its final cause, that God has endowed man with the capacity
for taking delight in that which overflows his mind (*S.* 412,
413) .[62] "At one side of the walks you have a near prospect of
the Alps, which is broken into so many steps and precipices,
that they fill the mind with an agreeable kind of horror, and
form one of the most irregular, misshapen scenes in the
world." [63] Earlier, in the middle of a long, objective description
of Alpine scenery, he had written of the "irregularity and con-

[59] Marjorie Nicolson, *Mountain Gloom and Mountain Glory*, pp. 279, 307.
[60] *Dennis*, II, 380. See Clarence D. Thorpe, "Two Augustans Cross the Alps:
Dennis and Addison on Mountain Scenery," *SP*, XXXII (1935) , 463–482.
[61] *Dennis*, II, cxv.
[62] Tuveson, *MLQ*, XII (1951) , 35, 37.
[63] Addison, *Works*, I, 510–511.

fusion" of the mountains.[64] Dennis's description of the Alps is more immediate, more of the author's real or apparent reactions and fears. Addison, as always, is more self-conscious about his status as a gentleman-traveller. He notes that his trip was an easy one, because the roads were clear of snow, but then he cannot resist the temptation so prevalent among Augustan writers of travel books to cite the appropriate stories from Roman history and quote Silius Italicus on the peaks breaking through the clouds.

The difference between Dennis's and Addison's reactions to the great in nature is summarized in the phrases they use to describe their reactions: "agreeable horror" and "enthusiastic passion." If Addison's reaction seems to be less intense, it is no less honest. And the moderation of his reaction, which avoids the apparent extreme of "enthusiastic passion," is at least partially responsible for the popularity of Addison's view of the sublime. The minds of the gentleman and the journalist are frequently one in their eclecticism. They gather and mould what is currently being thought, occasionally adding something of their own. Addison found support for his taste for greatness in nature not only in the religious and philosophical writings of Burnet, Dennis, John Ray, and the third Earl of Shaftesbury,[65] but in artistic and decorative fashions, as well.

[64] *Ibid.*, I, 507. Professor Thorpe writes, "Here he [Addison] felt tremendously the vastness, the incommensurable might of the forces of nature, the timelessness of the creation; he felt awe, horror, even, carrying with him long after he had left the mountain tops, vivid 'apprehensions' of their fearsome aspects" (*SP*, XXXII [1935], 469) . There is little evidence in Addison's reports that his emotional reactions were "tremendous" or in any way overpowering. The whole tenor of his reaction, especially his equation of greatness with thought rather than passion, would seem to indicate that Addison, unlike Dennis, did not have any overpowering emotions to explain in his critical writings. Furthermore, if Marjorie Nicolson is correct, and Addison began his papers on the imagination in 1704, then even this moderate reaction was not carried "long after he left the mountain tops." See above, Note 12.

[65] John Ray, *Wisdom of God Manifested in the Works of the Creation* (1701), 6th ed., corrected, pp. 260–261. Shaftesbury, like Dennis, speaks of losing himself in the "immense," of being overcome to a degree which is quite foreign to Addison. "Thy being is boundless, unsearchable, impenetrable. In thy Immensity all Thought is lost; Fancy gives o'er its Flight: and weary'd Imagination spends itself in vain. . . . Thus having oft essay'd, thus sally'd forth into the wide *Ex-*

Although Professor Nicolson is certainly correct in stating that contemporary religious thought is the most important influence upon Addison's view of greatness in Nature, this influence and that of Longinus are hardly the only ones. In gardening, there is a movement from the formal French ideal to more rustic ones. In design, there is a growing interest in Chinoiserie. In painting, mountain landscapes are beginning to take their place alongside the more popular "ideal" landscapes. Each of these movements is concurrent with that of the new belief in the vast universe of plenitude and, of course, is not independent of this concept. But the English merchants returning with Chinese and Indian fabrics and porcelain did not do so for the glory of an infinite God, and English purchasers of mountain scenes by Claude and Salvator Rosa, if they did their bidding with one eye on *The Sacred Theory of the Earth,* have left us with no record of this peculiar aspect of art collecting. One of the reasons for Addison's importance to the history of early eighteenth-century criticism is that he brought together and unified a number of tastes which, to earlier writers, had no apparent connection.

Addison is aware that his opinions are new ones here, as in his judgment of "Chevy Chase." Comparing the "artificial Rudeness" of foreign gardens with the "Neatness and Elegancy" of English ones, he writes, "there is generally in Nature something more Grand and August, than that we meet with in the Curiosities of Art . . . I do not know whether I am singular in my Opinion, but, for my part, I would rather look upon a Tree in all its Luxuriancy and Diffusion of Boughs and Branches, than when it is . . . cut and trimmed into a Mathematical Figure" (*S.* 414) .[66] Addison's opinion is, indeed, a new

---

panse, when I return again within *My-self,* struck with the sense of this so narrow Being, and the Fulness of that Immense-one; I dare no more behold the amazing Depths, nor sound the Abyss of *Deity*" (Shaftesbury, *Characteristicks,* II, 345–346; cited by Brett, *The Third Earl of Shaftesbury,* p. 146) .

[66] C. D. Thorpe, "Addison and Hutcheson on the Imagination," *ELH,* II (1935) , 220–221. See, too, the parallel in description with quotation from Burnet, above, pp. 111–112.

one. In the year when this *Spectator* was written, Dezallier's
book on gardening was translated into English.[67] Dezallier's
Theory is the epitome of more than forty years of French formal gardening.[68] The "parterre of embroidery," which Addison finds less delightful than an orchard in bloom (*S.* 414), is
the "finest and most magnificent of all" garden designs.[69] The
formal garden is to be laid out according to the principles of
geometry, with the prize for the greatest beauty going to the
garden made up of the parterres of the most intricate designs.[70]

A "correspondent" to the *Spectator,* after reading the papers on *The Pleasures of the Imagination,* drew the clearest
Addisonian parallel between the two arts of gardening and poetry.

> I think that there are as many Kinds of Gardening as of Poetry:
> Your Makers of Parterres and Flower-Gardens, are Epigrammatists
> and Sonneteers in this Art, Contrivers of Bowers and Grottos,
> Treillages and Cascades, are Romance Writers . . . As for my self,
> you will find by the Account I have already given you, that my Com-
> positions in Gardening are altogether after the *Pindarick* Manner,
> and run into the beautiful Wildness of Nature, without affecting
> the nicer Elegancies of Art. (*S.* 477)

Behind this mildly ridiculous comparison, at once both ironic
and serious, is Addison's opinion of Pindar or, if taken ironi-
cally, the "modern Pindarick" poets. Although Addison hardly
admired the modern imitators of Pindar, he placed Pindar with
Homer among the great geniuses who wrote without the aid of
rules (*S.* 160). The writers of epigrams and sonnets are little
wits, men of small imagination, who produce facile and regular works which reveal only their meanness of spirit and their

[67] [Antoine Joseph Dezallier d'Argenville], *The Theory and Practice of
Gardening . . . Done from the French Original . . . 1709. By John James.* This
work on pleasure gardens was written for owners of large estates, not novices.
See p. 16.

[68] See René Rapin, *Of Gardens. Four Books First Written in Latine Verse by
Renatus Rapinus . . . now made English by J. E.,* pp. 8–9, on the inadmissibility
of irregularity in pleasure gardens.

[69] Dezallier, p. 33.

[70] B. S. Allen, *Tides in English Taste,* I, 144–146.

inability to imitate the greater parts of Nature. Milton's irregularities, however, are but spots on the sun, minor blemishes
in a brilliant and sublime work.[71]

For Addison, the formal gardener is no better than his peer
in verse. His praise of Dryden's "poetic heat and rage," [72]
though modified upon mature reflection, finds its counterpart
in his preference for the "rude heaps of Stones" of the gardens
at Fontainebleau rather than the more regular gardens at
Versailles.[73] Although Addison is sometimes credited with having initiated the new style in English gardening,[74] he has done
little more than give this idea its first coherent popular expression. Sir William Temple had noted the Chinese disdain for
geometrical gardening: "a boy that can tell a hundred, may
plant walks of trees in straight lines . . . But the greatest reach
of imagination is employed in contriving figures where the
beauty shall be great, and strike the eye, but without any order
or disposition of the parts that shall be commonly or easily observed . . . And whoever observes upon the best India gowns,
or the painting upon their best screens or porcelains, will find
their beauty in all of this kind (that is) without order." [75]
Temple, unlike Addison, considers this "disorder" under the
category of beauty, emphasizing the fact that order and harmony are obscured in, not absent from, the artificial naturalness
of the Chinese garden, whose style is so difficult to imitate that
Temple discourages any English attempts to do so. Addison,
by removing this naturalness from the realm of the beautiful,
strikes upon the similarity between the artificial naturalness of

[71] Leonard Welsted, ed., The Works of Dionysius Longinus, p. 107. Welsted
most succinctly summarizes Addison's position: "To excel in other respects, is
Human; in the Sublime, God like: All that is gain'd by not committing Faults,
is freedom from blame; but the Sublime creates Admiration . . ."

[72] Addison, "To Mr. Dryden," Works, I, 1–2.

[73] To William Congreve, Blois, December 1699, Letters, pp. 10–11.

[74] Alexander Pope, Poems (Twickenham ed.), III, Pt. 2, p. 137 n. See Addison,
T. 161; S. 412, 414, 477. Pope, G. 173, "Epistle to Burlington," lines 47–98.

[75] Sir William Temple, Works (1757), III, 229–230; quoted by A. O. Lovejoy,
"The Chinese Origin of a Romanticism," Essays in the History of Ideas, p. 111.
See B. S. Allen, Tides in English Taste, II, 116 ff.

these gardens and the sublimity of physical nature, which it imitates (*S.* 414).[76]

Temple's preference for Oriental designs and paintings comes closest to the real source of this aspect of English taste for the diffuseness and greatness which are found in the imitations of natural wildness. Few Englishmen had seen Chinese gardens or had even read descriptions of them, but from the 1670's Oriental designs were to be found everywhere, on fabrics, porcelain, screens, and on English silver. "For the first time in European history clay was held in as high estimation as silver, and the smith accepted his designs from the potter. In England, where this tendency was most strongly felt, silver was engraved with designs in the Chinese taste at least as early as 1670."[77] B. S. Allen notes the unsymmetrical designs of the polychrome porcelains, often embellished with misshapen trunks, with an equilibrium of color masses, however. "But such nice balance did not compensate for the absence of perspective and proportion in the representation of landscapes."[78] These designs gained even wider circulation in fabrics used in gowns and draperies,[79] providing English audiences with representations of "natural" landscapes which were only beginning to become popular among European painters.

These seemingly isolated events in the history of English taste—the rise of the natural garden, the vogue of Oriental designs, the trend away from "ideal" landscape painting—are part of the movement away from beauty, the harmony of form, as the value *par excellence* of art. Although examples of "natural" landscapes may be found among the works of Titian, Tintoretto, and Rubens,[80] they are isolated works among the

[76] A. O. Lovejoy, *Essays in the History of Ideas*, p. 115.

[77] Joan Evans, *Pattern: A Study of Ornament in Western Europe from 1180–1900*, II, 67.

[78] B. S. Allen, II, 198. See Plate 40, facing p. 179.

[79] *Ibid.*, I, 220–222. See "Curtain of English embroidery in the Oriental Style," Plate 336, facing p. 64, in Joan Evans, *Pattern*. The curtain is dominated by a central tree, with a profusion of plants and animals about this vertical axis. There are rocks in the foreground, but the foliage runs to the other three edges.

[80] B. S. Allen, I, 119, cites the following examples of "natural" landscape which

many "ideal" landscapes produced during the seventeenth century. Titian's landscapes and engraved copies of them by Battista Pettoni Vincentino (1520–1584) and Angelo del Moro (*fl.* 1550) were well known in England and were praised by men whose artistic ideals were represented in the concept of beauty.[81] But paintings of irregular Nature were rare. Poussin and Salvator Rosa were among the few who painted landscapes of predominantly mountain scenes.[82] The great majority of the other landscapes were either "ideal" or topographical in their treatment. "The mood which most of these topographical landscapes evoke as a result of their esthetic qualities is basically the mood of diffused well-being which dominates ideal landscape." [83] Adrian van Dust's *Mountain Landscape* is one of the few paintings of the period to capture the mountain horror felt by Burnet, Dennis, and Addison.[84]

The slowness of the response of European painters to the claims of the greatness of Nature is to be explained largely by the fact that the taste for the natural sublime had its origins in England, where the native painters followed the fashions set by the more popular continental artists and critics, who defined beauty in geometrical terms,[85] just as the gardeners, their followers, had. When Addison wrote that the works of Nature are vaster than those of art (S. 414) , he was not only affirming the

appeared before *Paradise Lost:* Titian, *The Original Sin* (Prado) ; Tintoretto, *Adam and Eve* (Academy, Venice) ; Domenichino, *The Original Sin* (Palazzo Barberini, Rome) ; Rubens and Jan Breughel, *Garden of Eden* (Mauretshuis, The Hague) .

[81] Henry S. V. Ogden and Margaret S. Ogden, *English Taste in Landscape in the Seventeenth Century,* p. 104. See John Evelyn, *Sculptura; or the History and Art of Chalcography and Engraving in Copper,* ed. C. F. Bell, p. 50; Roger de Piles, *L'Art de peinture* (1673) .

[82] Ogden and Ogden, p. 140.

[83] *Ibid.,* p. 163.

[84] *Ibid.,* p. 146, Plate 69. See Elizabeth W. Mainwaring, *Italian Landscape in Eighteenth Century England: A Study Chiefly of the Influence of Claude Lorrain and Salvator Rosa on English Taste, 1700–1800,* pp. 96–97; C. V. Deane, *Aspects of Eighteenth Century Nature Poetry,* pp. 64 ff.

[85] Christopher Wren, *Parentalia: or Memoirs of the Family of the Wrens . . . chiefly of Sir Christopher Wren . . . In which is contained, besides his Works, A great Number of Original Papers and Records . . . Compiled by his Son Christopher,* p. 351; Roland Fréart, *An Idea of the Perfection of Painting . . . ,* pp. 4, 40 ff.; C. A. Dufresnoy, *The Art of Painting,* trans. John Dryden, pp. 7, 25.

superiority of Nature to art in this respect; he was also commenting, implicitly, upon the contemporary situation in European art, which presented so few representations of natural sublimity that he had to seek his ideal landscape in the Chinese garden. Because painting lacked that in which Nature was bountiful, *greatness*, Addison took his examples for the second pleasure of the imagination from nature, rather than from art.

Pastorals and Politics

> Your tragick Heroes shall not rant,
> Nor Shepherds use *poetick Cant:*
> Simplicity alone can grace,
> The Manners of the rural Race,
> *Theocritus* and *Philips* be,
> Your guides to *true* Simplicity.
>
> Swift, *Apollo's Edict* (1721).

WHEN AN anonymous writer for *The Lay Monk* described the pastoral as the poetic form of landscape painting,[1] he was particularizing the familiar belief that poetry and painting are sister arts whose affinity is greater than that between poetry and music, an art containing only a harmony of formal relationships without any reference to external nature or moral truth. "As moral truth is the conformity between our Thoughts and Assertions, so the Truth of Painting is founded in the Similitude between the Picture, and the Exemplar in the Mind of the Artist, where it is first imagin'd, and has an Ideal Existence previous to that on Canvas . . . The Painter is a Poet to the Eye, and the Poet is a Painter to the Ear." The end of both arts is to

---

[1] *The Lay Monk,* No. 30 (January 25, 1714) .

"For, as in Painting, so I believe, in Poetry, the Country affords the most Entertaining Scenes, and most delightful Prospects" (Ambrose Philips, *Poems,* ed. M. G. Segar, p. 3) .

On Horace's *ut pictura poesis,* Jean Hagstrum, *The Sister Arts: The Tradition of Literary Pictorialism and English Poetry from Dryden to Gray* (Chicago, 1958) ; Rensselaer W. Lee, "*Ut pictura poesis:* The Humanistic Theory of Painting," *Art Bulletin,* XXII (1940) , 197–269; Addison, *Works,* I, 140.

move the passions, "inspire generous Sentiments, and to convey to the Mind Moral and Divine Instruction." [2] *Enargeia* was thought of as a quality peculiar to those arts which "illuminated" nature through the embodiment of the values of harmony, order, and proportion.[3] The printed poem and the painted canvas are evaluated upon the degree of faithfulness with which they reproduce the "Exemplar in the Mind," the poet's or painter's conception of his subject as ideal Nature or essence.

This view of the relationship between the artist and nature was especially suited to pastoral poetry. The satirist and the comedian could belittle the follies of human life, but in doing so they had to represent this life. The elegist and the tragedian, though they were devoted to elevating real human nature, drew their subjects from "men like ourselves." The pastoral poet sought neither the end nor the materials for his art in contemporary life. Pastoral poems from Theocritus to Ambrose Philips are idealizations of the life which they portray. Even the realistic descriptions of rustic life in Theocritus's idylls had given way to the more generalized ones in the eclogues of the Virgilian school, which fused the two ideals of the pastoral life and the Golden Age. "Virgil's new conception of the pastoral poem was actually nothing more than the fusion of his own wish-fulfillment dream of peace with the propaganda for a policy for appeasement." [4]

From a sociological point of view Arnold Hauser's analysis of the appeal of the pastoral modes in art is very much to the point. Addison's Europe, torn by two wars, and feeling the first pains of growing commercial strife, found solace in visions of

[2] *The Lay Monk*, No. 30 (January 25, 1714); No. 32 (January 27, 1714). See Roland Fréart, *The Idea of the Perfection of Painting*, p. 3; Dryden, *Essays*, II, 137. On the influence of neo-Platonism upon the idea that genius in painting is a gift of God, see R. W. Lee, pp. 220–221.

[3] Rosamund Tuve, *Elizabethan and Metaphysical Imagery*, p. 29: "This resultant 'light' is simply that 'illumination'—revealing harmony, order, proportion —which had been indicated time out of mind as an attribute of works of art achieving formal excellence, by Cicero, by Augustine, by Aquinas."

[4] Arnold Hauser, *The Social History of Art*, II, 517.

rustic peace and simplicity provided by pastoral art and poetry. Watteau's paintings of rural life, dominated by figures of courtiers in modern dress, are parallel to the world of Pope's *Rape of the Lock*. Both portray social ideals which are designed "to keep love at a distance, to divest it of its directness and passionateness." [5] The harmony of social motive and aesthetic mode ceased to be universal, however, long before the pastoral's decline as a popular literary form in England. And the change in poetic form, unaccompanied by a corresponding shift in pastoral social values, cannot be explained in terms of the transformation of mores during the eighteenth century.

Undoubtedly, *le beau monde* was not everywhere admired by English men of letters. The *Tatler* and the *Spectator,* as well as *The Rape of the Lock* and the first book of *Gulliver's Travels,* are aimed, at least in part, at the follies of court life. But this is not the life depicted by pastoral poets, who admired the life of the Golden Age of Greece or England, but had few illusions about living in it.[6] The debate between Alexander Pope and Ambrose Philips about the superiority of Virgil's or Theocritus's pastorals did not call into question the values of naturalness and simplicity, the values *par excellence* of the Golden Age. But the defenders of the idylls of Theocritus and the eclogues of Spenser did not agree that the names, language, and descriptions of Virgil's pastorals were proper vehicles for conveying these values in English poetry. Unlike the Virgilians, who maintained their position from a definition of the pastoral as a genre, Ambrose Philips, Addison, and Thomas Tickell argued that the representation of nature by the imitators of Virgil did not produce the effects which both parties agreed were valuable. The fundamental disagreement was not over the ends of this genre, but over the means by which they could be most readily achieved.

[5] *Ibid.*, II, 521.

[6] The compilers of the *Athenian Gazette,* XI (1693), 25, admirably expressed educated opinion on this subject:
"*Q. Whether this ben't the Golden Age?*
A. Not with us; We don't know what it may be with you."

I

The French critics, here as elsewhere, are the fathers of debates which occupied the center of the English literary stage. Rapin had based his pastoral criticism upon classical practice, noticing especially that heroic numbers are best for this genre because Virgil used no others.[7] He hesitates about defining the nature of this genre, because neither Aristotle nor Horace had offered precedents for pastoral criticism. "And I am of the opinion that none can treat well and clearly of any kind of poetry if he hath not helps from these two."[8] Having only poetic examples to guide him, Rapin finds his models in the decorous simplicity of the shepherd of the Golden Age. The filthy goatherd of Theocritus, who is too close to the real shepherds of the seventeenth century, is not a fit subject for poetic representation.[9]

Fontenelle, however, places less emphasis upon the pastoral as a depiction of the Golden Age than upon the primitiveness, leisure, and tranquility of the lives of the early shepherds. The shepherds of the second age of man are the products of a perverted time, and they produced a homely, artless poetry. "And indeed nothing is more certain, than that no real Shepherds could be like those of Theocritus."[10] Fontenelle's praise of Theocritus is qualified in his objections to the depths to which Theocritus occasionally took his art, especially when he had a shepherd yearning to be a goat when he saw them copulating.[11] By making his shepherds more polite and agreeable, Virgil surpassed his model.

Fontenelle's pastoral theory differs from Rapin's, first, in the former's greater concern with the affective workings of the

[7] J. E. Congleton, *Theories of Pastoral Poetry in England, 1684–1798*, pp. 53–54, 61. See René Rapin, "A Treatise de Carmine Pastorale," *Idylliums of Theocritus*, trans. Thomas Creech (Oxford, 1684). For the influence of Rapin on Pope, see Émile Audra, *L'Influence française dans l'oeuvre de Pope*, p. 168.

[8] Rapin, p. 16.

[9] *Ibid.*, pp. 25–26, 33.

[10] Bernard Fontenelle, "A Treatise of Pastorals," in Le Bossu, *Treatise of the Epick Poem*, II, 317.

[11] *Ibid.*, II, 319. See II, 320–321, 322.

pastoral art. He praises the idea of quietness as the pastoral ideal. The two strongest passions of the pastoral life are laziness and love: "what makes this kind of Poetry please, is the Idea which it gives of the Tranquility and Innocence of that Life." [12] Although Fontenelle agrees with Rapin that the vulgarity and misery of real country life are unfit subjects for pastoral poetry, he does not defend this position by arguing from the example of Virgil or the ideal of pastoral as representation of the Golden Age, but from the fact that the inclusion of pastoral misery or vulgarity prevents the poet from arousing the passions of laziness and innocent love. Fontenelle thinks this argument from effect strong enough to apply it with equal force to both Theocritus and Virgil, condemning both of them when they step beyond the bounds of pastoral decorum to imitate the lives of real shepherds or to reach above these lives to depict gentlemen in language appropriate only to heroic poetry.[13]

J. E. Congleton has characterized the English followers of Rapin as "neo-classical" critics of the pastoral and the followers of Fontenelle as "rationalistic" critics.[14] Insofar as this division is used to describe the difference between the methods of approach used by these two groups, Professor Congleton's analysis tends to be misleading. Although the battle of the ancients and the moderns figures in the debate over pastoral poetry,[15] it is not the central issue which divides the two camps. Rapin does not defend Virgil's eclogues because they are ancient, but because they best exemplify his conception of the pastoral as a representation of the Golden Age. Rapin's argument is typical of the rationalistic neoclassical criticism of the last half of the seventeenth century.[16] This type of argument, moving from the definition of the genre to a consideration of individual speci-

---

[12] *Ibid.*, II, 328. See II, 324–326.

[13] *Ibid.*, II, 351.

[14] Congleton, *Theories of Pastoral Poetry*, p. 75; see his "Theories of Pastoral Poetry in England, 1684–1717," *SP*, XLI (1944), 544–575. Professor Congleton modifies his judgment of Rapin as an authoritarian critic by placing him in the "School of Sense" (*Theories of Pastoral Poetry*, p. 53).

[15] Congleton, *Theories of Pastoral Poetry*, p. 53.

[16] See above, p. 32.

mens of it, is an example of deductive reasoning in the most literal sense of that term; ". . . as a result of their deductively rather than empirically constructed aesthetics they [the neoclassicists] recognized only one acceptable kind of artistry for each genre." [17]

The followers of Fontenelle, rather than being rationalistic in their pastoral theory, are inductive and empirical. It is certainly true that Fontenelle advances the supremacy of reason, not authority, on the assumption that man's reason is not decayed,[18] but an adherence to faith in reason does not distinguish Fontenelle's argument from that of his opponents; Rapin and, later, Chetwood, Pope, and Gay are no less convinced of the rational basis of their own criticism. Fontenelle, Addison, and Ambrose Philips, by arguing affectively, reject the deductive argument from the definition of "genre" for one which sets the value of individual examples of the genre in terms of their ability to arouse the pastoral passions.[19]

Two distinct external influences made themselves felt in this aspect of neoclassical criticism. The first is the general influence of Cartesian psychology in France and Hobbesian and Lockean psychology in England, which led to a closer inspection of the relationship between the nature of the human mind and its affective workings in literature.[20] The second and more specific source is the inductive "method" of argument developed by the natural philosophers and popularized in nonscientific circles by the Whig politicians. When Addison censured Virgil's eclogues because they contain "a purity of style as is not entirely agreeable with the dialect of shepherds; and

[17] Earl R. Wasserman, *Elizabethan Poetry in the Eighteenth Century*, p. 49.

[18] Congleton, *SP*, XLI (1944), 549. See above, Note 13.

[19] Congleton, *Theories of Pastoral Poetry*, notes that Fontenelle's criticism is rationalistic and subjective (p. 66) and later adds that "his only criterion is subjective" (p. 70).

[20] See *The Works of Thomas Purney*, ed. H. O. White, p. 1. Professor White notes that Purney took the cue for his psychological treatment of literary problems from Addison's *Spectators* (*ibid.*, p. 2). See above, Chapter 1, Note 19. Because the influence of contemporary psychology upon early eighteenth-century criticism extends beyond pastoral theory, the discussion of this aspect of Addison's cultural milieu will be discussed in the following two chapters.

frequently the dignity of his verse is in no way consonant with the rural pipe," [21] his comment would have been appropriate to either Rapin or Fontenelle. The next year he laid down the principles which were to become the basis of his and Ambrose Philips's pastoral criticism in the decade to come. "Theocritus and Homer have still disputed for the advantage over him [Virgil] in pastoral and heroics . . . The truth of it is, the sweetness and rusticity of a pastoral cannot be so well expressed in any other language as in Greek." [22] This theme is later picked up and expanded by Philips in the preface to his own pastorals:

> *Gassendus, I remember, tells us,* that Piereskius *was a great lover of Musick, especially that of Birds; because their artless Strains seem to have less of Passion and Violence, but more of a natural Easiness, and therefore do they befriend Contemplation. This after the same manner that* Pastoral *gives us a sweet and gentle Composure to the Mind; whereas the* Epick *and* Tragick *Poem put the Spirits in too great Ferment by the Vehemence of their Motions.*
>
> *To see a stately, well-built Palace strikes us, indeed, with Notions of Grandeur. But when I view a Country Dwelling, advantageously situated amidst a beautiful Variety of Fields, Woods, and Rivers, I feel an unspeakable kind of Satisfaction, and cannot forebear wishing, that my good Fortune would place me in so sweet a retirement.*[23]

In both of these statements the critics have based their judgments upon their own responses to pastoral poems or scenes, using the ability of the pastoral to elicit a subjective response or express pastoral emotion as a criterion for objective evaluation.

There are two reasons for characterizing the inductive approach to pastoral criticism as a phase of "Whig" aesthetics. In

---

[21] Addison, *Works,* VI, 588.

[22] Addison, *Works,* I, 154.

[23] Ambrose Philips, *Poems,* p. 3. Addison wrote to Philips on March 10, 1704: "Your first pastoral is very much esteemed by all I have shown it to tho the best Judges are of Opinion you should only Imitate Spencer in his beautys and never in the Rhime of the Verse for there they think it looks more like a Bodge than an Imitation . . . I am wonderfully pleas'd with your little Essay of Pastoral in your Last, and think you very Just in the Theory as well as in the practical part" (*Letters,* p. 49).

England the development of this form of analysis outside of the sciences is peculiar to those men whose political leanings were Whiggish. Secondly, the debate between the inductive and deductive pastoral critics is parallel in method to the contemporaneous one being waged between Tory and Whig politicians.[24]

The more common practice has been to identify "Whig" aesthetics with particular issues in both politics and criticism. The Tories were identified with a defense of the *status quo* and security, and the Whigs with "progress and an expanding future," which the Tories held to be an argument for excessive irregularity.[25] Evidence of the dangers implicit in this application of party names to critical positions in the late seventeenth and early eighteenth centuries is supplied by Professor Kliger himself.[26] By 1710 many Whig doctrines had been adopted by the Tories. Both Dryden and Pope held French tyranny in contempt. With all of their Tory leanings, they accepted the superiority of English freedom to continental absolutism as the foundation of English greatness. And both men were instrumental in helping to liberalize and rationalize the hold of the rules upon English criticism.[27]

[24] There is no one-to-one correspondence between political Toryism and deductive aesthetics or between Whiggery and inductive aesthetics. Of the men Professor Congleton lists as "neo-classical" pastoral critics (*Theory of Pastoral Poetry*, p. 75) Chetwood, Gay, and Pope are Tories; Temple, Walsh, and Congreve are Whigs. Swift and Parnell switched parties. All of the men Congleton lists as "rationalistic" critics (Addison, Ambrose Philips, de la Roche, Tickell, Purney, Dennis, Thomas Pope Blount, and St. Évremond) were Whigs or had Whig leanings. Certainly, it is possible to divorce one's literary thinking from one's political thinking, but it is curious that there are no avowed Tories among the inductive pastoral critics. It is not being suggested here that the political debates determined the outcome of parliamentary voting; see Robert Walcott, *English Politics in the Early Eighteenth Century*. Members of Parliament were rarely influenced by London political debates and party tags.

[25] Samuel Kliger, "Whig Aesthetics: A Phase of Eighteenth-Century Taste," *ELH*, XVI (1949), 135–150; "The Goths in England: An Introduction to the Gothic Vogue in Eighteenth Century Aesthetic Discussion," *MP*, XLIII (1945), 107–117. On "Whig" aesthetics and relativism, see Wellek, *History of Modern Criticism*, pp. 24–25.

[26] In the articles cited above Professor Kliger is primarily concerned with "Whig" aesthetics during the middle of the eighteenth century. He discusses earlier critics by way of introduction.

[27] Kliger, *ELH*, XVI (1949), 144–145, 148. See Sir William Temple, *CESC*, III,

Although it would be foolhardy to minimize the differences between Whigs and Tories on political issues, these issues, Popery and the Junto, and a National Mortgage,[28] cannot be clearly related to the problems of literary criticism. Tory opponents of rebellion in England frequently found support among the Whigs, including Addison, who used what had been a Tory argument to defend the Hanoverian dynasty, at the same time that he attacked the Pretender and the Pope.[29] This pattern of crossing party lines in key issues is prominent enough to make the use of differences of opinion on general political questions an uncertain guide to the definition of Tory or Whig aesthetics.[30]

The reasons for the inadequacy of such a definition lie in the nature of party divisions in England during the early years of the eighteenth century. Not only were the issues which gave rise to the party divisions no longer as clearly defined as they had been during the last quarter of the preceding century, the desire for moderation tended to curb the party instinct and impel leading politicians and diplomats to abjure the party

---

104, who ascribes the multiplicity of English humors to English freedom and describes the effects of tyranny upon comedy.

The Whigs frequently made use of the identification of the Tories with the Jacobite cause and Romanism in literary as well as political debates, as Oldmixon does in his reply to Swift's *Proposal for correcting, improving and ascertaining the English Tongue.* Swift wanted Harley and the Tory Party to get credit for the project, to which Oldmixon replied: " 'Tis amazing that he shou'd be so foolish as to fancy, that Learning which always goes by the Stile of Commonwealth, would submit to the Arbitrary Government of an Ignorant and Tyrannical Faction." "Reflections on *Dr. Swift's Letter to Harley*" (1712) , pp. 6–7. Both Oldmixon and Mainwaring (*The British Academy, ibid.*) hoped to kill the plan by associating it with the French Academy and its absolutism. The Tories, however, were conscious of the value of the word "liberty" and held that it was not the exclusive property of the Whigs. See *Mr. Addison turn'd Tory* . . . , pp. 6, 21.

Addison's objections to religious and political tyranny in France and Italy may be found in *Letters*, pp. 12–13, 14–15; *Works*, I, 35, 362–363, 390, 420–421, 428. See Smithers, pp. 54–55, 62–63; Audra, p. 37.

28 *The Examiner*, No. 27 (March 1, 1714) .

29 Addison, *Freeholder* 12, in *Works*, IV, 443–444, 446.

30 Matthew Prior, who combined a life of letters with diplomacy within the Tory ranks, wrote a verse epistle to Boileau after the British victory at Blenheim, condemning that poet's servile devotion to the French king. *Works*, ed. A. R. Waller, I, 125–126.

label. In spite of all the name-calling by both factions, party lines and issues were no longer the strong rallying points which they had been during the reign of William III. Harley was closer to Addison in his political beliefs than he was to the more conservative members of his own party. The identity of interest of the crown and the bishops was felt by the Tory Party, but Addison, the Whig, thought that "an honest Englishman is a Tory in Church matters and a Whig in politics." [31] Jacobitism widened the split in the Tory camp, which already harbored men who had joined the cause for a variety of reasons, many unrelated to the defense of the royal prerogative. The fall of the Earl of Clarendon was, indeed, the end of the old order of Tories.[32] "From the fall, as King James II wrote, 'one may date the beginning of all the misfortunes, which happened since, and the decay of the authority of the Crown; he generally supported the prerogative, which his successors never minded.' " [33] Only the most reactionary Tories had failed to become constitutionalists by the beginning of the eighteenth century. William, the Whig king, promoted a policy of moderation which made Royalists of the Whigs and drew support from the "modern" Tories who no longer seriously espoused the claims of James II.[34]

It was in this sense that Addison and his contemporaries in both parties found labels misleading. These labels had lost their original meaning and were used chiefly to arouse "cabal and faction." [35] The *Tatler* and the *Spectator* were successful

[31] Smithers, p. 28. See pp. vi–vii, where Smithers argues that Addison's biographers have been too preoccupied with Addison as a man of letters though Addison saw himself primarily as a political figure.

The low opinion of party politics was common throughout the first half of the eighteenth century. "A party he [Lord Halifax] judged to be at best a kind of conspiracy against the rest of the nation, and party-discipline he felt to be incompatible with the liberty of private opinion. This low estimate of political parties was typical until the publication of Burke's *Present Discontents* in 1770" (George H. Sabine, *History of Political Theory*, p. 522).

[32] Keith Feiling, *A History of the Tory Party, 1640–1714*, p. 45.

[33] *Ibid.*, p. 122. Quotation from James II is taken from James Macpherson, *Original Papers containing the Secret History of Great Britain*, I, 39.

[34] *Ibid.*, p. 275.

[35] *The Observator*, VII, No. 11 (March 24, 1708); see No. 23 (May 1, 1708); *Mercurius Reformatus*, II, No. 23 (May 14, 1690); *The Examiner* 44 (May 31,

not because they were apolitical, but because Steele and Addison disguised their moderate Whig position in allegory and fable or presented Whig programs in ostensibly nonpartisan essays. In this manner they were able to support the Junto while addressing an audience much larger than party loyalty commanded. At the same time, no reader who came to know Sir Roger de Coverley was tempted to think that the business of national government would be safe in the Tory squire's hands.[36] This indirect method of defending Whig principles, stripped of its literary dress, is derived from a Whig theory of government, however, and is to be found fully clothed in Addison's political tracts and in periodicals which appeared before and after he wrote for the more nearly nonpartisan *Tatler* and *Spectator*.[37]

It was the good fortune of Addison and the Whig faction to have Halifax and Locke to draw upon for their political theory.

1711) ; *The Entertainer* 5 (Dec. 4, 1717). *The Observator*, a Whig paper, identified British virtue with Whig principles, but admitted the common Tory complaint that the Whigs wished to load the House of Commons with pensioners and officers: "For he that acts contrary to *Magna Charta,* and *British* Liberty in any Thing, may call himself what he pleases; but in so far he is certainly a Tory, according to the true Meaning of that Word, and the Nature of the Thing; and he that acts for our fundamental Constitution, and does what tends to support it, may be call'd a Tory a thousand Times; but so far he is certainly a Whig, and deserves the Countenance and Approbation of all true Patriots." These are principles which most Tories, except Jacobites, supported. In this sense, A. de Grisy is closest to the truth when he wrote that most Englishmen of this period were Whigs at heart (*Joseph Addison, ou un Attique en Angleterre,* p. 32) .

[36] See Calhoun Winton, "Steele, the Junto and *The Tatler* No. 4," *MLN,* LXXII (1957) , 178–182; A. de Grisy, pp. 26–27; Alexandre Beljame, *Men of Letters and the English Public in the Eighteenth Century 1660–1744, Dryden, Addison, Pope,* ed. Bonamy Dobrée, trans. E. O. Lorimer, pp. 264–265, 277. Beljame denies that the *Spectator* is a partisan paper.

Addison upholds his moderate position even in *The Freeholder* (No. 34) , arguing against political parties and extremists in both camps. He was especially concerned about the mixture of literature and politics. See Addison's advice to Pope, in Spence, *Anecdotes,* p. 7; and in his *Letters,* p. 281.

The English newspapers and periodicals took up the cause of moderation as the way to truth (as *via media*) and as the best defense of the national welfare before the first *Tatler* was published. See *HWL,* III (February, 1701) , 105; Defoe, *Review,* II, 19, and III, 23; *Monthly Miscellany,* II (March, 1708) , 84. Thirteen months after the appearance of the first *Tatler,* the first *Moderator* (May 22, 1710) arrived on the scene, claiming that Defoe's *Review* and *The Observator* were not truly moderate papers.

[37] See Smithers, pp. 208–209.

"Nothing is clearer in the political thought of Halifax and Locke than the recession of doctrinal and ecclesiastical questions from the position of dominant interest which they had held." [38] The effect of these questions upon Tory political thought was to make them defend their view of government by deducing their aims from their conception of the nature of government and its relationship to the church.[39] The Whigs were more immediately concerned with questions about the practical functions and effects of government, as the "Whig" critics were to argue about the proper activity of the pastoral poet rather than the nature of pastoral poetry. Neither the true critic nor the true citizen entirely neglects the nature of the object of his inquiry and the need for rational order, but both must base their judgments upon palpable observations as well as upon established rules.

Those who set up for Criticks in Poetry, and are met with in ordinary Conversation, may be reduced to two Classes; such as judge by *Rule,* or such as judge by *Nature.* The first are Men of little or no Taste, who having read over the Mechanical Rules, and learned a few Terms of Art, are able to point out palpable Faults or Beauties in an Author, and thereby gain a Reputation for *Learning.* The others are generally Talkers, of glittering Fancies, and hurried Imaginations; who despise Art and Method, who admire what was never said before, and affect the Character of *Wits* . . .

To conclude this Comparison: the cautious Critics are like the Subjects of an Arbitrary Prince; and the Licentious are in a State of barbarous Anarchy; but the free Critick, like a free *Briton,* is governed by the Laws which he himself votes for; whose Liberty is checked by the Restraints of Truth, and the Monarchy of right Reason.[40]

The judge by rule believes nothing but his own rules; the judge by nature observes everything, but orders none of his experiences.

[38] George H. Sabine, p. 518.

[39] See *The Examiner* 9 (Sept. 28, 1710), for a typical early eighteenth-century moderate Tory defense of divine- as opposed to inalienable-rights theory as it applied to the Jacobite controversy.

[40] Sir Richard Steele, *The Englishman,* pp. 30–31.

The Whigs, because their political and economic aspirations were tied to an expanding Britain, were more inclined to base their political arguments upon their commercial and legal interests, which they identified with the national good, than upon established legal and theological principles. On the tariff issue Addison embodies the Whig interests in Goodman Fact, a plain-spoken Englishman, who opposes the French fop, Count Tariff. Goodman wears homespun clothes and possesses natural eloquence, both of which are superior to Latin and brocade.[41] The objections to French religion and tyranny are subordinated to the objection that French commercial interests are seriously conflicting with English ones.[42] The Tories blame "Lady Credit" for betraying Charles II, but they never directly relate their political theory to immediate English commercial and political interests.[43] The Whigs not only made their theory fit their interests, but they also equated these interests with empirically verifiable facts.[44]

The identification of Whig interests with that which could be confirmed by observations of nature had consequences which influenced the entire Whig political theory and extended beyond that realm into the world of poetry. Addison did not attempt to refute divine-right theory by showing its logical weaknesses, but reduced the controversy to statements of conflicting states of affairs. " 'Whether they would be governed by a prince that is obliged by laws to be good and gracious, just and upright, a friend, a father, and a defender of his people; or by one who, if he pleases, may drive away or plunder, imprison or kill, without opposition or resistance.' This is the true state of the controversy relating to passive obedience and non-resistance."[45]

[41] Addison, *Works*, IV, 364.
[42] Addison, *Works*, IV, 341–342, 343.
[43] *The Moderator* 28 (August 25, 1710).
[44] *The Whig-Examiner* 1 (September 14, 1710). See Edward A. Bloom and Lillian D. Bloom, "Joseph Addison and Eighteenth-Century 'Liberalism'," *JHI*, XII (1951), 560–583. Addison's later political writings are much less moderate than his *Spectator* papers; see *Freeholder* 22. On foreign trade and parliamentary elections, see Steele's *The Englishman*, p. 407 n.
[45] *Whig-Examiner* 5 (October 12, 1710). See G. M. Trevelyan, *The Peace and the Protestant Succession*, pp. 47 ff., 101; Edward and Lillian Bloom, *JHI*, XII

The intellectual frame of mind which conceives of its values as the resolution of conflicting factual situations rather than deductions from *a priori* principles, even when these conflicting "facts" are rationalizations of Whig interests, is suited for a scientific world-view, one which posits nature as empirical reality as its norm, replacing the older view of the closed universe of the microcosm-macrocosm analogy and Nature as essence or Platonic ideal. In literary criticism, the nonempirical conception of Nature did not lose its appeal, even among the "Whig" critics. But the conflict between the proponents of Virgil's and Theocritus's pastorals is founded, in large part, upon two distinct views of Nature, the ideal and the empirical.

II

The six papers on pastorals in the *Guardian* are the epitome of English debate on the subject during the opening years of the eighteenth century.[46] Ambrose Philips, had he read Pope's eclogues more carefully, would not have been surprised when he discovered that *Guardian* 40 was a parody of his own pastorals, rather than a serious exposition of his theory. But even an earlier awareness of Pope's intent would not have calmed the members of the "Little Senate" at Button's.[47] Pope and Gay had followed Rapin in setting the pastoral ideal in the Golden Age, denying that modern times provide fit subjects for pastoral poetry.[48] Descriptions of rustic life are rare and there is little action in the pastorals of Virgil and Pope.[49] In this respect, Pope stood at the end of the line of Virgilian pastoral

(1951), 565. Addison, while he sat in the House of Commons, voted with his party for Sacheverall's impeachment ([Abel Boyer], *History of the Reign of Queen Anne, Digested into Annals*, VIII, Appendix, 171. See account of the trial on pages 217–335 of text).

[46] G. 22, 23, 28, 30, 32, 40. The last paper is by Alexander Pope. The others are usually attributed to Addison's protégé Thomas Tickell, but there is no conclusive evidence of his authorship. See Congleton, *Theories of Pastoral Poetry*, p. 87 n.; J. E. Brett, "Notes for a Bibliography of Thomas Tickell," *Bodleian Quarterly Record*, V (1928), 302.

[47] Bonamy Dobrée, *Essays in Biography: 1680–1726*, pp. 269 ff.

[48] Congleton, *SP*, XLI (1944), 545–547.

[49] R. F. Jones, "Eclogue Types in English Poetry of the Eighteenth Century," *JEGP*, XXIV (1925), 35, 38.

criticism which emphasized the moral and allegorical elements of pastoral poetry at the expense of description.[50]

Ambrose Philips's imitation of the rusticity of description and diction of Theocritus's and Spenser's pastorals does not presuppose a denial of the neoclassical values of decorum and delightful instruction, but a desire "to describe nature more simply and factually and therefore somewhat more effectively than did many of his fellow pastoralists, who most frequently set their scenes in a golden age of bucolic gentility." [51] Throughout Pope's poetry we find generalized descriptions of Nature which correspond to his belief that "the first Rule of Pastoral [is] that its Idea should be taken from the Manners of the *Golden Age,* and the Moral form'd upon the Representation of Innocence . . ." (G. 40).[52] He parodies Ambrose Philips's use of English names, native flowers, and foreign animals in a mock effort to show that Philips comes closer to Pope's definition of the pastoral than even Theocritus and Virgil do.

Pope's most important objection to Philips's eclogues is only partially indicated in his sniping at details and inconsistencies. What disturbs Pope most is the "beautiful rusticity" of these poems (G. 40). "As there is a difference betwixt simplicity and rusticity, so the expression of simple thought should be plain, but not clownish." [53] That is, they should not imitate the manners, thoughts, and archaic language of Edmund Spenser. This English pastoralist's language and characters betray a want of innocent simplicity which is essential to the thought and pure diction of ideal pastoral life. The eclogue should appear to be the shepherd's own poem, but the poem of a shepherd who finds his pastoral existence his recreation, not his business.[54]

---

[50] See Congleton, *Theories of Pastoral Poetry,* p. 16 ff., for the history of Renaissance pastoral criticism.

[51] E. R. Wasserman, *Elizabethan Poetry in the Eighteenth Century,* p. 143. See C. V. Deane, *Aspects of Eighteenth Century Nature Poetry,* pp. 120–121.

[52] See Pope, "Discourse on Pastoral Poetry," *Prose Works* (1936), I, 297–299.

[53] *Ibid.,* I, 301. See Spenser's Epistle to Gabriel Harvey, *The Shepheardes Calender,* in which he offers as part of his aim the desire to imitate "rustical rudeness"; and John Hughes's edition of *The Works of Mr. Edmund Spenser,* I, xcix (cited by Wasserman, *Elizabethan Poetry,* p. 141).

[54] *Ibid.,* I, 198.

The conflicting attitudes toward the representation of empirical nature which divide the two pastoral camps have their source in two equally incompatible conceptions of the relationship between nature and the divine order. Not even the most extreme Whigs would have denied that natural law is the moral law, or that the conception of natural law as nothing but a "Connexion of Causes and Effects in the Visible World" is a gross impiety.[55] The difference lies, rather, in the thinking which leads Pope to write the *Dunciad* and Addison to write "The Spacious Firmament on High." Pope's poem "celebrates" the complete collapse of physical nature in the person of Dulness, the daughter of Chaos and eternal Night.[56] The nature of physical causes is completely cut off from harmony and divine order. "The traditional view of the relation of art to nature, as enunciated by Aristotle, broadened by the late Classical rhetoricians, and developed by Christianity, preserves a distinction that is much less clear in Pope. In this view there are two levels in nature. The lower one is the ordinary physical world, which is theologically 'fallen'; the upper one is a divinely sanctioned order, existing in Eden before the Fall, and mirrored in the Classical and Boethian myth of the Golden Age." [57] The distinctions are less clear in Pope because the discovery of change in the higher Nature, the Heavens, had challenged his age's picture of the divine order. For the more philosophically optimistic, the picture was even less distinct. They could not deny the meaningfulness and value of the higher Nature, and they were constantly aware of evidence of man's fall. Yet, their belief in the new science was instrumental in raising the status of the fallen physical nature.

The optimistic solution affirmed both the ideal and the real orders of Nature. The blemishes in physical nature, like the spots in the sun and the faults of *Paradise Lost,* are real, but

[55] Sir Richard Blackmore, "An Essay upon the Laws of Nature," *Essays upon Several Subjects,* I, 359–360.

[56] George Sherburn, "Pope and 'The Great Shew of Nature'," *The Seventeenth Century: Studies in the History of English Thought from Bacon to Pope,* ed. R. F. Jones, pp. 313–314. See *Essay on Criticism,* I, 68–73, 76–77, 88–89, on ideal Nature.

[57] Northrop Frye, "Nature and Homer," *Texas Quarterly,* I (1958), 192.

insignificant in terms of the greater divine harmony.[58] Addison celebrates the metaphorical, if not the literal, truth of the musical harmony of the spheres in "The Spacious Firmament on High." The scientific and religious interest in physical nature prompted a poetic one in the form of a more accurate description of nature and a more sceptical attitude toward the guises which ideal Nature had taken in earlier critical thought. Chetwood, follower of Rapin and master to Alexander Pope, wrote that the ancient shepherd did not live the impoverished life of the modern one, "without wit, or courage, or education." [59] The pastoral in English dress, he thought, was another example of that unpardonable pride which led modern poets to make their own age the measure of all things.

The followers of Fontenelle, as Chetwood noted, did not "represent that ancient innocence, and unpracticed plainness, which was then [in the Golden Age] in the world." [60] In England the sceptical Whig pastoral theorists were possessed more of an historical than a philosophical imagination. "Thus happy was the first Race of Men, but rude withal and uncultivated" (G. 22).[61] The pastoral life had to end before there could be any progress in the arts and sciences. This account of the pastoral life permitted the advocates of Fontenelle's pastoral theory to continue in their belief that the eclogues represented a primitive stage in human history which had been surpassed by modern learning and poetry.[62] At the same time, their longing for

[58] *Dennis*, I, 73, where Dennis advises the poet to copy "Universal Nature, which is always perfect."

[59] [Knightly Chetwood], "Preface to Pastorals with a Short Defence of Virgil against the Reflections of Monsieur Fontenelle," *The Works of Virgil: Translated into English Verse by Mr. Dryden*, p. li. This preface was published anonymously in the first edition (1697), but Dryden, in a letter to Tonson, written in December, 1697, credited Chetwood with the authorship (Hugh Macdonald, *John Dryden: A Bibliography of Early Editions and of Drydeniana*, p. 57 and note).

On Chetwood's influence upon Pope's "Discourse on Pastoral Poetry," see Audra, pp. 164–173. M. Audra is ambiguous about the relationship between Pope's and Fontenelle's theories, but finally admits that there is nothing in Pope's discourse which he could not have found in Chetwood's preface.

[60] *Ibid.*, p. lxii.

[61] See above, Note 47.

[62] "I hope you will follow the example of your Spencer and Virgil in making

the plain and unadorned pastoral life remained undiminished.

It was in the search for the best means of representing this life that the Whig pastoralists parted company with Pope and Gay.[63] Servile imitation of Greek and Roman models reduces the effectiveness of English pastorals, because foreign scenery, customs, and sports, like foreign theology or mythology, cannot move English readers. The English pastoralist should find his models in his own country (G. 30). The appeal to national sentiment and, indeed, the difference between the shepherds of Alexander Pope and those of Ambrose Philips are mirrored in Addison's contrasting characters, Count Tariff and Goodman Fact, the French fop and the homespun Englishman.[64] This appeal is not expanded upon, however; instead, the author of *Guardian* 30 insists that the modern English reader will not be moved by what is strange to him. "The Reasons why such Changes from the Ancients should be introduced is very obvious; namely, that Poetry being Imitation, and that Imitation being best which deceives the most easily, it follows that we must take up the Customs which are most familiar, or universally known, since no Man can be deceived or delighted with the Imitation of what he is ignorant of." The appeal to a form of realism as a means of arousing pleasure in the reader had the same logical basis as the more general condemnation of the use of pagan characters and devices had; nothing delights and instructs as well as the truth does.[65] Classical scenery and situations, like the religions of Greece and Rome, are not only inconsistent with contemporary English beliefs and experiences, but, in the falsification of the "rudeness" of pastoral life, are untrue to that life.

The proponents of the new pastoral aesthetic, as noted earlier, did not divorce their theory from the view of Nature as ideal

---

your Pastorals the prelude of something better" (To Ambrose Philips, [12 August, 1710], Addison, *Letters*, p. 230) .

[63] See G. 40; Pope, "Discourse on Pastoral Poetry"; Gay, *The Shepherd's Week* (1714) .

[64] Addison, *Works*, IV, 364.

[65] Addison, *S.* 419. See A. O. Lovejoy, " 'Nature' as Aesthetic Norm," *Essays in the History of Ideas*, p. 74.

essence. This much is clear in both their critical writings and in the poems themselves. Fontenelle criticized the low pursuits and "clownish" postures of the characters in the idylls of Theocritus, writing that "The chief Advantage of Poetry consists in representing to us in a lively manner the things that concern us, and in striking strongly a Heart which is pleas'd with being mov'd." [66] The author of *Guardian* 22 confirms Fontenelle's judgment by writing that the poet should not discover the less pleasant aspects of country life, but should conceal part of the truth by showing the tranquility and hiding the meanness of that life. If this writer was aware that the poet is concealing elements of the literal truth, he was willing to make this concession on the grounds that he served a still higher truth, one which is more pleasing because its values, innocence and tranquility, are more important than fidelity to physical nature.

The dual standard for representation of Nature had its effect upon both the form and the content of Ambrose Philips's pastorals. And Pope, even while his relations with the "Little Senate" were good, noticed the inconsistencies of his competitor's literary practice. He praised Philips's eclogues, but noted that the fifth one is closer to the manner of Virgil than to that of Theocritus.[67] Later, when his relations with Philips were less cordial, Pope aggravated the situation by writing the fortieth *Guardian*, which exposed what he thought to be the weaknesses of Philips's theory and practice. Philips had insisted upon the use of native scenes in his pastorals, but he had wolves in one of his eclogues. He mixed simple and elevated diction on more than one occasion. The fifth pastoral, with its particularized description of the nightingale, Pope found too lofty even for his Virgilian taste.[68]

---

[66] Fontenelle, "Treatise upon Pastoral," in Le Bossu, II, 332. See the objections to the coarseness of Theocritus's pastorals in G. 28.

[67] To Thomas Cromwell, 28 October, 1710, Alexander Pope, *Correspondence*, ed. George Sherburn, I, 100.

[68] C. V. Deane, p. 124. Pope never attempted to reproduce the naturalness of description sometimes found in Philips's pastorals. See, for example, *Spring*, lines 11–16, 23–26. *Summer* and *Winter* are written after the manners of Spenser and Theocritus, respectively. See Audra, p. 177.

The "Proeme" to Gay's *Shepherd's Week* is harsher and sometimes unjust in its satire on Philips's work. *"Great* marvel hath it been (and that not unworthily) to diverse worthy wits, that in this island of Britain, in all rare sciences so greatly abounding, more especially in all kinds of poesie highly flourishing, no poet (though otherways of notable cunning in roundelays) , hath hit on the right eclogue after the true ancient guise of Theocritus, before this mine attempt." [69] The diction, alliteration, rhyme, and syntax mark even the proem as the work of a "follower" of Spenser. Not even Philips was so uncritical in his admiration of Spenser and Theocritus, especially when the latter "maketh his louts give foul language, and behold their goats at rut in all simplicity." [70] Reading the eclogues alone, we can occasionally miss Gay's satirical intent. They are "imitations" which surpass the originals. But as a satire *The Shepherd's Week* must stand as a whole work, with its remarks on the need to translate the poems into a "modern *Dialect,*" its *"glosses and explications of uncouth terms,"* and "An Alphabetical Catalogue of Names, Plants, Flowers, Fruits, Birds, Insects, and other material Things mentioned by this Author." The last item, a list of four pages, is the final show of the realistic effects of which the followers of Fontenelle were so proud.

Philips, in the revisions of his pastorals, shows that he had taken pains to achieve many of the effects which Gay satirized. The imitation of Spenserian diction is unmistakable in the first pastoral, and Pope could not have selected more appropriate lines than the ones he ridicules in the *Guardian.*

> How would my Younglins round thee gazing stand!
> Ah witless Younglins! gaze not on her Eye:
> Such heedless Glances are the Cause I die.[71]

"Lamented" in the 1708 version of this eclogue became "plain'd" in the edition of the following year. Similar changes in the diction and syntax were made in the revisions of the

[69] John Gay, *The Shepherd's Week. In Six Pastorals,* Sig. A3^r.
[70] *Ibid.,* Sig. A3^v.
[71] Ambrose Philips, "The First Pastoral," lines 88–90, *Poems* (1937) , p. 5.

second and fourth pastorals. But even here not all of the changes were made to give the poems more archaic appearances. In the eighth line of the first pastoral, the spelling of "dreery" is modernized. "Bleatings" was replaced by the more dignified "Complaints" in the twenty-eighth line of the revised second pastoral.

The new pastoral theory was, at best, a compromise which was not entirely satisfactory because it embodied values based upon two distinct, though not contradictory, ways of perceiving the external world. The older, moral order, reasoning from above, sought its vehicle in elevated diction and a distant, ideal vision of pastoral life. The proponents of the newer divinely oriented empirical order were not fully aware of the implications of their reasoning from below, from the subjective response rather than from the objective work of art or genre.[72] Even if Addison had been able to develop a coherent aesthetic and poetic theory from Cartesian or Lockean psychology, it is not likely that the pastoral poets who shared his view of the world would have come nearer to a solution of their immediate literary problems. Their break with Rapin and the French neoclassicists would have been more complete, but even then they would not have been able to justify their use of archaic diction to an age which found its poetic values so largely embodied in those pleasures which even Whig pastoralists tried to arouse, ease and simplicity.[73] The same eighteenth-century English ear which found ballads too "Gothick" for its taste was not easily moved by the "enervating" ("softening")[74] qualities of archaic diction, but by its strangeness and barbarity, which philosophizing, neither from above nor from below, could justify.

[72] Shortly after the height of the Pope-Philips controversy, Thomas Purney, an unknown and uninfluential critic, came closer to seeing the implications of Addison's papers on *The Pleasures of the Imagination* than did any other critic of his time. See above, Note 20.

[73] Purney, *Works*, pp. 4–5. His discussion of the pastoral fable, which follows Fontenelle, is the most complete analysis to be found among the Whig pastoral theorists.

[74] *Ibid.*, pp. 59–60.

THE
EMPIRICAL
TRADITION

7

The Philosophical Background

> How doth such a Genius as Sir *Isaac Newton,* from
> amidst the Darkness that involves human Under-
> standing, break forth, and appear like one of an-
> other Species!
>
> Addison, *Spectator* 635.

ADDISON'S INTEREST in natural phenomena, especially the Nature of the new philosophy, reflects a more general concern about the scientific and philosophical developments of his day. His own experiments and his consideration of the experimental work of others [1] are counterbalanced by a healthy scepticism about the work done by certain members of the Royal Society. He shares the common prejudice that the natural philosopher is often the victim of his own enthusiasm, which leads him to investigate phenomena that are not proper subjects of human concern. He does not approve of the minute and the esoteric in nature, because they do not reflect the glory of God as well as immense objects do (*T.* 119, 216). These reservations about the activity of the Royal Society were minor, however, especially when compared with the more serious endeavors of Alexander Pope and Jonathan Swift. And there is certainly nothing in Addison like Boileau's early attack upon all of the anti-Aristotelian philosophers: *"Gens sans aveu,"* he called them, vagabonds, men without masters.[2]

[1] See, for example, Addison, *Works,* I, 436; *T.* 119, 229.
[2] Boileau, *Arrest Burlesque,* in *Oeuvres complètes,* ed. Charles-H. Boudhors, IV, 31. See above, Chapter 2. For Addison's early defense of the work of Descartes and Newton, see *Works,* VI, 607.

Addison's essential accord with the discoveries and moral implications of the new science appears in his participation in the shift from a belief in idealized human nature as reflected in the inner and outer harmony of the cosmos to a view of nature based upon common manifestations of human passions and actions. Essential Nature in the latter view is not a Platonic ideal in a limited universe, but is a set of data to be empirically observed and ordered. While it is still the product of the "universal artisan," God, and is worthy of artistic imitation ("representation"),[3] the operation of Nature can be discovered only through the reason and senses. Just as the natural philosopher is capable of discovering efficient causes only,[4] so the degree of naturalness in art, or faithfulness of representation, can be discovered only through a study of the affective workings of the art object upon the observer. The more empirical view of nature gives rise to a more literal interpretation of naturalness in art, leading to a "restriction of employment of supernatural apparatus or mythological figures to 'that which is universally agreed upon'; or an inner consistency even in the portrayal of the unreal" (S. 419).[5]

This scientific view of nature had many practical advantages for Addison. Because he shared contemporary disregard for Aristotle's philosophy, which he thought had been created entirely within Aristotle's brain without reference to empirical reality, he was amused by the absurdity of what he saw as the purely syllogistic battles between Aristotelian philosophers.[6] Since the nature of Descartes and Newton is not clouded by

[3] Lovejoy, *Essays in the History of Ideas*, p. 71. See C. D. Thorpe, "Addison's Contribution to Criticism," *The Seventeenth Century: Studies in the History of English Thought and Literature from Bacon to Pope*, p. 317.

[4] See Robert Boyle, *Works*, ed. Thomas Birch, V, 395–396, 443–444; cited by Rexmond C. Cochrane, "Francis Bacon in Early Eighteenth-Century English Literature," *PQ*, XXXVII (1958), 65. "Unlike Swift and Pope, who feared the giant groaning in its chains, Addison seems to have felt that all essential discoveries in nature had been made and only awaited their moral application by a new Plato" (*ibid.*, p. 66).

[5] Lovejoy, *Essays in the History of Ideas*, p. 74.

[6] Addison, *Works*, VI, 609–611.

metaphysics and metaphysical ideal-types, our knowledge of it through the understanding is potentially infinite.

The more extended our Reason is, and the more able to grapple with immense Objects, the greater still are those Discoveries which it makes of Wisdom and Providence in the Work of the Creation. As Sir *Isaac Newton,* who stands up as the Miracle of the present Age, can look through a whole Planetary System; consider it in its Weight, Number, and Measure; and draw from it as many Demonstrations of infinite Power and Wisdom, as a more confined Understanding is able to deduce from the System of an Human Body. (*S.* 543)

Addison had moved beyond the philosophical scepticism of John Dryden [7] to a belief in the possibility of progress in both the arts and the sciences.[8] If the secrets of Nature were discovered by the "Miracle of the Age," they soon became available to lesser intellects. They were, indeed, accessible to every man of intelligence. Again, opinion in the realm of natural philosophy was adapted to the needs of criticism. Natural beauty, like natural truth, was to become available to every man of good understanding. Nature became " 'Nature' as manifested in the artist's public; and therefore determining the appeal or aesthetic validity of the work of art . . . the universal and immutable in thought, feeling and taste; what has always been known, what everyone can immediately understand and enjoy; usually connected with the assumption that the universally valid is also the objectively beautiful" (*S.* 253) .[9]

This conception of nature comprehensible to the understanding, when applied to human nature and psychology, would tend to—and in Addison does—give rise to an empirical criticism, as opposed to the more formal criticism by the rules. Yet formal criticism flourished in the France dominated by the philosophy of Descartes, whom Addison greatly admired: "A

[7] Bredvold, *The Intellectual Milieu of John Dryden*, pp. 16, 20.

[8] Addison's philosophical optimism is reflected, too, in his theological liberalism, just as Dryden's scepticism in philosophy is reflected in his religious and political conservatism. See Lovejoy, *The Great Chain of Being*, p. 247.

[9] Lovejoy, *Essays in the History of Ideas*, p. 73.

great man indeed he was, and the only one we envy France." [10]
The rise of empirical criticism did not follow upon the fall of
the metaphysics of the macrocosm-microcosm analogy, but came
only after the triumph of the Baconian spirit in philosophy over
Cartesian rationalism.[11]

If Bacon missed the mathematical nature of the new philosophy, his theory of induction was to make him the prophet of the
experimental sciences in post-Restoration England. In his zeal to
free natural philosophy from the abstractions of logic and theology, Bacon envisaged a science in which all of the facts would
arrange themselves once they had been presented to our experience.[12] This faith in the ability of man's natural reason to order
his experience by induction, although not a workable basis for a
scientific method, turned Bacon's attention toward the operations of the human mind, and his approach to poetry has the
germ of the affective theory, which was to appear more promi-
nently in the literary criticism of the late seventeenth century.

So that this Poesy conduces not only to delight but also to magna-
nimity and morality. Whence it may be fairly thought to partake
somewhat of a divine nature; because it raises the mind and carries
it aloft, accommodating the show of things to the desires of the
mind, not (like reason and history) buckling and bowing down
the mind to the nature of things.[13]

[10] Addison, *Works,* VI, 608.

[11] "Aside from Robert Boyle there is no important thinker in England in the
seventeenth century whose primary allegiance was to Bacon rather than to Descartes" (Sterling P. Lamprecht, "The Role of Descartes in Seventeenth Century
England," *Studies in the History of Ideas,* III [1935], 183) . Descartes, not Bacon,
was seen as the champion of the new philosophy and principal foe of Aristotle.
Locke and Newton gave serious impetus to the rise of Bacon's reputation and
the decline of Descartes's. Cowley's ode, "To the Royal Society" (1667) , is one of
the early English literary works to present Bacon as the "Moses" of the new philosophy. Jeremy Collier, in the 1701 edition of his *Dictionary,* reflects this new
high reputation of Bacon: "It is said of him, That as *Socrates* brought Morality
to Discourse, so did he Philosophy from Speculation to Experience" (article on
Bacon) . See Addison, *T.* 133, 267; *HWL,* XII (August, 1710) , 495, on the declining reputation of the Cartesians in England.

[12] *Advancement of Learning,* Book I, "To the King," *Works,* ed. James Spedding, R. L. Ellis, D. D. Heath, III, 282 ff. See Bredvold, *The Intellectual
Milieu of John Dryden,* pp. 50–51, on the late awakening to the importance of
mathematical method for science in England.

[13] Bacon, *op. cit.,* II, xiii; in *Works,* IV, 316. Dennis (I, 326–327) uses this pas-

Descartes, on the other hand, maintained that the submission of the mind to its desires is the chief cause of error. Such a triumph over the reason could not be the product of clear and distinct ideas.

The entire tenor of Cartesian philosophy supports formal criticism. Descartes's *"Mathesis universalis"* minimizes the importance of sensation in cognitive activity. The world has a rational structure, and God has given us self-validating rational cognition. If we knew everything about the present, then we could mathematically predict all future events. Sense plays no part in gaining this absolute knowledge of fact in a rationally ordered world in which God is a great geometer (*De Reguli, IV*).

Descartes's epistemology reflects his conception of the nature of the physical world. The piece of wax in the *Meditations on First Philosophy* belies his real criterion for distinguishing between primary and secondary qualities. The secondary qualities are not necessarily less permanent than the primary ones, but they cannot be handled mathematically. *"Descartes' real criterion is not permanence, but the possibility of mathematical handling."* [14] The "real world" is composed of mathematically determinable qualities only. Whatever cannot be quantitatively studied is not the subject of real knowledge or a part of objective reality. [15]

The definition of body, "extended material substance," is refined still further. Material substance exists apart from its accompanying attributes. Of the mathematically determinable qualities, only extension is an essential quality of matter. This narrow conception of the primary qualities completely eliminates the senses and the imagination as means of acquiring knowledge. The idea of a triangle, or any other extended body, appears first in the mind. That is, we have ideas ("intellections"

---

sage from *The Advancement of Learning* to defend his view of poetry as a moral vehicle which teaches by moving the soul.

[14] E. A. Burtt, *The Metaphysical Foundations of Modern Physical Science*, p. 117.

[15] *The Passions of the Soul*, pp. 30, 31; in *Descartes*, I, 345.

or "conceptions") of many things which we have neither seen
nor imagined; therefore, intellection logically precedes both
sensation and imagination.[16] Descartes was not satisfied with
empirical probabilism. His vortex theory and universal mathesis made the mathematical harmony and simplicity of the world
independent of any cognizant being.

If all knowledge is unified in the universal mathesis, then we
may expect to find aesthetic "knowledge" subsumed under the
larger Cartesian whole. Despite the diversity of art objects, all
aesthetic judgments must be related to some common universal
principles.

. . . Descartes reduces "matter" to "extension" and physical body to
pure space; however, space in Cartesian epistemology is not subject
to the conditions of sensory experience and "imagination" but to the
conditions of logic and arithmetic. This criticism of the faculties of
sense and imagination is taken up and extended by Malebranche
. . . Here again imagination does not appear as a way to truth but
as a source of all the delusions to which the human mind is exposed, in the realm of natural science and in that of moral and
metaphysical knowledge.[17]

If the only truths are those which are clearly and distinctly
perceived (in the case of physical bodies, mathematically conceived) , then poetry is not concerned with truth at all, but with
fancy and pleasure. One may think as a philosopher and feel as
a poet does, producing an *Essay on Man,* but poetry and philosophy are essentially antithetical. The end of philosophical criticism is the rational control of the principal poetic faculty, the
imagination. The Cartesian criteria for judging poetry are also
nonpoetic, if not antipoetic. The imagination is reduced to the
position of finding ornaments for philosophically acceptable
ideas.[18]

Addison's "new criticism" is, in a sense, the result of a return

[16] *Descartes,* I, 179.
[17] Ernst Cassirer, *The Philosophy of the Enlightenment,* trans. Fritz C. A.
Koelln and James P. Pettegrove, p. 283; see pp. 279 ff.
[18] *Descartes,* I, 85.

to the empiricism of Sir Francis Bacon. While much of Cartesian philosophy is incorporated in the works of the English empiricists, the post-Restoration English philosophers fundamentally distrusted the rationalistic tradition of which Descartes was the most important representative. Addison's lavish praise of Descartes reveals his youthful philosophical naïveté. He uses Hobbesian and Lockean psychological theories later without recognizing that they conflict with Descartes's. Addison's essays on *The Pleasures of the Imagination,* wit, and genius indicate that his criticism is part of the record of the shift from "praise of and conformity to the fixed patterns and forms of the ancients and emphasis on learning and judgment" to "does this work please?" "why does it please?" and "is it the product of genius and native imaginative abilities?" [19] This affective approach to criticism is, for Addison, the result of the subjectively inclined "sensationalist" critique of Cartesian philosophy.

The Baconian philosophy of science is Aristotelian to the degree that it begins with sense experience and, therefore, is nonmathematical, as opposed to the Platonic orientation of Galileo's reduction of physics to Euclidean geometry and motion to mathematical formulae.[20] In the seventeenth century, especially in the philosophy of Descartes, this "Platonic" view of the epistemic value of mathematical abstraction deprived the senses and the imagination of their roles as mental activities, placing them in the realm of *"res extensa"* in the mind-body dualism.[21] This reduction of sensation and imagination to purely physiological activities,[22] rather than operations of the soul, disturbed both the champions of poetry and those who saw sensation as the first step in mental activity. The former, heirs of Aristotle and Sir Philip Sidney, in criticism, agreed with Bacon that imagination is the active mental faculty of the

[19] C. D. Thorpe, in *The Seventeenth Century,* p. 317.
[20] Alexander Koyre, "Galileo and the Scientific Revolution of the Seventeenth Century," *Philosophical Review,* LII (1943), 338, 347. See H. Butterfield, *The Origins of Modern Science,* pp. 3–5.
[21] *De Reguli,* XII; in *Descartes,* I, 36–38.
[22] *Descartes,* I, 341. See A. C. Crombie, "Descartes on Method and Physiology," *Cambridge Journal,* V (1951–1952), 178–186.

poet.[23] Kenelm Digby rejected Descartes's nerve theory of the conduct of sensory impulses, adding that we sense only that which the mind concentrates upon.[24] This view of both sense and imagination is expanded upon by Richard Burthogge, who writes that the two faculties conceive images and sentiments, just as the mind conceives ideas: "Sense and Imagination, as well as the Understanding and Reason, are Mental and Spiritual, not merely Mechanick and Material Powers." [25] Reason, he calls refined, sublimated sensation.[26]

Burthogge's separation of reason and sensation as a matter of degree, rather than kind, is representative of a growing English distrust of the continental rationalism which may be found in the principal sources of Addison's philosophical presuppositions—Hobbes, Locke, and Newton. Locke, while not granting that the lower animals have reason, contradicts Descartes by ascribing some forms of mental activity, perception and memory, to the brutes.[27] Locke's unwillingness to accept man's exclusive claim to mental activity is a reflection of his own distrust of the identification of mental activity with logic and abstract generalizations whereas Descartes had stripped all non-geometrical properties from *"res extensa,"* locating them in the mind.[28] Condillac later significantly notes that Locke is the better philosopher because he is not a geometer.[29]

Descartes had attempted to reduce physics to geometry. Newton, who also sought a mathematical order in Nature, did not

---

[23] See *De Augmentis*, V, i; VI, iii; *Advancement of Learning*, II, xii, i. Both cited by John L. Harrison, "Bacon's View of Rhetoric, Poetry, and the Imagination," *HLQ*, XX (1957), 109.

[24] [Kenelm Digby], *Two Treatises . . .* , pp. 275, 277–278.

[25] *An Essay upon Reason*, in *The Philosophical Writings of Richard Burthogge*, ed. Margaret Landes, p. 61. See Jakob Grünbaum, *Die Philosophie Richard Burthogges (1637–1698)* , p. 32.

[26] Burthogge, p. 63.

[27] *EHU*, II, ix, 12; cited by Kenneth MacLean, *John Locke and English Literature of the Eighteenth Century*, p. 69. Professor MacLean writes that Addison takes a Cartesian position in *S.* 120 and *G.* 89, where he writes that instinct is enough to explain animal behavior. While Addison denies that animals have even simple ideas, he does not think that the actions of animals can be described as properties of matter, as Descartes does (*S.* 120) .

[28] *Descartes*, I, 345.

[29] W. J. Bate, *From Classic to Romantic*, pp. 55–56.

find his order here. "He too seeks universal mathematical principles in nature but he no longer believes it possible to reduce
physics to geometry. He advocates rather the independent
function and unique character of physical investigation, and
this character is founded in the method of experimentation and
the method of inductive reasoning." [30] Here is the key to the
shift in aesthetic criticism, the double reversal from the induction of Bacon to the deduction of Descartes back to the inductive
method of Newtonian physics. *"The qualities of bodies, which
admit neither intensification nor remission of degrees, which
are found to belong to all bodies within the reach of our experience, are to be the universal qualities of all bodies whatsoever."* [31] Our knowledge of these bodies and of their epistemological status is not a function of our reason, but of our senses.
We are aware of extension, impenetrability, inertia, hardness,
and mobility, because we see and feel these qualities, not because we conceive them.

This shift in emphasis from mathematical method to experimentation narrowed the field of absolute knowledge. If scientific proof depends as much upon scientific principles as upon
mathematical certainty, then "the absolute certainty of a science
cannot exceed the certainty of its principles." [32] A science which
depends upon the senses for verification of its findings cannot
be as certain as the science which relies entirely upon rational
proof. Newton and his heirs did not search for the ultimate
nature of gravity (S. 120) ; this is beyond the scientist's realm
of investigation. The activity and behavior of physical objects,
not their ultimate natures, are the natural philosopher's proper
subject matter. [33]

The analysis of activity and behavior was carried over into

---

[30] Cassirer, *The Philosophy of the Enlightenment,* pp. 51–52. Even among
philosophers who did not accept sensation as the psychological foundation of
knowledge, induction was occasionally accepted as the method of operation of
the experimental sciences. See John Sergeant, *The Method to Science,* "Preface,"
with its attack upon Descartes's "methodical doubt."

[31] Newton, *Mathematical Principles of Natural Philosophy,* p. 398.

[32] E. A. Burtt, p. 220.

[33] *Ibid.,* p. 226.

psychology by the "sensationalists," who attempted to formulate empirical psychological laws founded upon common experience and responses. The concern about the relationship between the findings of natural philosophy and final causes is a real one in the eighteenth century, and Descartes's elimination of final causes from his philosophy was held to be an act of rashness by devout Englishmen.[34] But the trend of English philosophical psychology at the end of the seventeenth century is reflected in Addison's movement away from the philosophy of final causes to a study of effects, especially in his papers on *The Pleasures of the Imagination*. Even in his papers on *Paradise Lost*, however, we find Addison rejecting arguments about final causes in his unwillingness to accept the view that the moral is the "end" of poetry which exists before the fable is invented and is the principle which gives the fable its form (*S*. 369).

Addison's importance as a literary critic derives from his application of the psychology of Hobbes and Locke's "historical plain method" in his quest for the sources of the pleasures aroused in the imagination by Nature and art. While Addison believes that the objects which arouse these pleasures have intrinsic value, his principal concern, especially in the papers on the imagination, is with the responses themselves. Descartes, in formulating his theory of the primary and secondary qualities, had suggested that man cannot know the "substantial" basis of the physical world. His *"Cogito, ergo sum"* places the self in bold relief in modern philosophy. Man cannot know the world, but he can know his own self. Locke's rejection of faculty psychology and his description of the mind as the sum of its ideas carries Descartes's subjectivism one step further. By denying the validity of Descartes's and the Cambridge Platonists' conception of innate ideas, Locke had not only robbed himself of a good weapon with which to defend revelation; he had denied the existence of a pre-established mental order common

[34] John Ray, *Wisdom of God Manifested in the Works of the Creation*, p. 38.

to all men.[35] The "historical plain method" offered no meta-physical basis for the substantiality of the mind in its "non-speculative" study of the origins and structure of human thought.[36]

Locke did not deny the substantial nature of the soul. "But he characteristically blurs the sharp outlines of Descartes' definitions. He will not allow, for instance, that 'thought' is the 'essence' of the soul, but makes it rather the *function,* or activity, which may at one time be in operation and at another quiescent." [37] This view of the mind strips the "self" of its concreteness by identifying it with the sum of its ideas and processes.[38] On Addison's part, this meant a consideration of the responses which he called the "pleasures of the imagination," without relating them directly to the total experience of the people who feel these pleasures. The ego, which plays such an important part in Descartes's philosophy, is lost in Locke's *Essay* and in Addison's papers on *The Pleasures of the Imagination.* Neither of these men recognized how much he contributed to the "dissociation of the ego" by concentrating upon the psychological response rather than upon the nature of the responding mind.

[35] Henry Lee, *Anti-Scepticism: Or Notes upon each Chapter of Mr. Lock's Essay concerning Human Understanding,* Sigs. b 1ʳ–b 1ᵛ. See James Gibson, *Locke's Theory of Knowledge and Its Historical Relations,* p. 43; and Richard I. Aaron, *John Locke,* pp. 88–89.

Locke's theory of ideas was held to be damaging to both reason and religion. On the former, see John Sergeant, *Solid Philosophy Asserted* (London, 1697) , Epistle Dedicatory; Henry Lee, *Anti-Scepticism,* pp. 1–2; *Athenian Gazette,* II (May 26, 1691) , 1, III (July 21, 1691) , 17. On religion, see William Carroll, *A Dissertation . . . of Locke's Essay . . . ,* pp. vi–vii, 1 ff. John Witty, however, uses Lockean terminology to refute the Deists in *The First Principle of Modern Deism Confuted.*

The use of Locke's theory of primary and secondary qualities in theological disputes is described in John W. Yolton, *John Locke and the Way of Ideas,* pp. 183–193. The primary bibliography of this aspect of Lockean philosophy is derived almost exclusively from Mr. Yolton's work.

[36] *EHU,* I, i, 2. See Sterling P. Lamprecht, "Locke's Attack upon Innate Ideas," *Philosophical Review,* XXXVI (1927) , p. 149.

[37] Basil Willey, *The Seventeenth Century Background,* p. 277. See *EHU,* II, i, 10; IV, ix, 3.

[38] Ernest Tuveson, *MP,* LII (1954–1955) , 167–168. See James Gibson, pp. 116–117.

In seeking the general foundation of Addison's affective approach to aesthetic and literary questions in Locke's psychology, we need not suggest that Locke is the only important influence upon this area of Addison's thought. Those trends of Locke's philosophy described above were already present in the works of Thomas Hobbes, who contributed as much as Locke to Addison's theory of the imagination. Hobbes and Locke shared habits of mind inimical not only to Descartes and the Cambridge Platonists, but to the "notionalists"—Digby, Sergeant, and Burthogge—as well.[39] Although Addison, like Abraham Cowley, did not fully appreciate the "atheistic" and "materialistic" tendencies in the philosophy of Hobbes,[40] it was precisely these tendencies in the philosophies of Locke and Hobbes which provided the necessary milieu for the development of Addison's theory of the pleasures of the imagination. Descartes, the Cambridge Platonists, and the "notionalists," each in his own way, had stressed the substantiality of the mind. If Henry More found Descartes's theory of the mind as *"res cogitans"* inadequate because it made thought the only property of mind, he and Ralph Cudworth were more sympathetic to Descartes's view than they were to the "materialism and mechanism" of the new philosophers.[41] The Cambridge Platonists accepted and modified the Cartesian theory of innate ideas because they could use it to support their own metaphysical conception of the soul as essence or *persona*.[42]

The "notionalists," while providing many elements of Locke's theory of ideas, thought within a conceptual framework which subordinated epistemological questions to theological ones, which prevented them from breaking out of traditional modes of thought, obscured their originality, and

[39] See John Yolton, "Locke and Seventeenth-Century Logic of Ideas," *JHI*, XVI (1955), 431–452.

[40] See Robert Hinman, " 'Truth is Truest Poesy': The Influence of the New Philosophy on Abraham Cowley," *ELH*, XXIII (1956), 194–203. Addison did not accept Hobbes's theory of the state, but he did agree with his conception of human nature. See *S.* 47, 287; Smithers, p. 418.

[41] Basil Willey, *The Seventeenth Century Background*, pp. 159, 166–167.

[42] Tuveson, *MP*, LII (1954–1955), 164. See above, Notes 35, 36.

restricted their fame.[43] "Digbys philosophisches Interesse ist keineswegs in erster Linie auf die Analyse des Wissens, sondern auf den Beweis der Immaterialität und Unsterblichkeit der Seele berichtet." [44] Although Digby does not hold that "notions" are the "real nature" of the things which they represent, he believes, as Hobbes and Locke do not,[45] that they provide us with an absolute knowledge of things.[46] Digby's conceptualism is essentially that of Aristotle, a philosopher whose influence he acknowledges and whose perverters he condemns.[47] His discussion of the senses and the relationship between the senses and the reason is perfunctory. He sees the reason as a spiritual form and the senses as a material one, whose operation is to be explained, as in Descartes, in strictly physiological terms.[48]

John Sergeant goes even beyond Digby by denying Burthogge's and Locke's belief that sensation is psychologically prior to reflection in the process of gaining knowledge and by claiming that "notions" are the real essences of things in the mind.[49] Sergeant finds Descartes's systematic doubt as "fantastic" as the Cambridge Platonists saw it, but he maintains the Cartesian distinction between the material operations of the senses and the mental processes of the mind, a theory which worked, as it had in Descartes, to the disadvantage of both the senses and the imagination.[50] The entire tenor of Sergeant's philosophy, though he uses terminology common to Hobbes and Locke, is

[43] Yolton, *John Locke and the Way of Ideas*, pp. 20–21, finds this especially true of Richard Burthogge's *Organum Vetus et Novum* (1678) and *An Essay upon Reason* (1694). The former anticipated *EHU* by twelve years. See Burthogge's *Philosophical Writings*, pp. 19–22.

[44] Ernst Cassirer, *Das Erkenntnisproblem in der Philosophie und Wissenschaft der neueren Zeit*, II, 297–298.

[45] *Lev.* I, i; *EHU*, II, viii, 15.

[46] Yolton, *JHI*, XVI (1955), 433. See Kenelm Digby, *Two Treatises*, p. 356.

[47] Digby, *Two Treatises*, pp. 343–345. See pp. 13–14.

[48] Cassirer, *Das Erkenntnisproblem*, II, 298.

[49] Yolton, *JHI*, XVI (1955), 435, 448; *EHU*, I, ii; Burthogge, *Philosophical Writings*, pp. 11, 12, 60; Georges Lyon, *L'Idéalisme en Angleterre au XVIIIᵉ siècle*, pp. 72–96; Cassirer, *Das Erkenntnisproblem*, I, 464–474; John Sergeant, *Method to Science*, pp. 25–27.

[50] Sergeant, *Method to Science*, p. 20; *Solid Philosophy Asserted*, Sig. b 1ᵛ, p. 3. See Yolton, *John Locke and the Way of Ideas*, pp. 104–106.

contrary to that of English empiricism in its insistence upon the *sui generis* status of the reason among the operations attributed to the mind. A large part of his *Solid Philosophy Asserted* was written to clarify what he saw as Locke's confusion of "phantasms" and "notions."[51]

Of the three major "notionalists," Richard Burthogge was the most influential in the English empirical tradition. But his ideas, largely anticipated by Hobbes, found their public not through his own work, but in their adaptation by Locke, whose representative theory of perception, nominalism, and psychology appear, not fully worked out to be sure, in *Organum Vetus et Novum.* All available evidence points to the fact that his works were received as unexceptional additions to a plethora of theological tracts. His biblical quotations, his neo-Platonic digressions, and his theological aims served only to confirm this conclusion.[52] The failure of Burthogge to gain recognition suggests that serious readers of philosophical works were more attracted, though not necessarily persuaded, by the more radical statements of Hobbes and Locke than they were by the seemingly more orthodox philosophical works used to support Anglican religious principles.

This suspicion is confirmed, at least in Addison's case, with reference to the philosophy of Thomas Hobbes. Addison's allegiance to the Church of England and his dedication to the cause of moderation have already been treated. Hobbes's reputation among both Churchmen and moderates had not substantially improved since the restoration of Charles II.[53] Ad-

[51] Sergeant, *Solid Philosophy Asserted*, pp. 3, 5.

[52] Margaret Landes, ed. *Philosophical Writings of Richard Burthogge,* pp. xiii–xiv.

[53] For popular expressions of disapproval of Hobbes's philosophy and politics, see *Athenian Gazette,* III (September, 1691) , 15, 23, and V (January, 1692) , 14; *Memoirs of Literature,* I, No. 2 (March 20, 1710) ; *The Entertainer* 1 (November 6, 1717) . See Rosalie L. Colie, *Light and Enlightenment: A Study of the Cambridge Platonists and Dutch Arminians,* pp. 64–65.

Bayle, in his *Dictionary,* was one of the few men of his time to voice general approval of Hobbes, whom he called "one of the greatest genius's of the seventeenth century." See Smithers, pp. 83, 108, 205, 210, on Addison's relations with Bayle and Le Clerc.

dison either misunderstood or ignored the implication of Hobbes's philosophy for theology, but he sometimes shared Hobbes's low estimate of human nature [54] in spite of his belief in the possibility of progress in both the sciences and morality. But aside from his specific borrowings from Hobbes in his theory of the imagination, Addison's greatest debt is to that aspect of Hobbes's philosophy which reduced *"res cogitans"* to *"res extensa,"* explaining all of Nature in terms of "matter in motion" (*Lev.* I, v). By doing so, Hobbes was able to insist upon genetic definitions and causal explanations of all phenomena of Nature rather than scholastic definitions by specific differences.[55] The need for genetic definitions and explanations of cause-effect relationships outside of the physical sciences made itself felt even among men who, like Addison, did not accept Hobbes's materialism.

If we look for explicit literary criticism in Hobbes's works to support Professor Thorpe's remark, "To Hobbes, more than to any other single Englishman, later criticism owed its distrust for tradition and dogma and its gradual return to the spirit of Aristotle in basing its judgment on a close study of works of literature and on analysis of facts of mind in relation to literature," [56] we are likely to be disappointed. Hobbes's influence was more general, less specific, than this. We may see the implications of his treatment of the state as "body" extended not only to the political theory of his contemporaries who disagreed with his political philosophy, but to areas of thought outside of politics as well. The causal definition of the state, which Ernst Cassirer has so aptly described as the application of the mathematical method of Galileo to politics,[57] analyzes the state's acts and processes, not its "essence." Hobbes's method of argument appears with a less radical program in Locke's "Whig" theory

[54] See above, Note 40. Addison is more optimistic in *T.* 108.
[55] Cassirer, *Philosophy of the Enlightenment*, p. 254.
[56] C. D. Thorpe, *The Aesthetic Theory of Thomas Hobbes*, p. 8.
[57] Cassirer, *Philosophy of the Enlightenment*, p. 255. See A. Wolf, *A History of Science, Technology and Philosophy in the 16th & 17th Centuries*, p. 641, on Hobbes's appreciation of the importance of mathematical method to science.

of the state, opposed to the more Aristotelian "Tory" view which represented the state as "being" rather than "becoming." [58]

In criticism, we have seen how just such a distinction separated the "Tory" from the "Whig" critics of pastoral poetry. This conception of process, unlike Aristotle's idea of nature as "coming-into-being," is not defined in terms of a predetermined form, but with reference to human desires and motives. In Addison's papers on *The Pleasures of the Imagination* we find a similar functional definition of the human mind. This view of the mind, in both its details and its spirit, is faithful to the rising English empirical philosophy, which was less concerned about defending the unique position of the reason among the human faculties than about providing a satisfactory explanation of reason, imagination, and sensation as coordinated activities of the human mind.

[58] Cassirer, *Philosophy of the Enlightenment*, p. 254.

8

The Pleasures of the Imagination

> For, as for poesy, it is rather a pleasure or play of imagination, than a work or duty thereof. And if it be a work, we speak not now of such parts of learning as the imagination produceth, but of such sciences as handle and consider of the imagination.
>
> Sir Francis Bacon, *Of the Advancement of Learning*, II, xii, 1

THE FULL DEVELOPMENT of Addison's "psychological" criticism is to be found in his papers on *The Pleasures of the Imagination.* In the century following the publication of Ben Jonson's plays as *Works,* the question of whether poesy is a work or pleasure of the imagination gradually lost its significance in literary debate. Sir Francis Bacon discussed the imagination in terms of those sciences which used this faculty to make their discoveries. Addison's concern, in the papers on *The Pleasures of the Imagination,* is with the affective workings, not the epistemic value, of the imagination.[1] In these essays, "imagination," "taste," and "association of ideas" take on their greatest significance, and the impact of developments in English empirical

---

[1] See Ernest Tuveson, *The Imagination as a Means of Grace,* pp. 91–131, the chapter on "The Pleasures of the Imagination." The present work emphasizes the influence of Hobbes and Newton more than Professor Tuveson's does. The claim that Addison's papers on the imagination are "the first work ever written on aesthetics as a wholly autonomous subject" (p. 92) is belied by Addison's own remarks to the effect that one can know only the final, not the efficient or necessary causes of the pleasures of the imagination (S. 413); that is, Addison was aware that contemporary philosophical psychology did not provide a foundation for aesthetics as an independent subject. See below, Note 44; and Chapter 9, Note 3.

philosophy since the death of Bacon is most clearly in evidence. These papers are concerned not only with the affective relationship between the work of art and the observer, but, also, with the effect of any object, natural or artificial, upon the senses and imagination of the percipient. It is in this sense that Addison's fundamental critical interest in the principle of the association of ideas, in Locke's theory of primary and secondary qualities, and in the power of imagery over the mind is not an interest in the criticism of poetry only, but in aesthetic judgment in general.

I

The parallel of language between Locke's division of qualities and Addison's division of the pleasures of the imagination suggests that the basis of Addison's distinction is to be found in Locke's *Essay concerning Human Understanding*. Indeed, we are informed that "Addison himself assures the reader that the foundation of his idea of the imagination is Locke's distinction between the primary and secondary qualities of matter." [2] This assurance is found at the end of *Spectator* 413:

I have here supposed that my Reader is acquainted with that great modern Discovery, which is at present acknowledged by all the Enquirers into Natural Philosophy: Namely, that Light and Colours, as apprehended by the Imagination, are only Ideas in the Mind, and not Qualities which have Existence in Matter. As this is

[2] Victor M. Hamm, "Addison and the Pleasures of the Imagination," *MLN*, LII (1937), 499. See J. G. Robertson, *Studies in the Genesis of Romantic Theory in the Eighteenth Century*, pp. 247–248, for a statement of the theory which Professor Hamm criticizes. Walter J. Hipple, Jr., *The Beautiful, the Sublime, & the Picturesque in Eighteenth-Century Aesthetic Theory*, p. 15, writes that the two distinctions have only the words "primary" and "secondary" in common, but he does not expand upon this observation.

Parallels to the names of Addison's pleasures of the imagination are to be found not only in the theories of primary and secondary qualities of Locke and Hobbes, and in Bacon's distinction between the works and the pleasures of the imagination, but in Hobbes's philosophical psychology as well (see *Lev.* I, iv, where Hobbes distinguishes between the pleasures of the sense and those of the mind). It is likely that Addison found his name for "present objects" in this same section of the *Leviathan*. See below, p. 182. In each of these cases, however, Addison had adopted only the name and had modified or completely changed the concept to which the name refers.

a Truth which has been proved incontestably by many Modern Philosophers, and is indeed one of the finest Speculations in that Science, if the *English* Reader would see the Notion explained at large, he may find it in the Eighth Chapter of the second Book of Mr. *Lock's* Essay on Human Understanding.

Addison, however, is merely suggesting that a knowledge of this distinction, which may be acquired by an *"English* Reader" through a reading of Locke's *Essay,* would aid the reader's understanding of the matters previously discussed in this issue of the *Spectator.* This paper is concerned with the distinction between the primary and the secondary pleasures of the imagination. Addison comments upon the "colorlessness" of the natural world, noting that we cannot know the efficient causes of the pleasures of the imagination, because we do not know the nature of the soul. But we can know the final cause of these pleasures, and that is the *"Power"* given to material objects by God which allows them to produce the effects we know as the secondary properties of matter.

It is difficult to see how Addison, who was well acquainted with Locke's philosophy, could have derived his theory of primary and secondary pleasures of the imagination from Locke's theory of qualities. The primary qualities of an object are those modes or attributes which inhere in the substance of the object. The primary pleasures of the imagination are those which arise from the "perception of visual objects which are present to the beholder." A "present object" is any natural object or artifact which is not a representation. Gardens and buildings, though artifacts, excite primary pleasures of the imagination, because they do not "represent" ("imitate") anything in nature.

The secondary qualities, as Addison observes, are not, properly speaking, qualities of matter. They are "powers of bodies to produce ideas by means of [primary] qualities." [3] For Addison, as for Hobbes, Locke, and Berkeley, these secondary

---

[3] Reginald Jackson, "Locke's Distinction between Primary and Secondary Qualities," *Mind,* n.s. XXXVIII (1929), 58. See *EHU,* II, viii, xiii; John Yolton, *John Locke and the Way of Ideas,* p. 135.

qualities have no existence apart from the ideas which they produce. The secondary pleasures of the imagination, those produced by painting, sculpture, and poetry, are those pleasures aroused by objects which are presented to the sense of sight, but which are not "present objects," because they merely represent objects not present to the perceivers of the statues, paintings, and poems, objects which arouse primary pleasures of the imagination when a perceiver is present. Primary pleasures of the imagination arise from the direct perception of the "present object" while secondary pleasures of the imagination arise from the comparison of the representation with the represented object.

On the simplest level, Addison's distinction between primary and secondary pleasures of the imagination is based upon Aristotle's distinction between mimetic and nonmimetic arts, but the basis for this distinction is complicated by the fact that Addison does not see the imagination primarily in terms of Aristotle's formal criteria, but in terms of the philosophical psychology of Hobbes and Locke. Because Addison's theory of the imagination posits that this "faculty" is a visual one only (S. 411), both the primary and the secondary pleasures of the imagination are aroused by the secondary qualities of matter. "Things would make but a poor Appearance to the Eye, if we saw them only in their proper Figures and Motions: And what Reason can we assign for their exciting in us many of those Ideas which are different from any thing that exists in the Objects themselves (for such are Lights and Colours) were it not to add Supernumerary Ornaments to the Universe, and make it more agreeable to the Imagination?" (S. 413). Furthermore, neither primary nor secondary pleasures of the imagination may be said to be aroused by the primary qualities of objects, but by their secondary qualities only, while the distinctly secondary pleasures of the imagination are aroused not through the object at all, but through the power of the imagination, which compares the "representation" with the idea of the object itself. Addison may have adapted Locke's terminology to indicate his own distinction between the pleasures of the imagination, but the power which lies in the object in Locke's epistemology must be transferred to the perceiver in Addison's criticism.

The statement that the secondary pleasures of the imagination are aroused by "visions of things that are absent or fictitious" suggests that the ideas which arouse these pleasures are in some way less real than the ideas which they represent; in Platonic and Aristotelian terms, they are "imitations." If Addison's philosophy had not been indebted to English empiricism, our understanding of his distinction would be complete. However, while our knowledge of "present objects" is also representative, we can gain no pleasure from comparing the idea of the present object with its original, because we cannot know anything but our own ideas. The "representation" of the secondary pleasures of the imagination, being twice removed from nature, is most nearly related to a corresponding theory of objects and their representations, Locke's distinction between words and ideas.

Awareness of the artificial nature of language, its origins and life in social conventions, was not new in seventeenth-century thought. Aristotle had written, "Spoken words are the symbols of mental experience and written words are the symbols of spoken words. Just as all men have not the same writing, so all men have not the same speech sounds, but the mental experiences, which these directly symbolize, are the same for all, as also are those things of which our experiences are images" (*De Interpretatione,* 16a 4–8). The author of *The Arte of English Poesie* was aware of this aspect of Aristotle's philosophy when he wrote that "speech it selfe is artificial and made by man." [4] Later, Bacon's "Idols of the Marketplace" exposed the errors produced by mistaking commonly used words for their real conceptions. If reason is the father of language, it is also the victim of words, which when vulgarly defined "rendered philosophy and the sciences sophistical and inactive." [5]

[4] Puttenham, *The Arte of English Poesie,* p. 8.
[5] *Novum Organum,* I, lix. See *Advancement of Learning,* II, xiii, 4; Sir Kenelm Digby, *Two Treatises,* pp. 2, 5, 6, 48; Sir Matthew Hale, *Primitive Originations of Mankind,* p. 162.

Both Bacon and, later, Descartes believed, however, that man could gain a real knowledge of the external world through the use of his reason and that this knowledge could be conveyed by symbols, words, which directly represented the conception of things in the mind.[6] In this, both philosophers were closer to Aristotle's conceptualism than they were to the philosophies of Hobbes and Locke. When Aristotle wrote that "Actual knowledge is identical with its object" (*De Anima*, 430a 20), he did not mean that the sun described by the astronomer is in the mind of the percipient, but that the *form* of the sun is potentially, not actually, in man's intellectual soul (*De Anima*, 429a 29).[7]

In his denial of the reality of "substance" and of the power of reason to give us real knowledge of the external world, Hobbes denied man's ability to develop any objective sciences (*Lev.* I, v, ix). Mathematics gives infallible knowledge, but it is analytic rather than synthetic in nature. Sense experience, too, is infallible, but it does not necessarily conform with external reality. The subjective status of human knowledge is at the bottom of not only Hobbes's epistemology and political theory, but is the basis for his theory of language, as well. Universals are not the forms of nature, but are merely the *names* given to our abstracted conceptions of a set of particulars, without which we could have neither truth nor falsity, knowledge nor error.[8]

This fragment of a theory of language, the product of Hobbes's scientific world-view, became part of the new philosophy of seventeenth-century England and, like other parts of Hobbes's materialistic philosophy, was influential even among men who abhorred Hobbes's dismissal of spiritual substance. One of the paradoxes of seventeenth-century English philosophy is that the implications of Hobbes's scientific philosophy were more fully developed in his contemporaries' low estimate

---

[6] *The World; or, Essay on Light*, in *The Philosophy of Descartes in Extracts from His Writings*, trans. Henry A. P. Torrey, pp. 207–208.

[7] See *Metaphysics* 981b; *Descartes*, II, 10.

[8] Hobbes, *Human Nature*, in *Works*, IV, 22, 25. See *Lev.* I, iv.

of poetry and rhetoric than they were in his own. Although rhetoric had begun to lose its intellectual respectability among men who regarded improvement of the understanding more than they did the moving of the passions before Hobbes became widely influential,[9] the effects of the distrust of the affective use of language and apprehension about the artificial nature of language were not felt until the presentation of the Royal Society's plan for language reform.[10]

Locke, however, is the first English philosopher to fully explore the implications of Hobbes's theory that words, like governments, are artificially contracted. Maintaining that there is no real connection between words and their meanings or referents,[11] Locke adopts Hobbes's theory of universals when he writes that most of our words are general names which stand for classes of objects in a world of nothing but particulars. Through the process of abstraction, one analyzes the common properties, eliminating those qualities which are not essential to the meaning of the term. The class names do not stand for Platonic Ideas or Aristotelian forms; they represent only the nominal essences, the crucial properties of the terms artificially defined (*EHU,* III, iii, 2). As in Hobbes, these words are the sources of both our knowledge and our error.

Words, by long and familiar use, . . . come to excite in men certain ideas so constantly and readily, that they are apt to suppose a natural connexion between them. But that they signify only men's peculiar ideas, and that *by a perfect arbitrary imposition,* is evident, in that they often fail to excite in others (even that use the same

9 George Williamson, *The Senecan Amble,* p. 277, quotes Alexander Ross, *The Philosophical Touch-stone* (1645) , p. 92: "If you lay the fault of this upon your *Rhetoricall* expressions, I must answer you, that *Rhetorick* in such a subject may well be spared; use your *Rhetorick* when you work upon the *affections,* but not when you will *informe* the understanding; for in this regard you do but cloud, not cleere the intellect."

10 Sprat, *History of the Royal Society,* Pt. I, Sec. xx. See Williamson, *Senecan Amble,* pp. 294–296; John Wilkins, *An Essay Towards a Real Character, And a Philosophical Language,* pp. 2, 19–20.

11 *EHU,* III, ii, 8. See John Sergeant, *Solid Philosophy Asserted,* pp. 33–34. Sergeant agrees that there is no real connection between *words* and their *meanings* ("things") , but, unlike Locke, he argues that the meaning of a word points to the thing itself, not merely to our idea of it.

language) the same ideas we take them to be the signs of: and every man has so inviolable a liberty to make words stand for what ideas he pleases, that no one hath the power to make others have the same words in their mind that he does. (*EHU*, III, ii, 8)

But all men, including poets, wish to communicate with their audiences; therefore, they use conventional modes of expression. Addison notes a similar difficulty in poetic communication: "It may be worth our while to examine how it comes to pass that several Readers, who are all acquainted with the same Language, and know the Meaning of the Words they read, should nevertheless have a different Relish of the same Descriptions. We find one transported with a Passage, which another runs over with Coldness and Indifference, or finding the Representation extremely natural, where another can perceive nothing of Likeness and Conformity" (*S.* 416). The similarity of the errors in the understanding of words and the objects of the secondary pleasures of the imagination may be traced to a similarity in their epistemological statuses.

Although Locke is vague about the nature of the relationship between ideas and words, he does see it as one of "representation." [12] The *idea-word* relationship provides the basis for the *present object-representation* [13] relationship, as the similarities between the two passages quoted above suggest, in that both are founded upon artificial conventions, or rules, governing the meaning of the word or the effect of the work of art. The *present object-representation* relationship may be compared to that between *substance* and *idea* in that both are iconic in the visual arts, though not necessarily in poetry, while the *word-idea* relationship generally is not, except in the case of onomatopoeia.[14] However, the analogy of the *present object-representation* and the *substance-idea* relationships soon breaks down.

[12] D. J. O'Connor, *John Locke*, p. 141.

[13] *Present object* is used as an abbreviated form for the "idea" aroused by the power of any object of the primary pleasures of the imagination. We cannot know the real "present object" any more than we can know any other real substance. The "idea" of the object, not the object itself, is the immediate cause of the pleasure of the imagination (*S.* 411).

[14] D. J. O'Connor, p. 141.

Since the substance is never known, the iconic idea is the closest we may ever come to a knowledge of the real essence of the "thing." We never have more than ectypes of complex ideas of substances, and these are not perfect representations of the substances, but merely collections of simple ideas (*EHU*, II, xxxi, 13). Still, these ideas are sometimes mistaken for the substance, but the statue of Moses is never mistaken for its model, and the word "Aeneas" is never taken to be the real hero of the *Aeneid*.

The difficulty which arises in the comparison of *substances* (primary qualities and their substrata) -*ideas* (secondary qualities) and *present objects-representations* is resolved when one realizes that the *present object,* which is composed of secondary qualities, cannot be comparable to *substances,* which are unknowable. The primary pleasures of the imagination are aroused by the secondary qualities of objects presented directly to the senses. The secondary pleasures of the imagination, however, are aroused through the comparison of "imitations" which, like words, stand for, but are not mistaken for, the ideas they represent. To this degree, then, the most likely source of Addison's distinction between the primary and the secondary pleasures of the imagination is Locke's theory of language and the idea-word relationship.

II

The sources of Addison's description of the operations of the imagination are not as specific as those for his distinction between the primary and the secondary pleasures of the imagination. Addison's conception of the imagination, which he equates with the fancy, represents an attempt to explain the nature of the appeal of "pleasant" objects in a manner which is alien to both the tenor and critical vocabulary of European neoclassicism. "Addison's study of the imagination is an attempt to discover this 'something more essential' to art than the Rules can explain. He proposes, he writes, to enter upon an 'Essay on the Pleasures of the Imagination which though it shall consider the subject at large, will perhaps suggest to the Reader what it is

that gives Beauty to many Passages of the finest Writers in both
Prose and Verse' " (S. 409) .[15] His purpose is to discover which
objects in nature and art arouse imaginative responses, how
they do this, and what the nature of such an experience is.

Addison's "imagination" lies somewhere between Descartes's
and Locke's conceptions of this faculty. Strictly speaking, the
imagination is not a faculty at all, but represents one of the
ways in which the unified soul operates. "The Soul consists of
many Faculties, as the Understanding, the Will, with all the
Senses both outward and inward; or to speak more Philosophically, the Soul can exert her self in many different Ways of Action" (S. 600) .[16] Addison, however, continues to speak of the
parts of the soul (memory, imagination, will, and reason) as if
they were independent faculties, but this expression is a product of convenience and custom. The entire soul wills, remem-
bers, and imagines. Here he is doing nothing more than following Locke's precept: "For if it be reasonable to suppose
or talk of faculties as distinct beings that can act . . . it is fit that
we should make a speaking faculty . . . and a dancing faculty,
by which these actions are produced, which are but several
modes of motion." [17] Addison rejects the faculty psychology in
theory, with its concomitant identification of the parts of the
soul, even when he speaks in terms of this popular psychology
in his papers written for a more general and less philosophically
sophisticated audience.

[15] C. D. Thorpe, "Addison's Theory of the Imagination as 'Perceptive Response'," *Papers of the Michigan Academy of Science, Arts and Letters,* XXI
(1936) , 510–511; hereafter, Thorpe, *PMASAL,* XXI (1936) .
   Many of the passages cited from the works of Thomas Hobbes were first cited
by Professor Thorpe in this article or in his *Aesthetic Theory of Thomas Hobbes.*
Repeated references to these citations would be burdensome. If the reader assumes that all such references are from Professor Thorpe, he will be correct ap-
proximately half of the time. These two works on English neoclassical aesthetics
and criticism are among the most important ones on the subject, and there is no
adequate way of expressing my debt to them.
   [16] Thorpe, *PMASAL,* XXI (1936) , p. 513.
   [17] *EHU,* II, xxi, 17. See "Faculty," John Harris, *Lexicon Technicum,* I. Harris
gives the ancient and medieval division of the three types of faculties and their
members, adding, "But these like most other Distinctions of the Ancient Philosophers, are both useless and ill-grounded." The entire entry is dropped from
the 1710 edition of the *Lexicon.*

Addison, unlike his philosophical predecessors, Descartes, Hobbes, and Locke, added dignity to the position of the imagination. Descartes had equated imagination with the senses, making it distinctly inferior to the understanding. For Hobbes and Locke, the imagination performs functions which are independent of sensation, but imagination untempered by reason tends to be wild and a source of error.[18] Addison takes something from each of these views. "The Pleasures of the Imagination, taken in their full Extent, are not so gross as those of the Sense, nor so refined as those of the Understanding" (S. 411).[19] If the pleasures of the imagination are not so enlightening as those of the understanding, they are as transporting as those of the understanding, and more easily comprehended and conducive to health by being less taxing to the mind.

The dominant view of the imagination in post-Restoration England is the one expressed in Hobbes's *Answer to Davenant.* Here, the imagination is the image-finder for the judgment, which supplies the invention and structure of the poem.[20] This distrust of unbridled and irrational fancy is the rule in late seventeenth-century criticism though Hobbes and, later, Dryden assigned more exalted tasks than that of ornamenter to this function of the mind.

In Addison's writings the imagination has three distinct functions. First, the imagination may serve as the "selective faculty," a conception which elevates the imagination through its as-

[18] *Descartes,* I, 185, 187; *Lev.* I, viii; *EHU,* II, xi, 11.

[19] The hierarchical arrangement of sense, imagination, and reason may be traced to the Aristotelian and neo-Platonic distinction made by Boethius (*Consolations,* Book V, Prosa IV) , in which the imagination is placed above the senses and below the reason and understanding. Both the order of these faculties and the reasons for the distinctions are maintained in the same general form in Aquinian philosophy. Locke's rejection of Aristotelian forms and Platonic essences led him to base his hierarchy upon epistemological and psychological, rather than upon metaphysical grounds. However, while Locke consistently maintained that imagination is always inferior to reason, Addison contended that the speed with which the imagination reacts makes it superior in the aesthetic realm.

One may note that Boethius's "understanding," which gives man a knowledge of ideal forms, disappears as an independent faculty with the decline of the belief in these forms in modern philosophy.

[20] *CESC,* II, 59. See Rymer, *Critical Works,* p. 20; John Sheffield, *Essay upon Poetry,* p. 3.

sociation with Bacon's theory of ideal imitation.[21] Bacon, calling
poetry "feigned history," remarks on the ability of the imagination to "join that which nature hath severed, and sever that
which nature hath joined." "The use of this feigned history
hath been to give some shadow of satisfaction to the mind of
man in those points wherein the nature of things doth deny it,
the world being in proportion inferior to the soul; by reason
whereof there is, agreeable to the spirit of men, a more ample
greatness, than can be found in the nature of things." [22] For
Bacon, imagination is *the* poetic faculty, just as the memory is
the historical faculty, and the reason the philosophical one.[23]
If the fruits of the imagination are not literal truth, poetry embodies truths of the reason in allegorical and sensual forms
which provide "illumination" unknown to readers of only history and philosophy.[24]

Addison, in his discussion of the pleasures of the imagination,
attempts to explain the delights which the mind derives from
seeing representations of natural objects and actions. All secondary pleasures of the imagination proceed from a comparison
of ideas of the original objects with the ideas received from the
representations (*S.* 416). The particular value of representation lies in the fact that the mind searches for perfection in imperfect nature. Therefore, this perfection must be supplied by
the poet's mind itself: ". . . on this account it is the part of the
Poet to humour the Imagination in its own Notions, by mend-
ing and perfecting Nature where he describes a Reality, and by
adding greater Beauties than are put together in Nature, where
he describes a Fiction" (*S.* 418). In Addison's view, the "Imagination can fancy it self things more Great, Strange or Beautiful
than the Eye ever saw." The poet or painter, seeing the flaws in
the natural world, selects and combines the great, new, and

[21] The names for Addison's functions of the imagination are taken from
Thorpe, *PMASAL*, XXI (1936).

[22] *Advancement of Learning*, II, xiii.

[23] *Ibid.*, II, i.

[24] Bacon, *De Augmentis*, in *Works*, VIII, 441; cited by Robert Hinman, *ELH*,
XXIII (1956), 196. See George Williamson, "The Restoration Revolt against Enthusiasm," *SP*, XXX (1933), 573; John L. Harrison, *HLQ*, XX (1957), 109–111.

beautiful materials presented to his imagination, presenting scenes more perfect than those provided by nature.

This function of the imagination represents the combined functions of two distinct faculties, called by Dryden "fancy" and "imagination." In his early essays Dryden agreed with Hobbes that judgment should be the master in poetry and drama, but, contrary to the position taken in *Answer to Davenant,* he assigned invention to the imagination, charging fancy with the responsibility for providing images and ornaments for the inventive imagination.[25] Addison, following Bacon rather than Dryden, combines the two roles in a single "faculty" which he called either "fancy" or "imagination." It was Thomas Hobbes, however, who provided Addison with the analysis of the operations of the imagination which he did not find in Bacon.

The imagination may serve, also, as the "agency of creative response." [26] Here Addison's break with the Cartesian philosophers and his debt to Hobbes and Locke are most evident. In this capacity the imagination is the active receiver of the secondary qualities of an object. "It is in this Sense [the sight] which furnishes the Imagination with its Ideas; so that by the Pleasures of the Imagination or Fancy (which I use promiscuously) I here mean such as arise from visible Objects, either when we have them actually in our View, or when we call up their Ideas into our Minds by Paintings, Statues, Descriptions, or any the like Occasions" (S. 411). In Cartesian philosophy these external senses play an entirely passive role in sense perception. Although the external senses are stimulated by physical

---

[25] *Essays,* I, 14. Addison, by assigning the power of invention to the imagination, follows Bacon and Dryden, rather than Hobbes. See John M. Aden, "Dryden and Imagination: The First Phase," *PMLA,* LXXIV (1959), 28–40. Professor Aden writes that fancy and imagination have "swept the stakes" in the *Essay of Heroic Plays* (p. 39). "The climactic character of the essay is reflected in its vocabulary. It has already been pointed out that neither *judgment* nor *wit* appear, but only *fancy* and *imagination. Fancy,* moreover, for the first time appears without unfavorable connotations" (p. 40). An exception to this statement is given (Dryden, *Essays,* I, 155). One must note, however, that even eight years later, in 1682, Dryden was wary of the "false applause of Fancy" (*Essays,* I, 237).

[26] Thorpe, *PMASAL,* XXI (1936), 512.

objects, the figure conveyed is "carried off to some other part of
the body, that part called the common sense, and in the very
same instant and without the passage of any real entity from
one to another." [27] The "common sense" impresses the imagination as if the latter were wax. The fancy or imagination has no
creative role in the act of perception; it is simply the function
of the body. Imaginations, like the passions, are not actions of
the intellectual soul, because they are not controlled by the
will.[28] Most often, pleasure is found to be good by the mind,
which sends an impulse to the imagination, located in the heart,
exciting a motion there. Apart from this, there is no connection
between the intellect and the imagination.[29] The imagination's
power to arouse the passions is not dependent upon the mind,
because the former can directly excite sensations of pleasure
and pain. In all of these operations, however, the imagination
engages in no creative activity; it remains the passive recipient
of perceptual responses.

The imagination, as the image-forming faculty, takes a much
more active role in Hobbes's philosophy.[30] Rejecting Cartesian
dualism, Hobbes subsumed *"res cogitans"* under *"res extensa"*;
thought became another result of physical activity, "matter in
motion." "Motion is the essential cause of sensation whether it
be external to the senses or internal . . . The sensible qualities
which arise from this process are not objective qualities which
can be predicated of the object, since they 'are in the object that
causeth them, but so many motions of the matter, by which it
presseth our organs diversely'." [31] Sense perception is infallible, but it does not necessarily conform to the world which it
depicts. Here, imagination, as original perception, is indistin-
guishable from "phantasms." Hobbes was not concerned about

[27] *Descartes*, I, 38. See Donald F. Bond, "The Neo-Classical Psychology of the
Imagination," *ELH*, IV (1937), 249–251.
[28] *Descartes*, I, 341. Peré Malebranche accepted Descartes's explanation of the
operation of the imagination in terms of animal spirits, but added an "active"
operation to the imagination. This apparent innovation merely posits that the
will causes the spirits to flow (*Search after Truth*, p. 46). See, too, pp. 66–67, 85.
[29] *Descartes*, I, 290.
[30] *Lev.* I, i; *Elements of Philosophy*, IV, xxv, 2–3.
[31] Yolton, *JHI*, XVI (1955), 437.

the problem of the reality of our perceptions, as Descartes and Locke were, and he never established a tangible relationship between "phantasms" and their objects; however, he was never uncertain about the nature of these products of the senses.

All appearances, or phantasms, of bodies are products of the fancy. Pressing a closed eye makes one "fancy" a light. The light could not be the pressure itself; therefore, it must be the product of motion within the percipient. "Sense in all cases is nothing else but original fancy, caused . . . by the pressure, by the motion of externall things upon our Eyes, Eares, and other organs thereunto ordained" (*Lev.* I, i). The motion, however, cannot be in the object alone; then the pressure on the eye would not cause the light to be perceived. While the imagination can hardly be said to be making a "creative response" in any sense which would have been meaningful to Descartes, the Hobbesian "imagination" may be said to be active in a way in which the Cartesian faculty is not.

Space is the phantasm existing without the mind simply; that is to say, that phantasm, in which we consider no other accident, but only that it appears without us . . . The *extension* of a body, is the same with the *magnitude* of it, or that which some call *real space.* But this magnitude does not depend upon our cogitation, as imaginary space doth; for this is an effect of our imagination, but *magnitude* is the cause of it; this is an accident of the mind, that of a body existing outside the mind.[32]

Imagination, as the organ of perception, gives us our knowledge of space. It is not a knowledge of real space, but of psycho-

---

[32] *De Corpore,* II, vii, 2; II, viii, 4. This explanation of imaginary space is, in part, a criticism of atomistic philosophy, which is one of the precursors of Hobbesian mechanism. See Robert Boyle, *The Origine of Formes and Qualities,* where the author reduces the nonspiritual world to matter and motion, but believes that man can know the real qualities of matter, which are the active causes of our sensations.

For the influence of atomism on Hobbes, see Frithiof Brandt, *Thomas Hobbes' Mechanical Conception of Nature,* pp. 73–76. See, too, on atomism in English philosophy, A. J. Snow, *Matter and Gravity in Newton's Physical Philosophy: A Study in the Natural Philosophy of Newton's Time,* pp. 16–26; Richard I. Aaron, *John Locke,* pp. 31–34.

logical space, which is as much a product of the motion of the imagination as it is of the motion of the object of the imagination. This, however, is but one step in the making of Addison's view of the imagination as "creative response."

Locke's epistemology, like Hobbes's, begins with a critique of Descartes's philosophy. The "historical plain method," a nonspeculative study of the origins of the human mind, rejects Descartes's "innate ideas" along with Leibniz's "necessary propositions." All knowledge begins with sense experience even when it does not have its logical roots there. The idea, which is any mental content whatsoever, comes directly from the senses or from reflection, the operation of the mind upon what the senses have given it.[33] The soul begins to have ideas only after it begins to perceive: "perception of ideas being . . . to the soul, what motion is to the body, but one of its operations . . ."[34] Although Locke refuses to reduce the world to Hobbes's "matter in motion," he agrees that man never perceives anything directly. In this representative theory of perception, we apprehend only *ideas* of primary qualities and their *powers,* the secondary qualities, to make impressions upon our minds.

Perception is, generally, a passive inlet for sense impressions. The imagination becomes active, as a form of reflection, in the contemplation of retained ideas.[35] Locke, however, is fundamentally antipoetic in his philosophy. He has little to say about the imagination, and his judgment of wit as a wild and erroneous faculty is much less flattering than Addison's view of the imagination.[36] Addison's "imagination" as "creative response" combines Hobbes's perceptual imagination with Locke's explanation of the secondary qualities of matter.

The imagination, in the papers on *The Pleasures of the Imagination,* assumes an unusual character. It is entirely dependent upon light and the sense of sight for its images.

[33] *EHU*, II, i, 2.
[34] *Ibid.*, II, i, 10. See Tuveson, *Imagination as a Means of Grace*, pp. 16–20, on Locke's epistemology and its influence on the theory of the imagination.
[35] *EHU*, II, i, 25.
[36] *EHU*, II, xi, 2.

Our Sight is the most perfect and most delightful of all our Senses
. . . The Sense of Feeling can indeed give us a Notion of Extension,
Shape, and all the other Ideas that enter at the Eye, except Colours;
but at the same time it is very much streightned and confined in its
Operations . . . Our Sight seems designed to supply all these Defects,
and may be considered as a more delicate and diffusive kind of
Touch, that spreads its self over an infinite Multitude of Bodies,
comprehends the largest Figures, and brings into our reach some of
the most remote Parts of the Universe . . . We cannot indeed have a
single Image in the Fancy which did not make its first Entrance
through the Sight. (S. 411)

The description of the sight as a "diffusive kind of touch" shows
Addison's indebtedness to Descartes and Malebranche for his
theory of light.[37] Addison's interest in the theory of colors may
be traced through a letter to Bishop Hough written from Mar-
seilles in 1700.

When I was at Paris I visited the Pere Malebranch, who has a
particular Esteem for the English nation, where I believe he has
more admirers than in his own. The French dont care for following
him through such deep Reserches, and look upon the New Philosophy in General as Visionary or Irreligious. He told me himself
that he was five and twenty years old before he had so much as
heard of the name of Des Cartes. His book is now Reprinting with
Additions, among which he read to me a very pretty Hypothesis of
Colours, which is very different from that of Cartesius or Dr. Newton, tho they may all three be True.[38]

There is no indication that Addison ever resolved his doubts
about the three theories of light, but the influence of Newton
seems to be clearest. Descartes neglected color and light because they are not primary qualities; that is, they cannot be
measured on a mathematical scale. While Newton did not attempt to return color to the realm of primary qualities, he re-

[37] *The World; or, Essay on Light,* in *The Philosophy of Descartes in Extracts
from His Writings,* pp. 214–218, 265.

[38] *Letters,* p. 25. Malebranche's *Discourse upon Light* was translated in the year
in which it was published. It was printed in England with the "second edition"
of *Search after Truth.*

stored the respectability of the study of color by reducing it to mathematical principles.[39]

Addison's identification of the pleasures of the imagination with the sense of sight cannot be wholly or even largely attributed to the influence of Newtonian physics, however. As Professor Nicolson has noted, sight was "the most comprehensive of all our senses" to both Descartes and Locke.[40] Although Addison's argument is a psychological rather than a metaphysical one, his restriction of the inlets of the imagination is hardly a new one.[41] Indeed, we come much closer to the truth if we see *Spectator* 411 as an explicit statement of the unique position of the sense of sight in criticism and philosophy from Plato to Addison's own day.[42] Addison, however, supported the traditional belief in the superiority of sight among the five senses with explanations from Locke's and Newton's theories of primary and secondary qualities.

Citing Locke's *Essay* (II, viii), Addison repeats what had

[39] Marjorie Hope Nicolson, *Newton Demands the Muse: Newton's Opticks and the Eighteenth Century Poets*, p. 22.

[40] *Ibid.*, p. 82. See Tuveson, *Imagination as a Means of Grace*, pp. 72–73.

[41] Wimsatt and Brooks, *Literary Criticism: A Short History*, p. 257.

[42] Plato called sight "the most piercing of senses" (*Phaedrus* 250). Aristotle falsely derived *"phantasie"* from the word for light. See Murray W. Bundy, *The Theory of Imagination in Classical and Medieval Thought*, Illinois Studies in Lang. and Lit., XII, Nos. 2–3 (1927), 69–70; *De Anima* 429a; *Metaphysics* 980a. Aristotle, in *De Memoria* 450a, writes that a *phantasm* is a picture of the object it represents (Bundy, p. 74).

On sight and hearing as the highest senses, see Aquinas, *Summa Theologica*, i–ii, q. 27, a. 1, *ad* 3. Dante (in *Purgatorio*, XVII, 31 ff.) describes the imagination as the inner eye (cited by Bundy, p. 240). In religious tracts of the Middle Ages, the sight was frequently mentioned as the most pleasing and, consequently, the most misleading sense (see *Ancrene Riwle*, EETS 232, pp. 2 ff.). The belief that sight is the most pleasing sense and hearing the most useful one continued throughout the seventeenth century. See *Athenian Gazette*, II (July 25, 1691), 18; *HWL*, VI (April, 1704), 225.

Henry Lee, in his Lockean *Anti-Scepticism* (p. 39), places heavy emphasis upon the visual activity of the imagination. Lee's references to visual images in both poetry and the fine arts bring to mind the belief in the similarity between the poet's and the painter's imaginations, which is summed up in the Horatian *"ut pictura poesis."* See Jean Hagstrum, *The Sister Arts: The Tradition of Literary Pictorialism and English Poetry from Dryden to Gray*, especially for the development of the concept of *enargeia* from Plutarch through the seventeenth century (p. 11 *passim*). Professor Hagstrum calls Addison's identification of imagination with the sense of sight "the definitive statement in English of the doctrine of *enargeia*" (p. 136). See *Lev.* I, ii–iii; Addison, *Works*, I, 293.

been said before Locke by Descartes, Hobbes, and Newton: [43]
". . . Light and Colours, as apprehended by the Imagination,
are only Ideas in the Mind, and not Qualities which have any
existence in Matter" (S. 413). At this point Addison's views
become eclectic. Color, the source of a great part of the beauty
presented to the sight, is not a property of matter, at all. Locke,
whose artistic interests were limited, did little to explain the
evocation of pleasure by the secondary qualities, while Hobbes
discussed the pleasures of the sense and mind without reference
to the question of secondary qualities (Lev. I, iv). Addison
adapted Locke's conception of the secondary qualities and
Hobbes's theory of the active "original fancy" to explain the
reception of the pleasure-producing secondary qualities.

Beauty, which most of Addison's predecessors thought of as a
primary quality of objects, is, for Addison, induced by a subjective response through the operation of the primary qualities
of matter upon the imagination. "There is not perhaps any real
Beauty or Deformity more in one piece of Matter than another,
because we might have been so made that whatsoever now appears loathsom to us, might have shewn it self agreeable; but we
find by Experience, that there are several Modifications of Matter which the Mind, without previous Consideration, pro-
nounces at first sight Beautiful or Deformed" (S. 412). Because
God has created the world as he has, beauty, like sound and
color, is received as if it were a secondary quality (S. 413). [44]
The imagination, far from being a passive recipient of the secondary qualities which give it pleasure, participates in the per-

[43] Newton, Opticks, based on the 4th ed. of 1730, p. 124. See Hobbes, Works,
IV, 4.
[44] Tuveson, Imagination as a Means of Grace, pp. 107–108: Professor Tuveson
writes that Addison views beauty as an "illusion," a product of "subjective consciousness." This is true insofar as Addison sees the secondary qualities as illu-
sory. Addison, however, follows Locke and Newton in his view of the secondary
qualities and believes, therefore, that beauty and deformity elicit responses because of the manner in which God has constructed the mind (S. 413). In his
view of the imagination as the "organ of perceptive response," Addison attempts
to explain deviations from this "normal" reaction and ways of "cultivating" the
imagination. See Jerome Stolnitz, " 'Beauty': Some Stages in the History of an
Idea," JHI, XXII (1961), 188–189; "On the Origins of 'Aesthetic Disinterestedness,' " JAAC, XX (1961), 139–141.

ceptual activity. "Our Imagination loves to be filled with an Object, or grasp at anything that is too big for its capacity" (*S.* 413). For Addison, as for Hobbes, the imagination seems to be an interpreter of the "pressure" applied by the primary qualities through their *power* to produce the secondary ones. The world would be pleasureless without the active mediation of the imagination. And it is, indeed, the quality and education —the *taste*—of the responding imagination which largely determines the critic's evaluation of paintings, statues, and poems.

The final operation of the imagination takes the form of what Clarence Thorpe calls the "organ of taste and perceptive response." This pleasure of the imagination comes from the "spontaneous recognition of certain elements in its objects." [45] This response is independent of any practical interest which the perceiver may have in the object and is the precursor of what has come to be known as "aesthetic distance." The response is as immediate as that of the senses, but is stimulated by the imagination, which is not so "refined" as the understanding. The imagination does not add to man's knowledge or improve his mind, but its pleasures are as "great and transporting" as those of the mind. While accepting part of Locke's description of the imagination, Addison finds it necessary to defend his own view of the dignity of the imagination from Locke's theory. "Because its beauty appears at first sight, and there is no required labor of thought to examine what truth there is in it . . . the mind, without looking any further, rests satisfied with the agreeableness of the picture and the gaiety of the fancy" (*EHU,* II, xi, 2). Addison concedes that the response of the imagination is immediate, but objects to the denigration of it. "A beautiful Prospect delights the Soul, as much as a Demonstration; and a Description in *Homer* has charm'd more Readers than a Chapter in *Aristotle*" (*S.* 411). That the pleasures of the imagination are more immediate and easily acquired than those of the mind is to the advantage of the imagination.

More important, this imaginative response becomes a crite-

[45] Thorpe, *PMASAL*, XXI (1936), 512, 513.

rion of literary judgment. This is one beginning of the appeal to the imagination, not the reason or judgment, in aesthetic questions.

A Man of Polite Imagination is let into a great many Pleasures, that the Vulgar are not capable of receiving. He can converse with a Picture, and find an agreeable Companion in a Statue. He meets with a secret Refreshment in a Description, and often feels a greater Satisfaction in the Prospect of Fields and Meadows, than another does in the Possession. It gives him, indeed, a kind of Property in every thing he sees, and makes the most rude uncultivated Parts of Nature administer to his Pleasures: So that he looks upon the World, as it were, in another Light, and discovers in it a Multitude of Charmes, that conceal themselves from the generality of Mankind. (S. 411)

This disinterested immediate response to beauty is a "sort of nervous excitation." [46] It is part of Hobbes's "original fancy," which perceives the secondary qualities, but this "perceptive response" goes beyond the perception to respond favorably or unfavorably to the received impression.

This aspect of the imagination as "perceptive response" is hardly distinguishable from Addison's notion of taste.[47] All men have imagination and taste in some state of development. Addison, in his essays on ballads, is delighted by the songs and fables of the "vulgar" people. Expressing some confidence in untutored popular taste, Addison suggests that "it is impossible that any thing should be universally tasted and approved by a Multitude, tho' they are only the Rabble of a Nation, which hath not in it some peculiar Aptness to please and gratifie the Mind of Man" (S. 70).

Addison is more concerned with the man of fine taste and imagination, however. This man will discern all the general beauties and imperfections of an object immediately through

[46] *Ibid.*, p. 514.
[47] "Most Languages make use of this Metaphor, to express that Faculty of Mind, which distinguishes all the most concealed Faults and nicest Perfections in Writing. We may be sure that this Metaphor would not have been so general in all Tongues, had there not been a very great Conformity between that Mental Taste . . . and that Sensitive Taste which gives us a Relish of every different Flavour that affects the Palate" (S. 409).

his imagination, the taste being *"that Faculty of the Soul, which discerns the Beauties of an Author with Pleasure, and the Imperfections with Dislike"* (S. 409). There are no direct antecedents for this approach to the imagination. The criterion of disinterestedness, mentioned earlier, appears nowhere in Addison's critical or philosophical milieu. At best, one may trace parts of this theory to Hobbes: "Of Pleasures or Delights, some arise from the sense of an object Present; and those may be called *Pleasures of the Sense* . . . Of this kind are all Operations and Exonerations of the body; as also all that is pleasant, in the *Sight, Hearing, Smell, Taste* or *Touch*" (*Lev.* I, iv). Hobbes's approach is essentially physiological, and this approach explains not only the primary pleasures of the imagination, which are produced by "present objects," but the pleasures derived from all sense perceptions. Pleasure is the result of quickening motions to the heart. If the flow of vital fluids is slackened, the result is displeasure or pain. The passions are linked to the perception of pleasure and pain through these vital fluids.[48]

This is hardly an adequate explanation of the secondary pleasures of the imagination. Here, the imagination pleases with its constructions, which are represented in sculpture, painting, and literary images: ". . . we have the Power of retaining, altering and compounding those Images, which we have once received, into all Varieties of Picture and Vision that are most agreeable to the Imagination; for by this Faculty a Man in a Dungeon is capable of entertaining himself with Scenes and Landskips more beautiful than any that can be found in the whole Compass of Nature" (S. 411). This raises an immediate problem in Addison's criticism. Many people who are acquainted with the same language and know the meanings of the words they are reading do not make the same imaginative response to a given passage. Some will be indifferent while others will be deeply moved. One reader will be impressed by the likeness of the representation; another will think it false and artificial (S. 416). Addison, in a passage in which he anticipates

[48] *Lev.* I, vi; *Elements of Philosophy*, in *Works*, I, 406. See Thorpe, *PMASAL*, XXI (1936), 516–517.

the theories of "irrelevant associations" and "stock responses" of I. A. Richards, attributes these differences to the differences in human experience, which cause the diversity of ideas associated with a given word, and to differences in individual imaginations.

This difference in association and imagination serves as the criterion for judging *good taste*. A man who makes false analogies and has a weak imagination can hardly be expected to be a reasonable critic of the pleasures of the imagination. He may improve his imagination by furnishing it with images from literary classics and great art, but, Addison believes, a good imagination, like sound organs of sense, is the property of its owner from birth. Proper education can repair some defects of a faulty imagination, but it is not likely that an imagination so repaired will make its owner a critic of great ability.

Addison begins to describe the physiology of the imagination by stating the theory of retention of ideas inherited from Descartes.[49] The set of ideas received from the "present objects" is given a corresponding set of adjacent traces in the brain. When the imagination gives rise to one of these ideas, animal spirits flow to the proper traces and all of the adjacent associated ones. These associations are not limited to identical ideas, but include, as Locke suggests, all analogous and associated ones.

When I say the Ideas we receive from Statues, Descriptions, or such like Occasions, are the same that were once actually in our View, it must not be understood that we had once seen the very Place, Persons, or Actions in general, which bear a Resemblance, or at least some remote Analogy with what we find represented. Since it is in the Power of the Imagination, when it is once Stocked with particular Ideas, to enlarge, compound, and vary them at her own Pleasure. (*S.* 416)

This accounts for the awakening of ideas of the same set. The traces associated with pleasurable ideas are wider than those associated with painful ones. The latter may be "stopt up," allowing no flow of spirits whatsoever (*S.* 417).

Addison does not explain the operation of this power of the

[49] *Descartes,* I, 343.

imagination any further. The stronger imagination may be the function of a more perfect soul or a finer brain.[50] However, the sources of this view of the association of ideas may be traced to the idea of knowledge as the fitting together of congruous ideas and the separation of incongruous ones. The association of ideas means nothing more than the immediate calling up or suggestion of sets of ideas by an idea from direct perception or reflection.[51] Whether these ideas are ordered or not does not depend upon the imagination. The association may be natural, when there is some rational or "real" affinity between the ideas. To Hobbes, the ideas of such a "train of imaginations" would have to possess similar qualities or be causally related (*Lev.* I, iii). The unnatural association is nothing more than a set of contiguous ideas, such as one has in dreams. The connection between these associated ideas is not a causal one. "They are determined by relations established by the original sensation." [52] That is, they depend entirely upon our senses and memory. The "natural" train of ideas is directed by some passion to an end established by the judgment.[53]

Although Hobbes admits the need for similitudes and imagi-

[50] In *S.* 413, Addison writes that we cannot know the necessary cause of the pleasure of *greatness*, "because we know neither the Nature of an Idea, nor the Substance of a Human Soul." This limitation leads him to concentrate upon the operations of the mind, rather than its essence. Thomas Purney, complaining about the rigidity of French critics, used Locke's philosophy and Addison's papers on *The Pleasures of the Imagination* in his own critical program, in which he would have investigated "the Nature and Constitution of the human Mind, and what Pleasures it is capable of receiving from Poetry" (*Works*, p. 48). Purney adds the "gloomy" to Addison's list of the pleasures of the imagination, but he comes no closer to finding the "efficient causes" of the pleasures of the imagination than Addison had. H. O. White (pp. 81–82) finds Purney's originality in his awareness of the need to answer the questions which Addison refuses to discuss and in his differentiation between sublime images and sentiments. Neither Longinus nor Addison provided a sure method for identifying the former, but then neither of these critics would have recognized a sublimity of imagery independent of sublimity of thought. See above, Chapter 6, Note 20.

[51] Martin Kallich, "The Association of Ideas and Critical Theory," *ELH*, XII (1945), 290–291; W. J. Bate, *From Classic to Romantic*, p. 98. See Kallich, "The Association of Ideas and Critical Theory in Eighteenth Century England: A History of the Psychological Method in English Criticism," unpublished dissertation, pp. 33–63, on Hobbes and Locke.

[52] Kallich, *ELH*, XII (1945), 292.

[53] *Human Nature*, iii, iv; *Elements of Philosophy*, in *Works*, IV, 10–11, 15; and *Works*, I, 399–400. Cited by Kallich, p. 293.

native associations in art, these associations must be ordered by the judgment. Hobbes combines these two functions in the intellectual faculty which he calls the "natural wit." "The *Naturall Wit,* consisteth principally in two things; *Celerity of Imagining* (that is, swift succession of one thought to another) ; and *steddy direction* to some approved end" (*Lev.* I, viii). Without the steadying influence of judgment, fancy verges on madness. The thread of discourse is lost, destroying the beauty of the work. Judgment, by separating incongruous ideas, tempers the extravagance of fancy.

If Hobbes would restrain the fancy with judgment, he does not deny the pre-eminence of fancy in poetry (*Lev.* I, viii). Locke, on the other hand, calls this association of ideas by the fancy "something unreasonable in most men" and a "degree of madness" (*EHU,* II, xxxiii, 1, 4). Locke ascribes this "unruly passion" partially to self-love and the lack of proper education. The associated ideas have no connections with each other, but are joined only through chance, custom, or superstition. Therefore, they are the source of error, not knowledge. Constant repetition, not its veracity, makes association a habitual mode of thought.

Locke, although he does not contribute to the prestige of wit and the association of ideas, offers Addison a more systematic theory of association than Hobbes does. First, Locke has a more settled theory of ideas. The idea is an element of the mind; that is, the mind is the sum of its ideas. Fancy and wit can neither make nor destroy simple ideas. They can only compound them, not fancy new ones (*EHU,* II, ii, 2). Here, the wit acts as the organ of secondary perceptual response. "For wit lying most in the assemblage of ideas, and putting those together with quickness and variety, wherein can be found any resemblance or congruity . . ." (*EHU,* II, xi, 2). Addison accepts this definition almost without qualification (*S.* 94). He commends Locke's "admirable reflection," but his exception marks the difference between Locke's conception of the imagination and Addison's "organ of taste and perceptive response." Not every resemblance of ideas is an example of wit; only those which surprise and delight are. "They must not lie too near one another in the nature of things; for where the likeness is obvious, it gives no surprise" (*S.* 62). In the association of ideas lies the explanation for the difference between good and bad wit. Addison, like Hobbes, believes that a good wit must be coextensive with a good imagination: "from thence proceed those grateful similes, metaphors, and other tropes, by which poets and orators have it in their power to make things please and displease . . ." [54] Locke may have made use of Hobbes's definition of wit, but Hobbes made the two essential distinctions which Addison uses in his criticism of Locke; that is, the similitude must be surprising and rare.

Addison denies that wit depends entirely upon a degree of verbal facility. The true forms of wit—allegory, metaphor, similitude, parable, fable, and vision—require a critical imaginative response. Rejecting Dryden's definition of wit, "a propriety of words and thoughts adapted to the subject," [55] Addison suggests that such a definition would make Euclid the greatest wit, Dryden wittier than Cowley, and Virgil the most facetious of the Roman poets (*S.* 62). Addison's objections to Dryden's definition are moral as well as philosophical. Restoration comedy had reduced the decorum of wit to a propriety of character to its own class whether or not such characters were praiseworthy or despicable.[56] False wit and false humor, which are based upon tricks of language and action, are irrational in that neither instructs or improves mankind.[57] Addison did not agree that wit and humor are incapable of winning men to virtue, as Sir Richard Blackmore was to maintain. He had hoped that his *Tatlers* and *Spectators* effectively diverted men while exposing vice and folly.[58]

---

[54] *Elements of Law*, I, x, 4.

[55] *Essays*, I, 190, 270.

[56] Thomas H. Fujimura, *The Restoration Comedy of Wit*, pp. 20–22.

[57] See *S.* 35, 58–62. The first paper is on buffoonery and humor. The others, on wit, condemn puns, anagrams, acrostics, hieroglyphs, and other forms of false wit.

[58] *Freeholder* 45. See Sir Richard Blackmore, *Essay upon Wit* (1716), *Series One: Essays on Wit*, No. 1. Addison is writing at a time during which wit and wisdom were thought to be antithetical. As Blackmore notes, wit and immorality were commonly linked (pp. 190, 197). For other moral and religious objections to wit, see Malebranche, *A Treatise of Morality*, trans. James Shepton, p. 114;

Addison's definition of wit is derived from his understanding of the operations of the pleasures of the imagination. True wit, the resemblance of ideas rather than the propriety of words, requires an ability to discover real connections between ideas. Even an accurate representation of a dunghill will please the mind with its likeness. Such a pleasure, however, is aroused in the understanding, rather than in the imagination, which is moved only by representations of great, beautiful, and novel objects (S. 418).[59] False wit and "mixt wit" also require a degree of intellectual concentration and a kind of analysis which are foreign to the imagination and are appropriate only to the understanding, the slower-moving of the two higher functions of the mind.

In denying that every representation, or imitation, arouses a pleasure of the imagination, Addison is not controverting Aristotle's statement that man takes delight even in the imitation of the painful (*Poetics* 1448b 13).[60] He is expressing the neoclassical desideratum that the artistic imagination selects and combines its ideas in a manner more appealing than that of the scenes provided by the natural world (S. 418).[61] "It has something in it like Creation; It bestows a kind of Existence, and draws up to the Reader's View several Objects which are not to be found in Being. It makes Additions to Nature, and gives a greater Variety to God's Works. In a word, it is able to beautifie and adorn the most illustrious Scenes in the Universe, or to fill the Mind with more glorious Shows and Apparitions, than can be found in any Part of it" (S. 421). This view of the imagination is closer to Dryden's identification of wit with imagination than it is to Hobbes's wit as a function of the fancy and provider of verbal adornment.[62] The imagination, in the

---

Works of Samuel Clark (London, 1738), II, 603–604. Cited by E. N. Hooker, in *The Seventeenth Century*, pp. 228, 229.

[59] Robert Lee Morris, "Addison's *Mixt Wit*," *MLN,* LVII (1942), 666–667.

[60] See André Dacier, *Aristotle's Art of Poetry*, p. 36.

[61] John Sheffield, *Essay on Poetry*, p. 2; David Abercromby, *A Discourse of Wit*, pp. 7–8; Pope, *Essay on Criticism*, II, 89–104.

[62] John M. Aden, *PMLA,* LXXIV (1959), 32–33. See Dryden, *Essays*, II, 138. Pope, like Addison, does not join Hobbes and Locke in divorcing wit from judgment. See E. N. Hooker, in *The Seventeenth Century*, p. 237.

act of poetic invention or evaluation of such invention, assumes some of the attributes of judgment, but, at the same time, moves with much greater speed than does the understanding.

The physiology of Hobbes and Locke does not explain the operations of this critical faculty. Addison, while he uses Cartesian philosophical psychology to explain the effect of animal spirits upon the association of ideas, can offer no better explanation for this phenomenon. Addison's view of the imagination as the organ of perceptive response would hardly be possible in the context of Cartesian philosophy. The Cartesian "imagination" is too much a part of the sensory apparatus to register a critical response, which is, in part, intellectual. This view of the imagination as the organ of taste and perceptive response is made possible by Addison's eclecticism. The imagination has taken on some of the attributes of judgment, but its status between the senses and the understanding deprives this faculty of the ability to make a wholly objective response. Since the imagination as the organ of taste and perceptive response acts upon images of nature and art in the mind, there could be no objective, rational means of verifying such a "judgment" of the imagination as Locke would verify an ethical judgment. Addison cannot explain satisfactorily this aspect of the imagination, even to himself, but this awareness of the limitations of his understanding of the functions of the artistic imagination does not deter him from incorporating this view into his general critical outlook. "There appears something nobly wild and extravagant in these great natural Genius's, that is infinitely more beautiful than all the turn and polishing of what the *French* call a *Bel Esprit,* by which they would express a Genius refined by Conversation, Reflection, and the Reading of the most polite Authors" (*S.* 160). The something more wild and extravagant is the natural genius's boundless imagination, which responds, *"je ne sai que,"* on a scale and with a speed unknown to men who are not so favorably endowed.

CONCLUSION

9

Neoclassicism: The Last Phase

> They [many of our modern critics] are often led
> into those numerous Absurdities, in which they daily
> instruct the People, by not considering that, *1st,*
> there is sometimes a greater Judgment shown in de-
> viating from the Rules of Art, than in adhering to
> them; and *2ndly,* That there is more Beauty in the
> Works of a great Genius who is ignorant of all the
> Rules of Art, than in the Work of a little Genius,
> who not only knows, but scrupulously observes them.
>
> Addison, *Spectator* 592

ADDISON'S CRITICISM is the thematic, not the chronological, end of English neoclassicism and, though he did not know it, the beginning of a new critical theme and idiom which was to be expanded upon only many decades later. The death of Samuel Johnson seventy years after the publication of the last issue of the *Spectator* should serve as a reminder that the most notable figures in the history of English criticism have been her practical critics rather than her theoreticians. Johnson's view of poetry as moral discourse is closer to the Greek and Latin conceptions of poetry expressed in the terms *"poiēsis"* and *"ars"* than it is to Addison's discussion of natural genius in terms of a highly endowed imagination which functions creatively just as a gentleman of taste's imagination functions critically. As much as Addison's view of the poetic imagination owes to Plato's *Ion* and Longinus's *On the Sublime,* his papers on *The Pleasures of the Imagination* present a new interest in the workings of the imagination which is independent of its function implicit in the classical conception of a craft in which the maker creates with a pre-established end in view.

Addison's respect for natural genius, especially Shakespeare's, led him not only to hold "Mechanical Rules" in contempt, but, also, to waive the rule of reason and order where such genius was in evidence.[1] Nor is Addison entirely content with supernatural and physiological explanations of this phenomenon of the imagination.[2] Although both Dryden and Pope shared Addison's low regard for abjectly applied rules and his high opinion of the inventive powers of natural genius, neither of these critics examined the operations of the imagination in terms of the philosophical psychology of Hobbes and Locke. Addison did not pursue his affective argument to its logical conclusion, the rejection of genre criticism for the extensive analysis of subjective responses to works of art, because contemporary psychology provided no explanations for aesthetic responses to beauty, greatness, and novelty which were significantly different from those inherited from Aristotle and the Renaissance neoclassicists.

The danger of overestimating Addison's originality as a critic is, perhaps, greater than that of overlooking his accomplishment. When William Worsfold wrote that the difference between Aristotle's and Addison's criticism is that whereas Aristotle saw "the plot [as] the 'central principle and soul' of tragedy; Addison finds that the 'talent of affecting the Imagination' is the 'very life and highest perfection' of poetry," [3] he ex-

[1] See *S.* 160, 291, 409.

[2] "A happy genius is a gift of nature: it depends on the influence of the stars, say the astrologers; on the organs of the body, say the naturalists; it is the particular gift of Heaven, say the divines, both Christian and heathens" (Dryden, *Essays*, II, 138). The mysterious quality of genius, an Elizabethan commonplace (See Hooker, in *Dennis*, I, 481), is felt by John Sheffield (*CESC*, II, 286), Sir William Temple (*CESC*, III, 80), and René Rapin (*Whole Critical Works*, II, 136). Dennis is one of the few critics of the period to completely divorce genius from its divine source, calling it "a very common Passion, or a complication of common Passions" (*Dennis*, I, 46). See Paul Kaufman, "Heralds of Original Genius," *Essays in Memory of Barrett Wendell*, pp. 191–217.

[3] *The Principles of Criticism: An Introduction to the Study of Literature*, p. 82. Cf. Tuveson, *Imagination as a Means of Grace*, p. 94, where the author states that Addison gives "pleasure" a "new and truly ontological meaning." "Nowhere do we find the traditional and hitherto inescapable warning that imagination

plained the dynamics of Addison's criticism in terms which lead one to believe that Addison brought a *tabula rasa* to his study of Aristotle. Addison was not uninfluenced by the French classical critics; indeed, he believed, as most Renaissance and eighteenth-century readers did, that the fable is the "central principle and soul" not only of tragedy, but of all other genres, as well. And the Renaissance conceptions of the "soul" of poetry were far more mechanistic than that which Aristotle developed in his *Metaphysics*.

The largest part of Addison's criticism is derivative. His discussion of heroic and tragic poetry is based upon Le Bossu's interpretation of Aristotle's *Poetics,* though Addison's conception of the moral element in literature is more humanistic than that of his literally didactic contemporaries. Except when he is discussing that rare individual, the natural genius, Addison advises the poet to follow the well-illuminated path of reason and order. Even his remarks on the sublime and pastoral poetry are structured by his ties to mimetic-formal criticism.

In these last papers, on the sublime and pastorals, however, we begin to see changes in the context of neoclassical criticism. These changes have been called extrinsic, because the issues or arguments which prompted these writings are terminal points in English criticism. The theological argument explaining natural sublimity was of little consequence even in Edmund Burke's *Philosophical Inquiry into the Origins of Our Ideas of the Sublime and Beautiful.* The "Whig" theory of pastoral col-

---

must remain the faithful servant of reason. Nowhere does Addison assert that the pleasure obtained from imagination must be used in the service of truth. Nowhere does he make the compromise that, although poetry exists primarily for the sake of giving pleasure, the pleasure must disguise a rationally justifiable purpose."

Professor Tuveson minimizes the importance of the fact that the papers on the imagination are about the manner in which the imagination moves the mind. He seems to expect Addison to repeatedly remind the reader about the relationship between reason and imagination, art and morality. These essays supplement, rather than replace, Addison's earlier essays, however. In the following paragraph, Professor Tuveson briefly notes Addison's concern about "final" causes and purposes of the imagination. These purposes, the most important ones for Addison, must be stated in theological, not modern literary ontological, terms. See Chapter 8, Notes 1, 44; and the Appendix, "Opera and the Decline of English Virtue."

lapsed not from its own defects, but from the debility of pastoral poetry. Gay's parodies of Ambrose Philips's eclogues are better poems than their models. Pastoral composition continued to be popular after the middle of the century, but as a declining rather than as a growing form. Pastoral criticism did not leave the center of the literary stage, which it occupied for a few years in the first decades of the eighteenth century, because one theory had emerged victorious, but because both theories ceased to hold the attention of their audiences.

In one sense, issues underlying Addison's discussion of both the sublime and pastoral poetry are intrinsic to the more radical changes which literary criticism experienced in his papers on *The Pleasures of the Imagination.* The interest in empirical nature and the psychology of effects which appears in Addison's papers on poetic justice is re-enforced by the belief that physical nature is one of the glories of God. The universe is not a colorless and lifeless mass, but a true reflection of the greatness of its creator.[4] This appreciation of physical nature tended to encourage an examination of empirical nature and its effects upon the human mind in a manner which was foreign to those who supported the doctrine of poetic justice or the "Tory" theory of pastoral poetry. The conception of nature as a Platonic Idea is especially congenial to those who believe that the world of matter is a reminder of man's imperfection, rather than God's perfection. Addison's view of nature is not only more optimistic; it is also more scientific in its interest in the operations of the natural world and its relation to the mind of man.

The most significant aspect of this scientific approach is its concern with the psychology of effects. Whereas Dryden's concern is based upon the conviction that Shakespeare's and Fletcher's plays move us even though they do not follow the rules,[5] Addison's discussion has a more systematic foundation in contemporary philosophy and in a method of argument

[4] William Dampier, *A History of Science and Its Relations with Philosophy and Religion,* pp. 172–173.

[5] Thorpe, *The Aesthetic Theory of Thomas Hobbes,* p. 207.

based upon the "Whig" theory of government. Professor R. F. Jones has suggested that Dryden's scepticism is characteristic of the scientific attitude of his time and that Dryden occasionally moves from works to principles, rather than from principles to works, calling his method inductive.[6] But Dryden's scepticism is that of Sextus Empiricus and Cornelius Agrippa. There is no consciousness here of its scientific implications or of Bacon's sponsorship of induction as the chief methodological tool of empirical science. Rather, Dryden's induction is more strictly logical in the Aristotelian sense. When the occasion arises, Dryden supports his arguments with examples from Terence, Ben Jonson, or Fletcher. Virgil, Tasso, and Spenser are his models for the use of gods and spirits in his poetry.[7] It is difficult to see how this use of example is significantly different from Vida's or Boileau's citation of Virgil in support of their own critical principles.

Addison's own debt to English empiricism cannot be easily summarized. Addison made no contribution to the philosophy of his age, but he was an interested observer of developments in many of the most important philosophical issues of his time, and an intelligent commentator upon them. His limitations are manifest in the very purpose for which his essays were written. The *Spectator* was not meant to be studied, but to be read in a leisurely fashion in the coffee houses. He read Locke and Hobbes carefully, but if the *Spectator* had been a learned journal Addison would not have written for it.

To this degree, his essays are a mirror of his age. His philosophy is eclectic, because the philosophical tenor of his milieu was eclectic. The age of Hobbes and Newton was past. Addison and his contemporaries were not great synthesizers; they were merely intelligent consolidators of the important achievements which had been made during the century before.[8] Addison's gathering together of elements from diverse and, often, conflicting philosophies is not the work of a philosopher.

[6] *JHI*, I (1940), 384–386. See Dryden, *Essays*, I, 195; II, 250.
[7] *Essays*, I, 153.
[8] Alfred L. Kroeber, *Configurations of Culture Growth*, pp. 149, 711.

He is an intelligent layman trying to piece together the philosophical roots of his criticism. Addison praises Descartes lavishly in his earlier writings [9] and accepts his explanation of pleasure and pain in terms of animal spirits (*S.* 417). Yet, the entire movement of Addison's critical thought, at its best, is away from the physiological explanations of Descartes toward the psychological approach of Locke. Even here, he is critical in his use of philosophical arguments. Although he accepts Locke's theory of primary and secondary properties, Addison is unwilling to relegate the secondary ones, particularly color, to an inferior status in his discussion of the pleasures of the imagination. If his theory of the association of ideas is taken directly from Locke's *Essay,* Addison's conception of the role and degree of activity of the imagination is closer to Hobbes's thinking than it is to Locke's.

When we consider Addison's involvement with the issues of contemporary philosophy in terms of Samuel Johnson's ignorance of the relationship between Lockean philosophical psychology and *Tristram Shandy,* we come to a realization of the extent to which each critic's cultural milieu is determined by his own interests. Addison, when he escapes from the limits set by neoclassical critical theories, provides his readers with more than a good epitome of other men's thoughts. He proves his ability to think philosophically, as Pope and Swift did not, in his use of Locke's theory of primary and secondary qualities and in his discussion of wit. Addison's adaptation of Locke's theory marks one of the beginnings of subjectivism in literary criticism; for the reception of these qualities requires the operation of the private individual mind to receive and combine the "powers" of the primary qualities and "create" the secondary qualities. Therefore, one of the purposes of art became the evocation of the most pleasing forms of this activity.[10] The stimulus-response character of this approach to literature is most clearly seen in Addison's discussion of the sublime. Oceans, landscapes, and mountains provide a greater

[9] *Works,* VI, 608.
[10] W. J. Bate, *From Classic to Romantic,* p. 98.

stimulus to the imagination than smaller objects do. The mind is overcome by this "immense" stimulus which appeals to its natural, God-given propensity to expand (S. 412).

Locke, however, raises serious questions about the epistemic value of the imaginative responses to sense data in his deprecation of imagination and wit. Locke relates wit to the association of ideas, to the disadvantage of both of them, but Addison accepts the association of ideas as a normal operation of the mind and wit as a legitimate poetic device, basing his argument upon Locke's own claim of validity for ideas from simple sensation.[11] Addison's argument must be reconstructed, because he did not write with the care of a professional philosopher, but with the unencumbered ease of a periodical essayist. In this case, Addison's rejection of Locke's attitude toward wit and association of ideas is left unclear because he offers no reason for accepting the association of ideas as a normal mental process.

It is clear, however, that Addison went to Locke's fundamental doctrine of ideas to find the justification for his approach. Cartesian rationalism denies the epistemic value of sense experience. At best, the senses provide the mind with unreliable impressions of the external world. Only the reason can be relied upon to provide real knowledge. There is a residue of this distrust of sense data in Locke's own thinking, particularly in his opinion of the imagination and the association of ideas, but his theory of ideas as any mental content whatever provided a solid foundation for a more elevated conception of the imagination and wit. The ideas provided by simple sensation are the necessary precursors of ideas of reflection, and the latter can be no more valid than the ideas of the sense from which they were abstracted or compounded. Had Locke followed his own theory of ideas consistently, he would have held the ideas of the imagination in higher regard. Instead, he chose to emphasize the older rationalistic argument that the ideas of the imagination neither conformed to external reality nor proved to be verifiable by rational means.

[11] *Ibid.*, p. 57.

Addison, on the other hand, chose to view association as a legitimate mental process, attributing errors arising from false associations to undisciplined wit (*S.* 62). The difference in approach is plain. Where Locke tends to lean toward rationalism in his subordination of wit to judgment, Addison accepts the ideas of the imagination as the legitimate products of simple ideas of the senses. If Addison's most important reason for taking this position is his belief that sensation is the basis of the pleasures of the imagination, he has the support of Locke's belief in the validity of ideas of sensation. If the ideas from simple sensation are reliable, then knowledge may be gained by studying both the agreement and disagreement of our ideas. Here is Locke's distinction between wit and judgment. However, although Locke admits that one gains knowledge by studying the agreement of ideas, he does not believe that one gains knowledge through the use of wit.[12] Addison follows Locke's thought consistently, preserving the epistemic value of wit and, consequently, that of poetry. Wit may go astray when it becomes the instrument for punning or other forms of the false wit of words, but true wit, which is always tempered by judgment, discovers real connections between ideas of sense and ideas of reflection.[13]

The irony of Locke's position and the direction of Addison's thought become clear when one examines Locke's conception of the association of ideas. Locke's explanation of this mental process is the most complete one of its time. He rejected this process as a means of gaining knowledge, because it is illogical; this "degree of madness" cannot be objectively verified by a disinterested observer. Unwilling to become involved in a subjectivist dilemma, Locke attempted to preserve order and objectivity by eliminating that which is not verifiable. The precise reason for Addison's contention that the association of ideas is a normal mental process is obscure. However, it is certain that Addison does not believe that the association of ideas is any more logical than Locke did. The association of ideas is

[12] *EHU,* II, xi, 2. See *S.* 62.
[13] See Pope, *Essay on Criticism,* II, 99–100.

a normal mental process, not a valid philosophical one. This psychological bias is part of the growing interest in mental states, an interest aroused by Locke's own philosophy.

At the same time the English empiricists urged a closer inspection of the mind-nature dichotomy. In natural philosophy this meant an investigation of natural phenomena and the formulation of general physical laws. For Addison, as for Fontenelle and Thomas Purney, this scientific interest led to a closer inspection of phenomenal nature rather than ideal Nature. Art may be as strange and as beautiful as Nature is, but vaster Nature is better qualified to entertain the imagination: ". . . there is generally in Nature something more Grand and August, than what we meet with in the Curiosities of Art . . . I do not know whether I am singular in my Opinion, but, for my own part, I would rather look upon a Tree in all its Luxuriancy and Diffusion of Boughs and Branches, than when it is cut and trimmed into a Mathematical Figure" (S. 414). The English gardener, unlike the wiser Chinese one, refuses to humor nature and "loves to deviate from it as much as possible." The mathematical method of Newton, which made color philosophically respectable, has no place in poetry. Art must represent nature just as faithfully as our ideas mirror the things which they represent. Or, if we have fanciful fictions, then we must not violate decorum by adding realistic details.[14] Addison objects to the operatic antics of Signior Nicolini, backed by pasteboard seas and real ermine wraps, fake ships and real sparrows (S. 5). A lion roaring in High Dutch is beyond Addison's sense of decency and consistency. If we are to have nonsense and fantasy paraded across the stage, they must not be mixed with crude attempts at realism. Harmony and order are Nature's first laws.

In its broadest aspect, Addison's criticism is the beginning of the break which divorced criticism from the values of Renaissance and neoclassical humanism. The portrayal of Nature, both physical and human, is secondary to the overt or implicit

14 S. 419, on "The Fairy Way of Writing." See Dryden, *Essays,* I, 188–189.

depiction of human values. Indeed, the portrayal of landscapes and oceans remains in the background of Addison's criticism, but the importance of such scenes has increased. Terence's *"Homo sum, humani nil a me alienum puto"* was the motto of Renaissance humanism and neoclassical enlightenment. Locke and Hobbes did not consider philosophy to be the study of all fields of knowledge, but only those sciences which help man in the conduct of his life. "Our business here is not to know all things, but those which concern our conduct." [15] This moral tenor is present in the writings of Dryden, Swift, Pope and, later, Samuel Johnson. Addison's theory of the imagination presents the results of a growing interest in aesthetic values and a waning one in humanistic and didactic criticism.

An extreme preoccupation with aesthetic values leads to a neglect of humanistic ones in art. Addison can be accused of neither adopting nor anticipating this position. His most important achievement is his break with the formal canon of neoclassical criticism. Neither the rules nor the concept of poetry as imitation or formal structure could fully explain the pleasures of the imagination. Nor can they explain the minds of those great geniuses who give us these pleasures. The revised notion of the imagination as a psychologically explicable function of the mind reduced criticism in its mimetic-formal stage to only one of a number of possible ways of examining a literary work.

Emerging from this consideration of the cultural milieu of Addison's literary criticism, one must conclude that the English empirical philosophers provided the necessary intellectual background, if not the imagination, for one of the most important predecessors of romantic criticism. To the degree that Locke's philosophy supported the view that the mind is a blank tablet which passively receives impressions from the external world, Hobbes's and Addison's views of the mind are closer to Coleridge's and Wordsworth's belief that the mind is

---

[15] *EHU*, I, i, 6. See Leo Strauss, *The Political Philosophy of Hobbes*, trans. M. Sinclair, pp. 34–35, which cites Hobbes, *Works*, VIII, v; *Opera Latina*, IV, 487 f.; *Lev.*, "Introduction."

an active percipient of the world. One of Addison's tests of the success of a work of art is its ability to arouse a pleasurable activity in the mind, a test which was to become an end in itself in romantic criticism.

At the same time this examination of pleasurable responses shifts the grounds for determining good taste from objective criteria based upon a conception of beauty as rational order and harmony of form to subjective criteria based upon individual emotional reactions. When this pleasurable activity becomes an end in itself, beauty yields its place as the most important value of art to a triad of values: beauty, novelty, and greatness. The last, greatness, frees the mind from its usual limits and restraints, a state of affairs which anticipates William Hazlitt's conception of "suggestiveness," a sublime combination and comparison of ideas for its own sake, uncontrolled by Addison's neoclassical restraints.

Although intellectual history does not adequately present the whole of the cultural milieu of Addison's literary criticism, changes in thought are certainly responsible for the most striking changes which neoclassical criticism underwent at Addison's hands. National, political, and religious prejudices, changing tastes in painting, design and gardening, even when they do not emanate from an explicit ideological context, serve primarily to re-enforce or supply a need in a given current of ideas. Thus, Chinese gardens provided Addison with a natural "art form" which had no counterpart, to his knowledge, in the visual or verbal arts of the West. Similarly, political entanglements complicated and re-enforced the pastoral debate between Chetwood, Pope, and Gay, on one side, and Addison, Philips, and Tickell, on the other. That the respective parties to the dispute followed modes of argument peculiar to their party allegiances was no coincidence, but the partisan differences are not as important in themselves as they are significant of broader ideological conflicts which extend beyond the realm of political thought.

The nonintellectual elements of the cultural milieu of Addison's literary criticism, as well as many of the intellectual factors, either existed within the framework of Aristotelian-Horatian criticism or induced changes which could be reconciled within such a frame of reference. Addison's criticism of "Chevy Chase" in terms of Le Bossu's *Treatise of the Epick Poem* reveals the inherent limitations of the critical vocabulary and presuppositions of the system which Addison inherited. Neither the theory of the sublime nor the mode of argument of the "Whig" theory of pastoral offers a clear forecast of the changes which literary criticism was to experience during the following hundred years. Occasionally, Addison's prejudices, such as his English disdain for Italian "effeminacy," served only to confirm an already existing opinion, in this case that the English would be wise to follow their native "masculine" genius, which is closer to the virtue of Augustan Rome.

It is hardly surprising that the intellectual milieu, especially natural philosophy and philosophical psychology, looms so large in any attempt to describe the changes in the tenor of eighteenth-century literary criticism. While we must be aware of the total cultural milieu of Addison's literary criticism to understand its problems and his proffered solutions, the more profound changes in critical theory needed sources such as those provided by the new ways of viewing nature and man which we find in the philosophy and natural science of Hobbes, Locke, and Newton.

Opera and the

Decline of English Virtue

THE ANTIPEDANTIC STRAIN in Addison's thought appears in his moral criticism of literature as well as in his discussion of the scope and structure of the ideal critic's knowledge. His position in the argument about poetic justice reveals the practical, rather than theoretical, interests which Addison has in ethical questions, interests which align him with Cicero and Quintilian, rather than with Plato and the idealistic tradition in ethical philosophy and literary criticism. Addison agreed that the function of literature is to teach as well as delight, but he did not accept the overt didacticism which finds its most extreme expression in the tracts of Jeremy Collier and in the periodical press, especially John Tutchin's *Observator* and John Dunton's *Post Angel*. Addison, thinking of himself as a moderate Tory in church matters, was relatively free of that unreasoned sense of religious obligation which gave rise to the undiscriminating attacks upon the theatre on the grounds that the English stage offered its audience neither the precepts nor the examples for proper moral conduct.

Addison equated good criticism with good taste, and both with good morals and good sense. The relationship between these is most clearly seen in Addison's critique of Italian opera, a dramatic genre which he thought offensive to the sense and taste of a Christian gentleman. Basically, Addison's argument against Italian opera is neither original nor antimusical. He speaks of banishing music from the state "if it would exclude Arts that have a much greater Tendency to the Refinement of Human Nature" (*S.* 18), but the tradition of sacred and secular music in England was too strong to permit a successful revival of the Platonic criticism of music. Addison's first concern, which is occasionally St. Évremond's, Rymer's, and Dryden's, is to save the English stage from the singers, dancers, musicians, and set designers. This line of criticism stems directly from the Renaissance and Augustan belief that tragic and epic poetry are man's highest artistic achievements. If comedy is lower than tragedy, it remains above the other arts, because, as a form of poetry, it teaches public virtue.

Only after the turn of the century, following Collier's attack on the theatre and the arrival of Italian opera, did English opera criticism take on a distinctly moralistic and nationalistic bias. Dennis's *Essay on the Operas after the Italian Manner* (1706) is explicitly moral and patriotic while Addison's opera criticism is only implicitly so. Dennis does not attack music, which he considers a noble art when it is subservient to reason; his thesis is that Italian opera, not English dramatic opera, is likely to overthrow the English stage by putting the pleasures of the sense before those of the reason. These operas, unlike the drama which supports both reason and religion, are dangerous to both church and state. Italian opera is incapable of informing the reason or reforming the will, "a Diversion of more pernicious Consequence, than the most licentious Play that has ever appear'd upon the stage." [1] Italian opera, like Italian poetry of the time, was believed to be without the virtues of the poetry of ancient Rome. Opera reflects the effeminacy of the Italian language and nation while the more masculine English language is better suited to the needs of poetry and drama.

Addison agrees with Dennis that the Italians have the greater genius for music, a state of affairs more than compensated for by the English genius for higher artistic forms, espe-

[1] *Dennis*, II, 383.

cially tragedy (*S.* 18) . The most important difference between Addison's and Dennis's opera criticism is in keeping with the former's less literal interpretation of the didactic function of poetry and his greater interest in opera performances. Dennis had little to say about matters of production, and none of it is favorable. Although Addison's remarks are usually adversely critical, he does appreciate a good performance, especially good acting.[2] Addison is most critical of the use of scenes and machines, but they are not the primary objects of his distaste. This phase of his opera criticism is highly diverting instruction, on a higher plane Addison thought, than the object of his ridicule.

His opera criticism is based upon the premise that opera is a poetic form bound by the rules of tragic decorum and a conception of poetry as rational discourse.[3] Discussion of spectacle and the narrower rules, especially the unities, is subordinate to a view of poetry which has its origins in Aristotle's statement of the relationship between poetry and philosophy, and in Horace's injunction that poetry should instruct as well as delight. D'Aubignac, writing specifically of the function of the playwright, remarks that a play, whether it is seen or read, will make no impression upon the reason except through the words of the play: "the Reason can understand no more of it, than the Verses or Expressions do inform him, so that either way all the Decorations, Clothes, or necessary Motions, for . . . Understanding the Play, must be had in the Verses, or other expressions in Prose, which are by the Actors recited." [4] The same assumption, that the reason draws only upon the verbal parts of the play, is implicit in Dryden's observation that opera tends to subordinate poetic ornaments to sound, voice, and music. "It appears, indeed, preposterous at first sight, that rhyme, on any consideration, should take the place of reason;

<hr />

[2] See Addison's laudatory notice on the occasion of Nicolini's retirement, *S.* 405.

[3] See Dorothy Irene West, "Italian Opera in England (1660–1740) , and Some of Its Relationships to English Literature," (University of Illinois, 1938) , *DA* (1938) , p. 5. Dr. West notes that operas generally observed the unities, especially in England, and that they were criticized primarily for their lack of decorum of sentiment and language, and for unfit subject matter.

[4] *The Whole Art of the Stage,* I, viii, p. 53.

but, in order to resolve the problem, this fundamental proposition must be settled, that the first inventors of any art or science, provided that they have brought it to perfection, are in reason, to give laws to it; and, according to their model, all undertakers are to build." [5]

Dryden, although he admits that opera is an independent dramatic genre, is unwilling to grant that the vocal and instrumental music of opera contributes to man's understanding. This particular attack on opera is based upon the growing awareness that the reputation of poets and poetry was declining and, more important, upon the unique status which music held among the arts during the latter part of the seventeenth century. Opera, thought Dryden and many of his contemporaries, merely served to confirm the suspicion that poets, rhymers, serve no purpose in a society which placed such a high value upon reason.[6] Music, because it did not communicate truth but operated only upon the senses, was given an inferior place among the arts, a position which did not change, or even begin to change, before the middle of the eighteenth century.[7]

The crux of Addison's argument against opera is that music, unlike poetry, is merely entertainment. Since music appeals to the senses only, it tends to divert the listener from more reasonable entertainments. It is unlikely that Addison would have followed Plato in banishing music from the state,[8] but he would ban the more sensual forms of music and opera from the English stage on the grounds that sense is entirely subordinated to sound in these musical compositions.[9] Dennis, writing

[5] *Essays*, I, 271.

[6] Thomas Pope Blount, *De Re Poetica*, pp. 11–13.

[7] Herbert M. Schueller, "Literature and Music as Sister Arts: An Aspect of Aesthetic Theory in Eighteenth-Century Britain," *PQ*, XXVI (1947), 195. See *British Apollo*, III (April 5, 1710), 4, on the inability of men of the time to explain the affective workings of music. Further comments on opera music may be found in Thomas Rymer, p. 117; Thomas Pope Blount, pp. 121–125; St. Évremond, *Miscellanea*, pp. 42–45; Steele, *T*. 5; La Bruyère, *Works*, I, 18–19.

[8] Plato uses "music" as a generic term for both music and poetry.

[9] See *S*. 18, 31. Addison, in his complaints about the translations of Italian opera into English, provides specific examples of the errors the Earl of Roscommon had warned against in his *Essay on Translated Verse*, in *CESC*, II, 303–304, 307, 308.

earlier on this subject, is careful to note that he is not attacking music and harmony, but Italian opera only, which is
good for neither intellectual development nor moral reform.
Opera, he thought, would drive comedy and tragedy from the
stage, leaving it completely without means to teach public
virtue.[10]

Addison, unlike Dennis, was not concerned with the immediate threat of Italian opera to the English church and state,[11] but
conceived of the problem in more general moral and literary
terms. First, Addison did not agree with Dryden that opera is
an independent genre. Dryden would admit impossible actions
in operas, because their subjects are gods. The decorum of
opera, for Dryden, is determined by the propriety of the characters from Greek and Roman mythology.[12] Dryden, however,
had English dramatic opera in mind when he was writing, not
Italian musical opera. Addison, writing of an art form even
further removed from English tragedy and heroic drama than
dramatic opera is, made no such concessions. Jeremy Collier had
objected to the characters of Dryden's *King Arthur,* because the
author had combined pagan and Christian ideas and characters, a mixture which Collier found contrary to his religious
faith.[13] Addison condemns the use of pagan mythology in any
serious poetry for both literary and religious reasons. Because
myths are not true, they cannot command the belief of an
eighteenth-century reader, who will find them improbable.
"No thought is beautiful which is not just, and no Thought can
be just which is not founded upon Truth, or at least in that
which passes for such" (S. 523).

Although Addison's Platonism is not profound, it forms an
integral part of his Christian humanism, with implications for
both his ethics and his criticism. *"There is nothing, says Plato,
so delightful, as the hearing or the speaking of Truth"* (S. 557).
By asserting that there is an inextricable relationship between
truth, virtue, and beauty, Addison is not looking forward to

---

[10] *Dennis,* I, 385, 386.   [11] *Ibid.,* I, 382.   [12] *Essays,* I, 270–271.
[13] *Short View of the Immorality and Profaneness of the English Stage,* pp. 188–189.

Shelley, but is reaffirming the well-known humanistic values of
his time: "The classical direction of art to human actions and
potentialities mirrors the traditional humanistic stress upon
moral knowledge and cultivation rather than upon scientific investigation of the external world." [14] Because he saw Italian
opera as a radical departure from the classical values of truth,
virtue, and beauty, Addison could not criticize the new opera
in precisely the same terms which he had used for contemporary
tragedy. The latter, whatever its faults, was still being written
with these ideals in mind. Although Addison had condemned
the concept of poetic justice in tragedy because it did not conform to the facts of this world, empirical nature, his critique
of opera is made in terms of the concept of ideal Nature.
When Addison writes that music should be banned "if it
would exclude Arts that have a much greater Tendency to the
Refinement of Human Nature" (S. 18), he is thinking in
the same mode as Rymer had when he condemned Elizabethan and Jacobean tragedy in *The Tragedies of the Last Age*
(1677). Assuming that human nature, as ideal form or essence,
remains the same, Rymer thinks that if human nature is more
corrupt among the English than it was among the ancient
Greeks, then the English poet ought to imitate civilized, not
brutal, human nature in order to improve the manners and
morals of the English people.[15] To this abstract conception of
the relationship between morality and ideal Nature, Addison
adds the more strictly Christian interpretation of the Cambridge Platonists, who "have so just a Notion of the Almighty's
Aversion to every thing which is false and erroneous, that they
look upon *Truth* as no less necessary than *Virtue,* to qualifie
an Human Soul for the enjoyment of a separate State" (S. 507).
The emphasis upon truth, both moral and scientific, ideal and
empirical, pervades not only Addison's philosophy, but all aspects of his criticism, as well.

The intellectual issues which underlie the war against the
opera in early eighteenth-century England are not, as Profes-

[14] W. J. Bate, *From Classic to Romantic,* p. 3.
[15] Rymer, p. 19.

sor Hamelius would have it, reducible to a conflict between rationalism and antirationalism,[16] though, as we have seen, the idea that music is irrational did much to prejudice Addison and his contemporaries against opera. But after only a cursory examination of the musical aspects of this art, Addison hastened to a closer look at opera as a dramatic form. Had Addison lived in the age of Rymer it is possible that he would have taken a more literally didactic view of tragedy. But even Rymer, who was so literal in his application of the doctrine of poetic justice, saw the puritans as the chief threat to the poetic arts.[17] The largest part of Rymer's criticism was written when the majority of English dramatists, especially the comedy writers, were not concerned with the moral utility of their art.[18] When Addison was writing, sentimental comedy, with its direct appeal to the principles of neoclassical criticism, was evolving out of the moral climate which produced Jeremy Collier. The authors of these plays looked to the critics for support. They did not join Collier in his attack upon the stage, but saw him as a wrecker rather than a reformer. Their plays were the best new arguments for the continued life of the English stage. After the first sentimental comedies reached the stage, the chief enemy of the theatre was not the libertine, but the enthusiastic and fanatical reformer.

Thus, while he held most of Collier's moral and religious principles, Addison could not accept Collier's application of them to comedy and tragedy. However, he did apply them to the opera, which he found more irrational and immoral than the drama, but with much greater moderation than Collier had. As early as 1657, Abbé d'Aubignac had found it necessary to state and answer "The common belief that to frequent Plays is a sin against the rules of Christianity." [19] The argument of the Church Fathers and the medieval church was not yet dead.

---

[16] Paul Hamelius, *Die Kritik in der englischen Literatur des 17. und 18. Jahrhunderts*, pp. 117–119.
[17] *A Short View of Tragedy* (1692) ; cited by Thomas Pope Blount, *De Re Poetica*, p. 13.
[18] Joseph Wood Krutch, *Comedy and Conscience after the Restoration*, p. 86.
[19] Aubignac, p. 166.

But the indecency of the stage, Aubignac wrote, neglecting some of the more vulgar lines of the medieval plays, was characteristic of the pagan stage and not the modern one, which is "an Innocent Recreation," a fact of which contemporary audiences must be made aware.[20]

Although the greatest number of English theatre-goers were not especially concerned about the immorality of the Restoration theatre and were often delighted by it, the moral and religious criticism of the theatre was not new when Collier wrote his *Short View*.[21] When the middle classes attended the theatre with greater regularity, they were appalled by the immorality which they found there, and they found their voice in the tracts of Collier and his followers. Collier's criticism of music, like his criticism of the theatre, was immoderate. When he writes that sight and hearing are the highest senses, he was not thinking of music, but of the pleasures which are derived from listening to sermons and other enlightening discourses. "The Manner of the Conveyance of Sounds, which is as it were the basis of Musick, is unintelligible. For what can be more Strange, than the rubbing of a little *Hair* and *Cat-Gut* together, should make a mighty Alteration in a Man that sets at a Distance?" [22] Even church music is condemned as an unnecessary and undesirable adjunct to worship.[23] Opera, of course, fares even worse. Vocal music of all kinds is damned for its lewdness and impiety. And, in the supplement to his *Dictionary*, Collier's successors revealingly define opera as "A Comick Entertainment with Musick and Machines." [24]

Collier's chief complaint against music, which in a charitable moment he admits is not in itself vicious, is that which applies to his account of the theatre as a whole, that "thinking is out of doors." [25] "Now why should it be in the power of a few

[20] *Ibid.*, p. 167.
[21] See Krutch, pp. 94–95, where he cites Baxter's *Christian Directory* (1673); Robert Gould, *The Playhouse: A Satire* (1689); Richard Blackmore, "Preface" to *Prince Arthur* (1694).
[22] Jeremy Collier, *Essays upon Several Moral Subjects*, Pt. II, pp. 19–20.
[23] *Ibid.*, Pt. II, p. 24.   [24] Collier, *Dictionary*, under *Opera*.
[25] *Short View*, p. 278; *A Second Defence of the Short View* . . . , pp. 35–36.

mercenary Hands to play People out of their Senses, to run away with their Understandings, and wind their Passions about their Fingers as they list? Musick is almost as dangerous as Gunpowder; and it may be requires looking after no less than the *Press,* or the *Mint."* [26] Collier and his friends were inclined to see anyone who defended the theatre, however timidly, as a scribbler and a libertine,[27] and the more conservative of them were dismayed by the assertion that church music, even organ music, justifies its presence in the service by "assisting our senses" in worship. Only Roman Catholics and Jews, the editors of *The History of the Works of the Learned* reported, thought that bodily worship should accompany spiritual worship.[28]

The defenders of the theatre and music, Addison among them, were not easily dismayed by Collier's arguments, though they were forced to admit abuses by both actors and playwrights. Nor were they fooled by Collier's supposed desire for reform: "But in his last Chapter, he plainly tells us, his Designe is not *Reformation,* but *Eradication:* for here he throws by the Pruning Hook, and takes up the Axe." [29] Filmer adds that Collier's attacks are misplaced; he should be seeking to reform the society portrayed in *The Plain Dealer,* rather than the play.[30] The reviewer of Filmer's second *Defence* for *The History of the Works of the Learned,* in a more generous mood to Collier's enemies than his brethren had been seven years earlier, notes that Collier's attack had caused such a stir that the theatre had been left defenseless by everyone except those who would defend her worst abuses. The current work, he notes,

---

[26] *Short View,* p. 279.

[27] See review of Collier's *Second Defence* in *HWL,* II (February, 1700), 106.

[28] Review of *A Treatise concerning the Lawfullness of Instrumental Musick in Holy Offices, by Henry Dodwell. To which is prefix'd, a Preface in Vindication of Mr. Newte's Sermon concerning the Lawfullness and Use of Organs in the Christian Church, &c* . . . , in *HWL,* II (April, 1700), 229–233.

[29] [Edward Filmer], *A Defence of Dramatick Poetry: Being a Review of Mr. Collier's View of the Immorality and Profaneness of the Stage* (London, 1698), p. 1. See Colley Cibber's remarks to the same effect written years later, in *Apology for the Life of Mr. Colley Cibber,* pp. 158–159.

[30] Edward Filmer, *Defence of Dramatick Poetry,* pp. 32–33.

supplies the need for a more temperate defense of the stage, one admitting her profaneness and immorality. There is nothing new in Collier's attack, the reviewer adds, except the way in which it is presented.[31]

It is possible, even likely, that Collier would have carried the argument among all of those members of the upper and middle classes who were concerned about the immorality of the stage had he been less extreme in the statement of his argument. Dennis, in *The Usefulness of the Stage* (1698), writes that Collier's malice exceeds his ability and that he has not restricted himself to attacking corruption.[32] To this he adds that Collier does not show "the Meekness of a true Christian and the humility of an exemplary Pastor," and he does not have "*the Reasoning of a Man of Sense,*" "*the Style of a Polite Man,*" "the Sincerity of an Honest Man," or "*the Humanity of a Gentleman, or a Man of Letters.*" [33] The virtues of a polite man of sense were no less important to Dennis and, later, to Addison and Steele than were those which Collier espoused in his attack upon the theatre. Surely, both Addison and Steele would have agreed with Collier that Congreve's use of Aristotle's observation that there are more bad women in the world than good ones to justify the immorality of the women in his plays was an unreasonable appeal to authority and to the facts of empirical nature.[34] One does not legislate morality by counting the noses of the wicked. At the same time, it is a mistake to call either Addison or Steele popularizers of the Collier tradition of moral and religious criticism of the theatre without making a number of important qualifications.[35]

Although Steele had insisted, as Collier had, that the stage

---

[31] Review of Edward Filmer, *A Defence of Plays; or the Stage Vindicated, from several Passages in Mr. Collier's Short View* . . . , in *HWL*, IX (January, 1707), 48. Filmer's *Defence of Plays* drew Collier's *Farther Vindication* (1708), after the latter had thought that he had won the field when his *Second Defence* (1700) had gone unanswered for seven years.

[32] *Dennis*, I, 146–147.   [33] *Ibid.*, I, 147, Italics are mine.

[34] [William Congreve], *Amendments upon Mr. Collier's False and Imperfect Citations from the Old Batchelour, Double Dealer, Love for Love, Mourning Bride*, p. 17; Collier, *Defence of the Short View*, pp. 23–24.

[35] John Loftis, *Steele at Drury Lane*, pp. 20–21.

should be morally useful (*G.* 43) [36] and had condemned Congreve's *The Old Batchelour* (*T.* 9), he did so more in the spirit of Dennis than of Collier. Steele praises the acting of Doggett, Mrs. Bracegirdle, and Mrs. Barry in Congreve's *Love for Love* and writes of the play, "This unusual encouragement, which was given to a play for the advantage of so great an actor [Thomas Betterton], gives an undeniable instance, that the true relish for manly entertainments and rational pleasures is not wholly lost" (*T.* 1). Steele is careful, as Collier is not, to praise good acting even in a play which he finds morally lax. While objecting to Wycherley's failure to censor Horner's immorality in *The Country Wife,* Steele is quick to tell his readers that he cannot join his fellow members of the Society for the Reformation of Manners in their universal censure of the theatre (*T.* 3).

Collier's *Short View* and its successors no longer had the urgency of appeal which they had enjoyed during the first years of the century, but their influence and audience remained large enough, as is seen in Filmer's answer to Collier in 1707 and in Collier's reply of the following year. Addison, more than Steele, was concerned with the moral issues which provoked Collier, his friends, and his enemies.[37] Seeing religion as a structure consisting of faith and morality, Addison insisted that morality, based upon reason, will survive even when faith fails; this is a just state of affairs because man is better in the world without faith than without morals (*S.* 459). One of the chief values of art, as well as faith, is that it supports morality. Early in his career as a journalist, Addison had complained that man takes pleasure in seeing his own form degraded, especially in the theatre. "The very design of dress, good-breeding, outward ornaments, and ceremony, were to lift up human nature, and set it off to advantage. Architecture, painting, and statuary were

[36] *Ibid.,* p. 21.
[37] To Joshua Dawson (November 29, 1709), *Letters,* p. 194. Walter Graham notes: "It has been long suspected that Addison had a restraining influence on the scandal-mongering tendencies of the *Tatler.* This is concrete evidence that such was the case."

invented with the same design; as indeed every art and science contributes to the embellishment of life, and to the wearing off and to the throwing into the shades the mean or low parts of our nature. Poetry carries on this great end more than all the rest . . ." (*T.* 108). Later, he was to complain that if only the English stage imitated the virtue of the Greek and Roman stages, the result would be a more faithful and moral English people (*S.* 446).

There can be little doubt that Addison accepted the popular middle-class morality of his age. He tells stories of Xerxes and Hercules to illustrate the virtue of business and the horrors of idleness (*T.* 97). On a more mundane level, he ridicules an innovation in modern architecture, the sash window, because of its extravagance (*T.* 162).[38] However, Addison's objection to the immorality of the stage is not a plea for explicit moral instruction in the theatre. He does not join Collier in the hope that sermons will be delivered from the stage and that the good will always be delivered while the malicious are properly dispatched. He desires only that the good be presented in a light which would encourage the audience to admire them and despise the vicious, a state of affairs hardly prevailing among either the Restoration comedies or the Italian operas (*S.* 446).

[38] B. S. Allen, *Tides in English Taste*, I, 44–45.

BIBLIOGRAPHY

BIBLIOGRAPHICAL AIDS

Standard scholarly bibliographies such as those published by *PMLA* and *Philological Quarterly* have been omitted from this list.

Case, Arthur E. *Bibliography of English Poetical Miscellanies, 1521–1750*. Oxford: Printed for the Bibliographical Society at the University Press, 1935.

Crane, Ronald S., and F. B. Kaye. *A Census of British Newspapers and Periodicals, 1620–1800*. Chapel Hill: University of North Carolina Press, 1927.

Davies, Godfrey, ed. *Bibliography of British History: Stuart Period, 1603–1714*. Oxford: Clarendon Press, 1928.

Draper, John W. *Eighteenth Century English Aesthetics: A Bibliography*. Heidelberg: C. Winter, 1931.

Grose, Clyde Leclare. *A Select Bibliography of British History, 1660–1760*. Chicago: University of Chicago Press, 1939.

Henderson, G. P. "A Survey of Work Dealing with 17th and 18th Century British Empiricism, 1945–1950," *Philosophical Review*, I (1951), 254–268.

Macdonald, Hugh, and Mary Hargreaves. *Thomas Hobbes: A Bibliography*. London: Bibliographical Society, 1952.

Morgan, William Thomas, and Chloe Siner Morgan. *A Bibliography of British History (1700–1715), with Special Reference to the Reign of Queen Anne*. 5 volumes. Bloomington: Indiana University Press, 1939–1942.

Pargellis, Stanley, and D. J. Medley. *Bibliography of British History: The Eighteenth Century, 1714–1789*. Oxford: Clarendon Press, 1951.

Templeman, W. D. "Contributions to the Bibliography of Eighteenth-Century Aesthetics," *MP*, XXX (1933), 309–316.

Vowles, Richard B. "Dramatic Theory: A Bibliography," *BNYPL*, LIX (1955), 412–428, 464–482, 525–534, 578–585.

PRIMARY SOURCES

Books and Pamphlets

Abercromby, David. *A Discourse of Wit*. London, 1685.

Addison, Joseph. *A Discourse on Antient and Modern Learning*. London, 1734.

———. *The Letters of Joseph Addison*, ed. Walter Graham. Oxford: Clarendon Press, 1941.

———. *The Miscellaneous Works of Joseph Addison*, ed. A. C. Guthkelch. 2 volumes. London: G. Bell, 1914.

———. *The Works of the Right Honourable Joseph Addison, Esq.*, ed. Thomas Tickell. 4 volumes. London, 1721.

———. *The Works of the Right Honourable Joseph Addison*, ed. Richard Hurd. A new edition by Henry G. Bohn. 6 volumes. London: G. Bell, 1888–1892 (a reprint of the 1854–1856 edition).

Addison, Mr., turn'd Tory: or, The Scene Inverted: Wherein It is made appear that the Whigs have misunderstood that Celebrated Author in his applauded Tragedy, call'd Cato . . . London, 1713.

Aristotle. *The Works of Aristotle.* The Oxford Translation, ed. J. A. Smith and W. D. Ross. 12 volumes. Oxford: Clarendon Press, 1910–1952.

Ascham, Roger. *The Scholemaster,* in *The Whole Works of Roger Ascham,* ed. J. A. Giles. Volume 3. London: J. R. Smith, 1864.

Aubignac, Abbé François Hédelin de. *La Pratique du theatre,* ed. Pierre Martino. Paris: Alger, 1927.

———. *The Whole Art of the Stage. Containing not only the Rules of the Dramatick Art, but many curious Observations about it* . . . [1657]. London, 1684.

Bacon, Sir Francis. *The Works of Francis Bacon,* ed. James Spedding, R. L. Ellis, and D. D. Heath. 14 volumes. London: Longman, 1857–1874.

Bayle, Pierre. *Dictionaire historique et critique.* 2 volumes. Rotterdam, 1697.

———. *The General Dictionary, Historical and Critical* . . . *of the Celebrated Mr. Bayle.* 10 volumes. London, 1734.

Bedford, Arthur. *The Great Abuse of Musick.* London, 1711.

Bentley, Richard. *Matter and Motion cannot Think; or, a Confutation of Atheism from the Faculties of the Soul.* London, 1692.

———. *Works of Richard Bentley,* ed. A. Dyce. 3 volumes. London: F. Macpherson, 1836–1838.

Berkeley, George. *Works of George Berkeley, Bishop of Cloyne,* ed. T. E. Jessop and A. A. Luce. 9 volumes. London: T. Nelson, 1948–1956.

Blackmore, Sir Richard. *Essays upon Several Subjects.* 2 volumes. London, 1716–1717.

———. *Essay upon Wit,* Series One: Essays on Wit, No. 1, introduction by Richard C. Boys. Augustan Reprint Society, 1946.

Blount, Sir Thomas Pope. *De Re Poetica: or, Remarks upon Poetry. With Characters and Censures of the Most Considerable Poets, whether Ancient or Modern, Extracted out of the Best and Choicest Criticks.* London, 1694.

———. *Essays on Several Subjects.* London, 1691.

Boethius. *Of the Consolation of Philosophy.* 2nd edition, trans. Richard, Lord Viscount Preston. London, 1712.

Boileau-Despréaux, Nicolas. *Oeuvres completes,* ed. Charles-H. Boudhors. 4 volumes. Paris: Société des Belles Lettres, 1942–1952.

———. *The Works of Monsieur Boileau. Made English from the last Paris Edition* [1701]. *By Several Hands. To which is prefix'd His Life, Written to Joseph Addison, Esq.; By Mr. Des Maizeaux. And some Account of this Translation by N. Rowe.* 2 volumes. London, 1712.

Bouhours, Dominique. *The Art of Criticism: or, the Method of Making a Right Judgment upon Subjects of Wit and Learning.* London, 1705.

———. *Entretiens d'Ariste et d'Eugène,* ed. René Radouant. Paris: Bossard, 1920.

[Boyer, Abel]. *History of the Reign of Queen Anne, Digested into Annals.* 11 volumes. London, 1703–1713.

Boyle, Robert. *The Origine of Formes and Qualities, (According to the Corpuscular Philosophy,) Illustrated by Considerations and Experiments* . . . Oxford, 1666.

————. *Works,* ed. Thomas Birch. Volume V. London, 1772.

Brady,˙Nicholas. *Church-Musick Vindicated* (1697), introduction by James E. Phillips. Augustan Reprint Society, No. 49. 1955.

Burnett, Thomas. *The Theory of the Earth.* London, 1684.

Burthogge, Richard. *An Essay upon Reason, and the Nature of Spirits.* London, 1694.

————. *The Philosophical Writings of Richard Burthogge,* ed. Margaret W. Landes. Chicago and London: Open Court, 1921.

Butler, Samuel. *Characters and Passages from Notebooks,* ed. A. R. Waller. Cambridge: University Press, 1908.

Bysshe, Edward. *The Art of English Poetry,* 4th edition. London, 1710.

Carroll, William. *A Dissertation upon the Tenth Chapter of the Fourth Book of Mr. Locke's Essay concerning Human Understanding* . . . London, 1706.

Castiglione, Baldessare. *The Covrtyer of Covnt Baldessar Castilio diuided into foure bookes . . . done into Englyshe by Thomas Hoby.* London, 1561.

Cato Examin'd; or Animadversions on the Fable or Plot, Manners, Sentiments, and Diction of the New Tragedy of Cato. With a Comparison of the Characters of the Dramatical and Historical Hero . . . Dedicated to Joseph Addison, Esq. London, 1713.

The Character of a Whig under several denominations; to which is added the reverse, or the character of a true Englishman, in opposition to the former. London, 1709 (reprinted from 1700 edition).

[Chetwood, Knightley]. "Preface to the Pastorals with a Short Defence against the Reflections of Monsieur Fontenelle," *The Works of Virgil,* translated by John Dryden. Perth, 1791 (reprinted from edition of 1709).

Cibber, Colley. *An Apology for the Life of Mr. Colley Cibber, Comedian, and Late Patentee of the Theatre-Royal. With an Historical View of the Stage during his own Time.* London, 1740.

Cicero, Marcus Tullius. *Brutus,* with translation by G. L. Hendrickson. Cambridge, Massachusetts, and London: Loeb Classical Library, 1939.

————. *De Inventione. De optimo genere oratorum. Topica,* with translation by H. M. Hubbell. Cambridge, Massachusetts: Loeb Classical Library, 1949.

————. *De officiis,* with translation by Walter Miller. New York: Loeb Classical Library, 1913.

————. *De Oratore,* with translation by William Sutton and Harris Rackham. 2 volumes. Cambridge, Massachusetts: Loeb Classical Library, 1942.

————. *Orator,* with translation by H. M. Hubbell. Cambridge, Massachusetts, and London: Loeb Classical Library, 1939.

Cobb, Samuel. *Discourses on Criticism and of Poetry from "Poems on Several Occasions"* (1707). Essays on Poetry and Language, No. 1., introduction by Louis I. Bredvold. Augustan Reprint Society, 1946.

Collier, Jeremy. *A Defense of the Short View of the Profaneness and Immorality of the English Stage, &c. Being a Reply to Mr. Congreve's Amendments, &c* . . . London, 1698.

————. *Essays upon Several Moral Subjects.* London, 1698.

————. *A Farther Vindication of the Short View . . . of the English Stage, In which the Objections of . . .* [Edward Filmer's] *A Defense of Plays are Consider'd.* London, 1708.

Collier, Jeremy. *The Great Historical, Geographical, Genealogical, and Poetical Dictionary* [1688] . . . *mostly out of Lewis Morery, D. D. his Eighth Edition Corrected and Enlarged by Monsieur Le Clerc* . . . 2 volumes. London, 1701 (2nd edition with supplements to date, 1705, 1716, 1721) .

————. *A Second Defence of the Short View of the Profaneness . . . of the English Stage: being a reply to a Book, Entituled The Ancient and Modern Stages Surveyed, &c.* London, 1700.

————. *A Short View of the Immorality and Profaneness of the English Stage: Together with the Sense of Antiquity upon this Argument.* 2nd edition. London, 1698.

[Collins, Anthony]. *An Essay concerning the Use of Reason in Propositions. The Evidence whereof depends upon Human Testimony.* London, 1707.

[Congreve, William]. *Amendments upon Mr. Collier's False and Imperfect Citations, &c. from Old Batchelour, Double Dealer, Love for Love, Mourning Bride.* London, 1698.

Crane, Ronald, ed. *A Collection of English Poems, 1660–1800.* New York and London: Harper, 1932.

Cudworth, Ralph. *The True Intellectual System of the World.* London, 1678.

Culverwel, Nathanael. *An Elegant and Learned Discourse on the Light of Nature. With Several Other Treatises.* London, 1652.

Dacier, André. *Aristotle's Art of Poetry . . . Together With Mr. D'Acier's Notes Translated from the French.* London, 1705.

Dacier, Anne Lefèvre. *L'Iliade D'Homère traduite en François, avec des remarques par Madame Dacier.* 3 volumes. Paris, 1711.

Dennis, John. *The Critical Works of John Dennis,* ed. Edward Niles Hooker. 2 volumes. Baltimore: Johns Hopkins University Press, 1939–1943.

Descartes, René. *The Philosophical Works of Descartes,* trans. Elizabeth S. Haldane and G. R. T. Ross. 2 volumes. New York: Dover, 1955 (reprint of 1911 edition) .

————. *The Philosophy of Descartes in Extracts from his Writings,* trans. Henry A. P. Torrey. New York: Henry Holt, 1892.

[Dezallier d'Argenville, Antoine Joseph]. *The Theory and Practice of Gardening . . . Done from the French Original . . . 1709. By John James.* London, 1712.

Digby, Sir Kenelm. *Observations upon Religio Medici.* 3rd edition, corrected and enlarged. In Sir Thomas Browne, *Religio Medici.* 5th edition, corrected and amended. London, 1659.

[————]. *Two Treatises. In the One of which The Nature of Bodies; in the other, The Nature of Mans Soule; is looked into: in the way of discovery, of the Immortality of Reasonable Soules.* Paris, [1644].

Dryden, John. *The Essays of John Dryden,* ed. W. P. Ker. 2 volumes. Oxford: Clarendon Press, 1900.

————. *The Letters of John Dryden,* ed. Charles E. Ward. Durham, North Carolina: Duke University Press, 1942.

Dufresnoy, C. A. *The Art of Painting,* trans. John Dryden. London, 1750.

Durham, Willard Higley, ed. *Critical Essays of the Eighteenth Century: 1700–1725.* London: Oxford University Press, 1915.

Earle, John. *Microcosmography; or, A Piece of the World Discovered in Essays and Characters,* ed. Harold Osborne. London: University Tutorial Press, n.d.

Elyot, Sir Thomas. *The boke named the Gouernour.* London, 1531.

English Theophrastus, The: or the Manners of the Age. 3rd edition. London, 1708.

Estwick, Sampson. *The Usefulness of Church-Musick. A Sermon* (1696), introduction by James E. Phillips. Augustan Reprint Society, No. 49, 1955.

[Filmer, Edward]. *A Defence of Dramatick Poetry: Being a Review of Mr. Collier's View of the Immorality and Profaneness of the Stage.* London, 1698.

Fontenelle, Bernard Le Bovier de. *Entretiens sur la pluralitie des mondes. Digressions sur les Anciens et les Modernes,* ed. Robert Shackleton. Oxford: Clarendon Press, 1955.

———. *A Plurality of Worlds,* trans. Joseph Glanvill. London, 1702.

Freart, Roland, Sieur de Chambray. *An Idea of the Perfection of Painting,* trans. "J. E., Esquire, Fellow of the Royal Society." London, 1668.

———. *A Parallel of the Antient Architecture with the Modern . . . Made English . . . To which is added, An Account of the Architects and Architecture . . . With Leon Baptista Alberti's Treatise of Statues. By John Evelyn . . . The Third Edition, with the Addition of The Elements of Architecture; Collected by Sir Henry Wotton Knt. from the best Authors and Examples . . .* London, 1723.

[Gastrell, Francis]. *Some Considerations Concerning the Trinity: And The Ways of Managing that Controversy.* London, 1696.

Gay, John. *The Shepherd's Week. In Six Pastorals.* London, 1714.

Gildon, Charles. *The Complete Art of Poetry.* 2 volumes. London, 1718.

[———]. *The Life of Thomas Betterton.* London, 1710.

[———], ed. *Miscellaneous Letters and Essays on Several Subjects.* London, 1696.

Glanvill, Joseph. *Plus Ultra: or, the Progress and Advancement of Knowledge since the Days of Aristotle.* London, 1668.

———. *The Vanity of Dogmatizing.* London, 1661.

Hale, Sir Matthew. *The Primitive Origination of Mankind, Considered and Examined According to the Light of Nature.* London, 1677.

Harris, John. *Lexicon Technicum: or, an Universal Dictionary of Arts and Sciences: Explaining not only the Terms of Art, but the Arts Themselves.* London, 1704.

Hobbes, Thomas. *De Cive or The Citizen,* ed. Sterling P. Lamprecht. New York: Appleton-Century-Crofts, 1949.

———. *The Elements of the Law, Natural and Political,* ed. Ferdinand Tonnies. Cambridge: University Press, 1928.

———. *The English Works of Thomas Hobbes,* ed. William Molesworth. 11 volumes. London: J. Bohn, 1839–1845.

———. *Leviathan,* introduction by A. D. Lindsay. New York: Dutton, 1950.

Horace. *Ars Poetica,* with translation by H. Rushton Fairclough. London and Cambridge, Massachusetts: Loeb Classical Library, 1936.

Isocrates, with translation by George Norlin and Larue Van Hook. 3 volumes. London and Cambridge, Massachusetts: Loeb Classical Library, 1928–1945.

La Bruyère, Jean de. *The Works of Monsieur De La Bruyere.* 2 volumes. 6th edition. London, 1713.

Le Bossu, René. *Monsieur Bossu's Treatise of the Epick Poem . . . Made English from the French, with a Preface upon the same Subject, by W. J. To which is added, An Essay upon Satyr, by Mons. D'Acier; with a Treatise upon Pastoral, by Mons. Fontenelle. The Second Edition: With a Discourse on the Usefulness of the Work, and some Memoirs concerning the Life of the Author, not in the former Edition* [1695]. 2 volumes. London, 1719.

Le Clerc, Jean. *Mr. Le Clerc's Extract and Judgment of The Rights of the Christian Church asserted.* London, 1708.

Lee, Henry. *Anti-Scepticism: Or, Notes upon each Chapter of Mr. Lock's Essay concerning Humane Understanding.* London, 1702.

Locke, John. *An Essay concerning Humane Understanding*, ed. Alexander Campbell Fraser. 2 volumes. Oxford: Clarendon Press, 1894.

———. *Posthumous Works of John Locke.* London, 1706.

"Longinus." *An Essay upon Sublime . . . Compared with the French of Sieur Despreaux Boileau.* Oxford, 1698.

———. *On the Sublime*, trans. Benedict Einarson, introduction by Elder Olson. Chicago: Packard, 1945.

———. *The Works of Dionysius Longinus: On the Sublime . . . with some remarks on the English poets.* By Mr. [Leonard] *Welsted.* London, 1712.

Maidwell, Lewis. *An Essay upon the Necessity and Excellency of Education* (1705), introduction by J. Max Patrick. Augustan Reprint Society, No. 51, 1955.

Mainwaring, Arthur. *The British Academy* (1712), Series Six: Poetry and Language, No. 1, introduction by Louis A. Landa. Augustan Reprint Society, 1948.

Malebranche, Nicolas. *Father Malebranche. His Treatise. Concerning the Search after Truth . . . Together with His Animadversions upon the First Volume . . . All Translated by T. Taylor . . . The Second Edition. Corrected . . . With the Addition of A Short Discourse upon Light and Colours . . .* London, 1700.

Newton, Sir Isaac. *Mathematical Principles of Natural Philosophy and his System of the World*, Andrew Motte translation, revised by Florian Cajori. Berkeley and Los Angeles: University of California Press, 1946.

———. *Opticks*, based on the 4th edition (London, 1730). New York: Dover, 1952.

Oldmixon, John. *A Pastoral Poem on the Victories of Shellenburgh and Blenheim . . . With a large Preface, shewing the Antiquity and Dignity of Pastoral Poetry.* London, 1704.

———. *Reflections on Dr. Swift's Letter to Harley* (1712). *Series Six: Poetry and Language*, No. 1, introduction by Louis A. Landa. Augustan Reprint Society, 1948.

Philips, Ambrose. *The Poems of Ambrose Philips*, ed. Mary G. Segar. Oxford: Basil Blackwell, 1937.

Plato. *The Dialogues of Plato*, trans. Benjamin Jowett. 2 volumes. New York: Random House, 1937.

Pope, Alexander. *The Complete Poetical Works of Pope*, ed. Henry W. Boynton. Boston: Houghton, Mifflin, 1903.

———. *Correspondence of Alexander Pope*, ed George Sherburn. 5 volumes. Oxford: Clarendon Press, 1956.

———. *Poems of Alexander Pope* (Twickenham edition), ed. John Butt and others. 6 volumes. London: Methuen, 1939–1954.

———. *The Prose Works of Alexander Pope,* Volume 1., ed. Norman Ault. Oxford: Basil Blackwell, 1936.

Prior, Matthew. *The Writings of Matthew Prior,* ed. A. R. Waller. 2 volumes. Cambridge: University Press, 1905–1907.

Purney, Thomas. *A Full Enquiry into the True Nature of Pastoral* (1717). Series Two: Essays on Poetry, No. 4., introduction by Earl R. Wasserman. Augustan Reprint Society, 1948.

———. *The Works of Thomas Purney,* ed. H. O. White. Oxford: Basil Blackwell, 1933.

Puttenham, George. *The Art of English Poesie,* ed. Gladys Doidge Willcock and Alice Walker. Cambridge: University Press, 1936.

Quintilianus, Marcus Fabius. *The Institutio Oratoria of Quintilian,* with translation by H. E. Butler. 4 volumes. New York: Loeb Classical Library, 1921–1922.

Rapin, René. *De Carmine Pastorali,* Series Two: Essays on Poetry, No. 3. introduction by J. E. Congleton. Augustan Reprint Society, 1947.

———. *Of Gardens. Four Books First Written in Latine Verse by Renatus Rapinus. And Now made English By J. E.* London, 1672.

———. *Oeuvres du P. Rapin.* 3 volumes. The Hague, 1725.

———. *The Whole Critical Works of Monsieur Rapin,* trans. Basil Kennet and others. 2 volumes. London, 1716.

Ray, John. *Wisdom of God Manifested in the Works of the Creation.* 6th edition, corrected. London, 1714.

[Ridpath, George]. *The Stage Condemn'd, and Encouragement given to the Immoralities and profaneness of the Theatre, by the Schools, Universities and Pulpits, Censured . . .* London, 1698.

Rollins, Hyder Edward, ed. *The Pepys Ballads.* 8 volumes. Cambridge, Massachusetts: Harvard University Press, 1929.

Rowe, Nicholas. *Some Account of the Life of Mr. William Shakespear* (1709). Extra Series, No. 1., introduction by Samuel H. Monk. Augustan Reprint Society, 1948.

Rymer, Thomas. *The Critical Works of Thomas Rymer,* ed. Curt A. Zimansky. New Haven: Yale University Press, 1956.

Saint-Évremond, Sieur de [Charles de Marguetel Saint-Denis]. *Miscellanea: or Various Discourses upon Tragedy, Comedy, The Italian & English Comedy. And Operas . . . made English by Ferrand Spence.* London, 1686.

———. *Miscellaneous Essays.* 2 volumes. London, 1692–1694.

———. *The Works of Monsieur de St. Evremond made English from the French original . . . by Mr. Des Maizeaux . . .* 3 volumes. London, 1714.

Scaliger, Julius Caesar. *Select Translations from Scaliger's Poetics,* trans. Frederick Morgan Padelford. Yale University Studies in English, XXVI. New York: Yale University Press, 1905.

[Sergeant, John]. *The Method to Science.* London, 1696.

[———]. *Solid Philosophy Asserted, Against the Fancies of the Ideists: Or, The Method to Science Farther Illustrated. With Reflections on Mr. Locke's Essay concerning Human Understanding.* London, 1697.

———. *Transnatural Philosophy, or Metaphysicks.* London, 1700.

Shaftesbury, Anthony Ashley Cooper, third Earl of. *Characteristicks of Men, Manners, Opinions, Times.* 3 volumes. London, 1711.

Shaftesbury, Anthony Ashley Cooper, third Earl of. *Letters concerning Enthusiasm to my Lord* [Somers]. London, 1708.

[Sheffield, John (Earl of Mulgrave)]. *An Essay upon Poetry.* London, 1682.

Smith, G. Gregory, ed. *Elizabethan Critical Essays.* 2 volumes. London: Oxford University Press, 1904.

Spingarn, Joel E., ed. *Critical Essays of the Seventeenth Century.* 3 volumes. Oxford: Clarendon Press, 1908–1909.

Sprat, Thomas. *The History of the Royal Society of London.* London, 1667.

Steele, Sir Richard. *The Correspondence of Richard Steele,* ed. Rae Blanchard. Oxford: Clarendon Press, 1941.

Swift, Jonathan. *The Correspondence of Jonathan Swift,* ed. F. E. Ball and J. H. Bernard. 6 volumes. London: G. Bell, 1910–1914.

———. *The Poems of Jonathan Swift,* ed. Harold Williams. 3 volumes. Oxford: Clarendon Press, 1937.

———. *The Prose Writings of Jonathan Swift,* ed. Herbert Davis and others. Volumes 1–4, 6–12. Oxford: Basil Blackwell, 1939–1955.

Theocritus, edited with a translation by A. S. F. Gow. 2 volumes. Cambridge: University Press, 1950.

Theologica Ruris sive Schola et Scala Naturae (1686) , introduction by H. S. V. Ogden. Augustan Reprint Society, No. 56, 1956.

Tickell, Richard E., ed. *Thomas Tickell and the 18th Century Poets, 1685–1740: Containing numerous Letters and Poems hitherto unpublished.* London: Constable, 1931.

Vida, Marco Girolamo. *Art of Poetry,* trans. Christopher Pitt. In *The Art of Poetry,* ed. Albert S. Cook. New York: G. C. Stechert, 1926.

[Wagstaffe, William]. *A Comment upon the History of Tom Thumb* (1711) . Parodies of Ballad Criticism (1711–1787) , introduction by William K. Wimsatt, Jr. Augustan Reprint Society, No. 63, 1957.

Wesley, Samuel. *Essay on Heroic Poetry.* 2nd edition, 1697. Series Two: Essays on Poetry, No. 2., introduction by Edward N. Hooker. Augustan Reprint Society, 1947.

Wilkins, John. *An Essay Towards a Real Character, and a Philosophical Language.* London, 1668.

Wilson, Thomas. *The Arte of Rhetorique* (1585) , ed. G. H. Mair. Oxford: Clarendon Press, 1909.

Witty, John. *The First Principles of Deism Confuted.* London, 1707.

Wren, Christopher. *Parentalia: or Memoirs of the Family of the Wrens; Viz. Of Mathew Bishop of Ely, Christopher Dean of Windsor, &c. but chiefly of Sir Christopher Wren, Late Surveyor-General of the Royal Buildings, President of the Royal Society, &c. &c. In which is contained, besides his Works, A great number of Original Papers and Records . . . Compiled by his Son Christopher.* London, 1750.

Newspapers and Periodicals

The dates given for the following items are not necessarily for their complete runs. Only those years which are relevant to the present study have been listed. The place of publication is London unless otherwise indicated.

Athenian Gazette; Or, Casuistical Mercury. 20 volumes. 1690–1697.

British Apollo; or Curious Amusements for the Ingenious. 4 volumes. 1708–1711.

British Merchant; or, Commerce Preserv'd: In Answer to The Mercator, or Commerce Retriev'd. Nos. 1–103. 1713–1714.

Englishman, The (1713–1714), by Richard Steele, ed. Rae Blanchard. Oxford: Clarendon Press, 1955.

Entertainer, containing Remarks on Men, Manners, Religion, and Policy (1717–1718). Nos. 1–43. 2nd edition, a reprint. London, n.d.

Examiner; or Remarks upon papers and occurences, The. 6 volumes. London, 1710–1714.

Freeholder, The (1715–1716), in Addison, *Works*, IV, 396–508, V, 1–102.

Guardian, The. 3rd edition. 2 volumes. London, 1747.

History of the Works of the Learned; or an Impartial Account of books lately printed in all parts of Europe. 14 volumes. 1699–1712.

Lay Monk (1713–1714). Reprinted as *Lay Monastery*. "2nd edition" (reprint of 1st edition), 1714.

Medley, The (1710–1712). First and second series. First series reprinted in 1712.

Memoirs for the Ingenious; containing Several Curious Observations in Philosophy, Mathematicks, Physick, History, Philology, and other Arts and Sciences. Nos. 1–12. 1693.

Memoirs of Literature, Containing an Account of the State of Learning both at Home and Abroad. Volume I, 1710 (reprint of 1722).

Mercator: or, Commerce Retrieved. Nos. 1–181. 1713–1714.

Mercurius Reformatus; or The New Observator, continued as *Weekly Observator* (from January 9, 1692), as *Mercurius Britannicus* (from April 15, 1692). Volumes 1–4. 1689–1694.

Miscellaneous Letters, Giving an Account of the Works of the Learned, Both at Home and Abroad. Volume I, Nos. 1–22. 1694–1695.

Moderator, The. Nos. 1–50. 1710.

Moderator. No. 1. 1719.

Monthly Miscellany: or Memoirs for the Curious. Volumes 1–3. 1707–1709.

Monitor, The. Intended for the Promoting of Religion and Virtue, and the Suppressing of Vice and Immorality. Nos. 1–21. 1713.

Muses Mercury; or The Monthly Miscellany, The. Volume I. 1707.

Observator, The. Volumes I–XI. 1702–1712.

Old Whig, The (1719), Addison, *Works*, V, 247–267, 284–297.

Patrician, The. Nos. 1–4. 1719.

Plain Dealer. Nos. 1–17. 1712.

Plebeian, The (1719). Nos. 1–4, by Richard Steele. In Addison, *Works*, V, 237–247, 267–284, 297–307.

Protestant Post-Boy, The. Nos. 1–123. 1711–1712.

Review of the State of the British Nation, A (1704–1711). *Defoe's Review,* reproduced from the original editions with an introduction and bibliographical notes by Arthur Wellesley Secord. 22 volumes. New York: Columbia University Press (for the Facsimile Text Society), 1938.

Spectator, The (1711–1714), ed. G. Gregory Smith. 4 volumes. London: Dent, 1907. Checked for errors with original folio sheets by S. Buckley and J. Tonson, and the first octavo edition (1712–1713) of the first seven volumes (Nos. 1–555) , printed for S. Buckley and J. Tonson.

Tatler, The (1709–1711) , ed. George A. Aitken. 4 volumes. London: Duckworth, 1898–1899.

————, *New Letters to the Tatler and Spectator,* ed. Richmond P. Bond. Austin: University of Texas Press, 1959.

————, *Original and Genuine Letters Sent to the Spectator and Tatler.* 2 volumes. London, 1725.

Tory Tatler, The. Nos. 1–6. 1710–1711.

Town Talk. Nos. 1–9. 1715–1716.

The Weekly Comedy: or The Humours of a Coffee-House. Nos. 1–4. 1707.

Whig-Examiner, The (1710) , in Addison, *Works,* IV, 370–395.

SCHOLARSHIP AND COMMENTARIES

Books and Articles

Aaron, Richard I. *John Locke.* 2nd edition. Oxford: Clarendon Press, 1955.

Aden, John M. "Dryden and the Imagination: The First Phase," *PMLA,* LXXIV (1959) , 28–40.

Aikin, Lucy. *The Life of Joseph Addison.* 2 volumes. London: Longmans, Brown, Green, and Longmans, 1843.

Aitken, George A. *Life of Sir Richard Steele.* London: W. Isbister, 1889.

Aldridge, Alfred O. "The Pleasures of Pity," *ELH,* XVI (1949) , 76–87.

Allen, Beverley Sprague. *Tides in English Taste (1619–1800) .* 2 volumes. Cambridge, Massachusetts: Harvard University Press, 1937.

Allen, Robert J. "The Kit-Cat Club and the Theatre," *RES,* VII (1931) , 56–61.

Anderson, George L. "The Authorship of *Cato Examin'd* (1713) ," *PBSA,* LI (1957) , 84–90.

Anderson, Paul Bunyan. "Addison's *Letter from Italy,*" *MLN,* XLVII (1932) , 318.

Anthony, Sister Rose, S.C. *The Jeremy Taylor Stage Controversy, 1698–1726.* Milwaukee: Marquette University Press, 1937.

Atkins, J. W. H. *Literary Criticism in Antiquity.* 2 volumes. New York: Peter Smith, 1952.

————. *Literary Criticism: The Seventeenth and Eighteenth Centuries.* London: Methuen, 1951.

Atkinson, A. D. " 'The Spectator' No. 543," *N&Q,* CXCV (1950) , 275.

Audra, Émile. *L'Influence française dans l'oeuvre de Pope,* Travaux et memoires de l'Université de Lille. Paris, 1931.

Ault, Norman. *New Light on Pope.* London: Methuen, 1949.

————. "Pope and Addison," *RES,* XVII (1941) , 428–451.

Barker, Arthur. "And on his Crest Sat Horror: Eighteenth Century Interpretations of Milton's Sublimity and his Satan," *UTQ,* XI (1942) , 421–436.

Bate, Walter Jackson. *From Classic to Romantic: Premises of Taste in Eighteenth-Century England.* Cambridge, Massachusetts: Harvard University Press, 1946.

————. "The Sympathetic Imagination in Eighteenth-Century English Criticism," *ELH,* XII (1945) , 144–164.

Bateson, F. W. "The *Errata* in *The Tatler*," *RES*, V (1929) , 155–166.

Beljame, Alexandre. *Men of Letters and the English Public in the Eighteenth Century, 1660–1744: Dryden, Addison, Pope*, ed. Bonamy Dobrée, trans. E. O. Lorimer. London: Routledge & Kegan Paul, 1948.

Bertalanffy, Ludwig von. "The Theory of Open Systems in Physics and Biology," *Science*, III (1950) , 23–29.

Bloom, Lillian D. "Addison as Translator: A Problem in Neo-Classical Scholarship," *SP*, XLIV (1949) , 31–53.

———, and Edward A. Bloom. "Addison's 'Enquiry after Truth': The Moral Assumptions of his Proof for Divine Existence," *PMLA*, LXX (1950) , 198–220.

———. "Joseph Addison and Eighteenth-Century 'Liberalism'," *JHI*, XII (1951) , 560–583.

Bluck, R. S. *Plato's Life and Thought, with a Translation of the Seventh Letter.* London: Routledge & Kegan Paul, 1949.

Bond, Donald F. "Addison in Perspective," *MP*, LIV (1956) , 124–128.

———. " 'Distrust' of Imagination in English Neo-Classicism," *PQ*, XIV (1935) , 54–69.

———. "The First Printing of the *Spectator*," *MP*, XLVII (1950) , 164–177.

———. "The Neo-Classical Psychology of the Imagination," *ELH*, IV (1937) , 245–264.

———. "The Text of the *Spectator*," *Studies in Bibliography*, V (1952–1953) , 109–128.

Bond, Richmond P. "The Business of the Spectator," *University of North Carolina Extension Bulletin*, Eighth Series, Lectures in the Humanities (1951–1952) , pp. 7–19.

———. *English Burlesque Poetry, 1700–1750*. Cambridge, Massachusetts: Harvard University Press, 1932.

———. *Studies in the Early English Periodical.* Chapel Hill: University of North Carolina Press, 1957.

Borgerhoff, E. B. O. *The Freedom of French Classicism.* Princeton: Princeton University Press, 1950.

Bosker, Aisso. *Literary Criticism in the Age of Johnson.* 2nd edition, revised. Groningen: J. B. Wolters, 1953.

Boswell, Eleanore. *The Restoration Court Stage (1660–1702)* . Cambridge, Massachusetts: Harvard University Press, 1932.

Boys, Richard C. *Sir Richard Blackmore and the Wits.* University of Michigan Contributions in Modern Philology, No. 13. Ann Arbor, 1949.

Bradner, Leicester. "The Composition and Publication of Addison's Latin Poems," *MP*, XXXV (1938) , 359–367.

———. "An Earlier Text of Addison's Ode to Dr. Hannes," *MLN*, LII (1938) , 279–280.

Bragg, Marion K. *The Formal Eclogue in Eighteenth-Century England*, University of Maine Studies, Second Series, No. 6. Orono, Maine, 1926.

Brandenburg, Alice Stayert. "English Education and Neo-classical Taste in the Eighteenth Century," *MLQ*, VIII (1947) , 174–193.

Brandt, Frithiof. *Thomas Hobbes' Mechanical Conception of Nature.* Copenhagen: Levin and Munksgaard, 1928.

Bray, René. *La Formation de la doctrine classique en France.* Paris: Hachette, 1927.

Bredvold, Louis I. *The Intellectual Milieu of John Dryden.* Ann Arbor: University of Michigan Press, 1934.

———. "The Rise of English Classicism: Study in Methodology," *Comparative Literature,* II (1950), 253–268.

———. "The Tendency toward Platonism in Neo-classical Esthetics," I (1934), 91–119.

Brett, R. L. "The Aesthetic Sense and Taste in the Literary Criticism of the Early Eighteenth Century," *RES,* XX (1944), 199–213.

———. *The Third Earl of Shaftesbury: A Study in Eighteenth Century Literary Theory.* London: Hutchinson's University Library, 1951.

Broad, C. D. "The New Philosophy: Bruno to Descartes," *Cambridge Historical Journal,* VIII (1944), 36–54.

Broadus, Edmund K. "Addison's Influence on the Development of Interest in Folk-Poetry in the Eighteenth Century," *MP,* VIII (1910–1911), 123–134.

Brown, Harcourt. "The Utilitarian Motive in the Age of Descartes," *Annals of Science,* I (1936), 182–192.

Bullitt, John, and W. Jackson Bate. "Distinctions between Fancy and Imagination in Eighteenth-Century English Criticism," *MLN,* LX (1945), 8–15.

Bundy, Murray W. *The Theory of Imagination in Classical and Medieval Thought,* University of Illinois Studies in Language and Literature, XII, Nos. 2–3. Urbana, 1927.

Burney, Charles. *A General History of Music* (1789), ed. Frank Mercer. 2 volumes. New York: Dover, 1957.

Burtt, Edwin Arthur. *The Metaphysical Foundations of Modern Physical Science.* Reprint of 2nd edition. Garden City, New York: Doubleday, 1955.

Bush, Mary Delaney. "Rational Proof of a Deity from the Order of Nature," *ELH,* IX (1942), 288–319.

Butcher, Samuel H. *Aristotle's Theory of Poetry and Fine Art.* 4th edition. London: Macmillan, 1932.

Butterfield, H. *The Origins of Modern Science.* Revised edition. New York: Macmillan, 1957.

Cambridge History of English Literature. Volume IX, *From Steele and Addison to Pope and Swift,* ed. Sir A. W. Ward and A. R. Waller. Cambridge: University Press, 1912.

Canguilhem, Georges. "Fontenelle, philosophe et historien des sciences," *Annales de l'Université de Paris,* XXVII (1957), 384–390.

Carritt, E. F. "Addison, Kant, and Wordsworth," *Essays and Studies,* XXII (1936), 26–36.

Case, Arthur E. "Pope, Addison, and the 'Atticus' Lines," *MP,* XXXII (1935–1936), 187–193.

Cassirer, Ernst. *Das Erkenntnisproblem in der Philosophie und Wissenschaft der neueren Zeit.* Volumes 1–2. Berlin: B. Cassirer, 1906–1907.

———. *The Philosophy of the Enlightenment,* trans. Fritz C. A. Koelln and James P. Pettegrove. Boston: Beacon, 1955.

———. *The Platonic Renaissance in England,* trans. James P. Pettegrove. Austin: University of Texas Press, 1953.

Chapin, Chester F. *Personification in Eighteenth-Century English Poetry*. New York: Columbia University Press, 1955.

Clark, A. F. B. *Boileau and the French Classical Critics in England*. Paris: Champion, 1925.

Clark, G. N. *The Later Stuarts: 1660–1714*. Oxford: Clarendon Press, 1934.

Clark, Kenneth. *The Gothic Revival, An Essay in the History of Taste*. London: Constable, 1928.

Cochrane, Rexmond C. "Bacon in Early Eighteenth-Century English Literature," *PQ*, XXXVII (1958), 58–79.

Colie, Rosalie L. *Light and Enlightenment: A Study of the Cambridge Platonists and Dutch Arminians*. Cambridge: University Press, 1957.

Congleton, J. E. "Theories of Pastoral Poetry in England, 1684–1717," *SP*, XLI (1944), 544–575.

———. *Theories of Pastoral Poetry in England, 1684–1798*. Gainesville: University of Florida Press, 1952.

Connely, Willard. *Sir Richard Steele*. London: Jonathan Cape, 1934.

Cook, Albert S. *Addison's Criticisms on Paradise Lost*. Boston: Ginn, 1892.

Cornford, Francis Macdonald. *Plato's Cosmology: The Timaeus of Plato translated with a running Commentary*. London: Routledge & Kegan Paul, 1937.

Courthope, W. J. *Addison*. New York: Harpers, 1884.

Cragg, G. R. *From Puritanism to the Age of Reason. A Study of Changes in Religious Thought within the Church of England, 1660–1700*. Cambridge: University Press, 1950.

Crane, Ronald S. "Imitation of Spenser and Milton in the Early Eighteenth Century: A New Document," *SP*, XV (1918), 195–206.

———. "Literature, Philosophy, and Ideas," *MP*, LII (1954), 78–83.

Crombie, A. C. "Descartes on Method and Physiology," *Cambridge Journal*, V (1951–1952), 178–186.

Crum, M. C. "A Manuscript of Essays by Joseph Addison," *Bodleian Library Record*, V (1954), 98–103.

Cunningham, Robert Newton. *Peter Anthony Motteux: 1663–1718*. Oxford: Basil Blackwell, 1933.

Dampier, Sir William. *A History of Science and Its Relations with Philosophy and Religion*. 4th edition, revised and enlarged. New York: Macmillan, 1949.

Davis, Herbert, "Swift's View of Poetry," *Studies in English, University College, Toronto* (1931), pp. 9–58.

Deane, C. V. *Aspects of Eighteenth Century Nature Poetry*. Oxford: Basil Blackwell, 1935.

Dent, Edward. *Foundations of English Opera, A Study of Musical Drama in England during the Seventeenth Century*. Cambridge: University Press, 1928.

Dobrée, Bonamy. "The First Victorian [Addison]," *Essays in Biography: 1680–1726*. London: Oxford University Press, 1925. pp. 201–357.

———. *Restoration Tragedy, 1660–1720*. Oxford: Clarendon Press, 1929.

Draper, John W. "Poetry and Music in Eighteenth Century Aesthetics," *Englische Studien*, LXVII (1932), 70–85.

———. "The Theory of the Comic in Eighteenth-Century England," *JEGP*, XXXVII (1938), 207–223.

Draper, John W. "The Theory of Translation in the Eighteenth Century," *Neophilologus*, VI (1921), 241–254.

Durling, Dwight L. *The Georgic Tradition in English Poetry*. New York: Columbia University Press, 1935.

Dutton, George B. "The French Aristotelian Formalists and Thomas Rymer," *PMLA*, XXIX (1914), 152–188.

———. "Theory and Practice in English Tragedy, 1650–1700," *Englische Studien*, XLIX (1916), 190–219.

Else, Gerald. *Aristotle's Poetics: The Argument*. Cambridge, Massachusetts: Harvard University Press, 1957.

Evans, Frank B., III. "Platonic Scholarship in Eighteenth-Century England," *MP*, XLI (1943), 103–110.

Evans, G. Blakemore. "Addison's Early Knowledge of Milton," *JEGP*, XLIX (1950), 204–207.

Evans, Joan. *Pattern: A Study of Ornament in Western Europe from 1180–1900*. 2 volumes. Oxford: Clarendon Press, 1931.

Feiling, Keith. *A History of the Tory Party, 1640–1714*. Oxford: Clarendon Press, 1924.

Foerster, Donald M. *Homer in English Criticism: The Historical Approach in the Eighteenth Century*. Yale University Studies in English, CV. New Haven, 1947.

Freeman, Edmund. "A Proposal for an English Academy in 1660," *MLR*, XIX (1924), 291–300.

Friedland, Louis S. "The Dramatic Unities in England," *JEGP*, X (1911), 56–89, 280–299, 453–467.

Friedman, Albert B. "Addison's Ballad Papers and the Reaction to Metaphysical Wit," *Comparative Literature*, XII (1960), 1–13.

———. *The Ballad Revival*. Chicago: University of Chicago Press, 1961.

Frye, Northrop. *Anatomy of Criticism*. Princeton: Princeton University Press, 1957.

———. "Nature and Homer," *Texas Quarterly*, I (1958), 192–204.

Fujimura, Thomas H. *The Restoration Comedy of Wit*. Princeton: Princeton University Press, 1952.

Gallaway, Francis. *Reason, Rule, and Revolt in English Classicism*. New York: Scribner's, 1940.

Gibson, James. *Locke's Theory of Knowledge and Its Historical Relations*. Cambridge: University Press, 1931.

Gilbert, Allen H. "Aristotle's *tòn omóion* (*Poetics* 13. 53a 5)," *SP*, LVI (1959), 1–6.

Gilbert, Katherine E., and Helmut Kuhn. *A History of Esthetics*. Revised and enlarged. Bloomington: Indiana University Press, 1953.

Gilman, Margaret. *The Idea of Poetry in France*. Cambridge, Massachusetts: Harvard University Press, 1958.

Goad, Caroline. *Horace in the English Literature of the Eighteenth Century*. Yale University Studies in English, LVIII. New Haven, 1918.

Goodman, Paul. *The Structure of Literature*. Chicago: University of Chicago Press, 1954.

Göricke, Walter. *Das Bildungsideal bei Addison und Steele.* Bonner Studien zur englischen Philologie, XIV. Bonn, 1921.

Graham, Walter. "Addison's Travel Letters in the *Tatler* and *Guardian*," *PQ*, XV (1936) , 97–102.

————. *English Literary Periodicals.* London: Thomas Nelson, 1930.

————. "Some Predecessors of the *Tatler*," *JEGP*, XXIV (1925) , 548–554.

Gray, Charles Harold. *Theatrical Criticism in London to 1795.* New York: Columbia University Press, 1931.

Green, C. C. *Neo-classical Theory of Tragedy in England during the Eighteenth Century.* Harvard University Studies in English, XI. Cambridge, Massachusetts, 1934.

Greene, William C. "The Greek Criticism of Poetry, A Reconsideration," *Perspectives of Criticism,* ed. Harry Levin. Harvard Studies in Comparative Literature, No. 20. Cambridge, Massachusetts, 1950. Pp. 19–53.

————. "Plato's View of Poetry," *Harvard Studies in Classical Philology*, XXIX (1918) , 1–75.

Grisy, A. de. *Joseph Addison, ou en Attique en Angleterre.* Paris: C. Delagrave, 1873.

Grünbaum, Jakob. *Die Philosophie Richard Burthogges (1637–1698).* Bern: J. Kleiner, 1939.

Gunther, Robert W. T. *Early Science in Oxford.* 14 volumes. Oxford: Printed for the Author at the University Press, 1921–1945.

Hagstrum, Jean. *The Sister Arts: The Tradition of Literary Pictorialism and English Poetry from Dryden to Gray.* Chicago: University of Chicago Press, 1958.

Hamelius, Paul. *Die Kritik in der englischen Literatur des 17. und 18. Jahrhunderts.* Leipzig: Theodor Grieben's, 1897.

Hamm, Victor M. "Addison and the Pleasures of the Imagination," *MLN*, LII (1937) , 498–500.

Harris, Victor. *All Coherence Gone.* Chicago: University of Chicago Press, 1949.

Harrison, John L. "Bacon's Theory of Rhetoric, Poetry, and the Imagination," *HLQ*, XX (1957) , 107–125.

Hathaway, Baxter Levering. "John Dryden and the Function of Tragedy," *PMLA*, LVIII (1943) , 665–673.

Hauser, Arnold. *The Social History of Art.* 2 volumes. New York: Alfred Knopf, 1951.

Havens, Raymond Dexter. *The Influence of Milton on English Poetry.* Cambridge, Massachusetts: Harvard University Press, 1922.

————. "Romantic Aspects of the Age of Pope," *PMLA*, XXXVII (1912) , 297–324.

Herrick, Marvin T. *The Fusion of Horatian and Aristotelian Criticism, 1531–1555.* Illinois Studies in Language and Literature, XXXII, No. 1. Urbana, 1946.

————. *The Poetics of Aristotle in England.* Cornell University Studies in English, XVII. New Haven: Yale University Press, 1930.

Hinman, Robert. " 'Truth is Truest Poesy': The Influence of the New Philosophy on Abraham Cowley," *ELH*, XXIII (1956) , 194–203.

Hipple, Walter John, Jr. *The Beautiful, the Sublime, & the Picturesque in*

Eighteenth-Century British Aesthetic Theory. Carbondale, Illinois: Southern Illinois University Press, 1957.

Hodgart, M. J. C. "The Eighth Volume of the *Spectator*," *RES*, n.s. V (1954), 367–387.

Hooker, Edward Niles. "Pope on Wit: *The Essay on Criticism*," *The Seventeenth Century: Studies in the History of English Thought and Literature from Bacon to Pope*, ed. Richard Foster Jones. Stanford: Stanford University Press, 1951. Pp. 225–246.

Horn, Robert D. "Addison's *Campaign* and Macaulay," *PMLA*, LXIII (1948), 886–902.

Howell, A. C. "*Res et verba:* Words and Things," *ELH*, XIII (1946), 131–142.

Hubbell, Jay B. "Some Uncollected Poems by Joseph Addison," *MP*, XXXVI (1939), 277–281.

Hussey, Christopher. *The Picturesque: Studies in a Point of View*. London and New York: G. P. Putnam's, 1927.

Hustvedt, Sigurd Bernhard. *Ballad Criticism in Scandinavia and Great Britain during the Eighteenth Century*. New York: American Scandinavian Foundation, 1916.

Jackson, Reginald. "Locke's Distinction between Primary and Secondary Qualities," *Mind*, n.s. XXXVIII (1929), 56–76.

———. "Locke's Version of the Doctrine of Representative Perception," *Mind*, n.s. XXXIX (1930), 1–25.

Jaeger, Werner. *Aristotle: Fundamentals of the History of his Development*, trans. Richard Robinson. 2nd edition. Oxford: Clarendon Press, 1948.

———. *Paideia: The Ideals of Greek Culture*, trans. Gilbert Highet. 2nd edition. 3 volumes. New York: Oxford University Press, 1945.

James, D. G. *The Life of Reason: Hobbes, Locke and Bolingbroke*. London: Longmans, Green, 1949.

Johnson, Samuel. *Lives of the Poets*, ed. G. Birkbeck Hill. 3 volumes. Oxford: Clarendon Press, 1905.

Jones, Richard Foster. *Ancients and Moderns: A Study of the Background of the "Battle of the Books."* Washington University Studies, New Series, Language and Literature, No. 6. St. Louis, 1936.

———. *The Background of "The Battle of the Books."* Washington University Studies, VII, Humanistic Series II. St. Louis, 1920.

———. "Eclogue Types in English Poetry of the Eighteenth Century," *JEGP*, XXIV (1925), 33–60.

———. "Science and Criticism in the Neo-classical Age of English Literature," *JHI*, I (1940), 381–412.

Kabelman, Karl. *Joseph Addisons literarische Kritik im "Spectator."* Rostock: C. Hinstorff, 1900.

Kallich, Martin. "The Association of Ideas and Critical Theory: Hobbes, Locke, and Addison," *ELH*, XII (1945), 290–315.

Kaufman, Paul. "Heralds of Original Genius," *Essays in Memory of Barrett Wendell*. Cambridge, Massachusetts: Harvard University Press, 1926. Pp. 191–217.

Kliger, Samuel. "The 'Goths' in England: An Introduction to the Gothic Vogue in Eighteenth Century Aesthetic Discussion," *MP*, XLIII (1945), 107–117.

———. "Whig Aesthetics: A Phase of Eighteenth-Century Taste," *ELH*, XVI (1949), 135–150.

Koyre, Alexander. "Galileo and the Scientific Revolution of the Seventeenth Century," *Philosophical Review*, LII (1943), 333–348.

Krapp, Robert M. "Class Analysis of a Literary Controversy: Wit and Sense in the Seventeenth Century," *Science and Society*, X (1946), 80–92.

Kroeber, Alfred L. *Anthropology: Race, Language, Culture, Psychology, Prehistory*. New edition, revised. New York: Harcourt, Brace, 1948.

———. *Configurations of Culture Growth*. Berkeley and Los Angeles: University of California Press, 1944.

Krutch, Joseph Wood. *Comedy and Conscience after the Restoration*. New York: Columbia University Press, 1924.

Lamprecht, Sterling P. "Locke's Attack upon Innate Ideas," *Philosophical Review*, XXXVI (1927), 145–165.

———. "The Role of Descartes in Seventeenth Century England," *Studies in the History of Ideas*, III (1935), 181–240.

Lancaster, Henry Carrington. *A History of French Dramatic Literature in the Seventeenth Century*. 9 volumes. Baltimore: The Johns Hopkins University Press, 1929–1942.

Lannering, Jan. *Studies in the Prose Style of Joseph Addison*. Essays and Studies on English Language and Literature, IX. Uppsala: University Press, 1951.

Lawrence, W. J. "The Early Years of the First English Opera House," *Musical Quarterly*, VII (1921), 104–117.

Lee, Rensselaer W. "*Ut pictura poesis:* The Humanistic Theory of Painting," *Art Bulletin*, XXII (1940), 197–269.

Lewis, C. S. "Addison," *Essays on the Eighteenth Century Presented to David Nichol Smith in Honour of his Seventieth Birthday*. Oxford: Clarendon Press, 1945. Pp. 1–14.

Litz, Francis Edward. "Richard Bentley on Beauty, Irregularity and Mountains," *ELH*, XII (1945), 327–332.

Loewenberg, Alfred. *Annals of Opera, 1597–1940*. 2nd edition, revised and corrected. 2 volumes. Cambridge: W. Heffer, 1955.

Loftis, John. *Steele at Drury Lane*. Berkeley and Los Angeles: University of California Press, 1952.

Lovejoy, Arthur O. *Essays in the History of Ideas*. Baltimore: The Johns Hopkins University Press, 1948.

———. *The Great Chain of Being: A Study of the History of an Idea*. Cambridge, Massachusetts: Harvard University Press, 1936.

Luce, Arthur Ashton. *Berkeley and Malebranche: A Study in the Origins of Berkeley's Thought*. London: T. Nelson, 1934.

Lyon, Georges. *L'Idéalisme en Angleterre au XVIIIᵉ siècle*. Paris: F. Alcan, 1888.

Macaulay, Thomas Babington. *Essay on Addison*, ed. Herbert Augustine Smith. Boston: Ginn, 1898.

Macdonald, Hugh. *John Dryden: A Bibliography of Early Editions and of Drydeniana*. Oxford: Clarendon Press, 1939.

MacLean, Kenneth. *John Locke and English Literature of the Eighteenth Century*. New Haven: Yale University Press, 1936.

Mallet, Sir Charles Edward. *A History of the University of Oxford.* Volumes 2–3. London and New York: Methuen, 1924–1927.

Mannheim, Karl. *Essays on the Sociology of Knowledge,* ed. Paul Kecskemeti. London: Routledge & Kegan Paul, 1952.

———. *Ideology and Utopia: An Introduction to the Sociology of Knowledge,* preface by Louis Wirth. New York: Harcourt, Brace, 1949.

Manwaring, Elizabeth Wheeler. *Italian Landscape in Eighteenth Century England.* New York: Oxford University Press, 1925.

Marburg, Clara. *Sir William Temple: A Seventeenth Century "Libertin".* New Haven: Yale University Press, 1932.

Marks, Emerson R. *Relativist and Absolutist: The Early Neoclassical Debate in England.* New Brunswick, New Jersey: Rutgers University Press, 1955.

Marni, Archimede. *Allegory in the French Heroic Poem of the Seventeenth Century.* Princeton: Princeton University Press, 1936.

Marsak, Leonard M. "Bernard de Fontenelle: In Defense of Science," *JHI,* X (1959), 111–122.

McKeon, Richard. "Literary Criticism and the Concept of Imitation in Antiquity," *MP,* XXXIV (1936), 1–35; reprinted in *Critics and Criticism, Ancient and Modern,* ed. Ronald S. Crane. Chicago: University of Chicago Press, 1952. Pp. 147–175.

———. "Imitation and Poetry," *Thought, Action, and Passion.* Chicago: University of Chicago Press, 1954. Pp. 102–221.

Miller, Perry. "Edwards, Locke, and the Rhetoric of Perception," *Perspectives of Criticism,* ed. Harry Levin. Harvard Studies in Comparative Literature, No. 20. Cambridge, Massachusetts, 1950. Pp. 103–123.

Monk, Samuel H. " 'Grace beyond the Reach of Art'," *JHI,* V (1944), 131–150.

———. *The Sublime: A Study of Critical Theories in XVIII-Century England.* New York: Modern Language Association, 1935.

Monroe, B. S. "An English Academy," *MP,* VIII (1910), 107–122.

Moore, Cecil A. *Backgrounds of English Literature, 1700–1760.* Minneapolis: University of Minnesota Press, 1953.

Morris, Robert L. "Addison's *Mixt Wit,*" *MLN,* LVII (1942), 666–668.

Muller, Herbert J. *Science and Criticism: The Humanistic Tradition in Contemporary Thought.* New Haven: Yale University Press, 1943.

Nethercot, Arthur H. "Abraham Cowley's *Discourse concerning Style,*" *RES,* II (1926), 385–404.

———. "The Reputation of the 'Metaphysical Poets' during the Age of Pope," *PQ,* IV (1925), 161–179.

Neumann, Joshua H. "Shakespearian Criticism in the *Tatler* and *Spectator,*" *PMLA,* XXXIX (1924), 612–623.

Nicoll, Allardyce. *A History of Early Eighteenth Century Drama: 1700–1750.* 3rd edition. Cambridge: University Press, 1952.

———. *A History of Restoration Drama: 1660–1700.* 4th edition. Cambridge: University Press, 1952.

———. "Italian Opera in England: The First Five Years," *Anglia,* XLIV (1922), 257–281.

Nicolson, Marjorie Hope. *The Breaking of the Circle: Studies in the Effect of the*

"New Science" upon Seventeenth Century Poetry. Evanston, Illinois: North-western University Press, 1950.

──────. "The Early Stage of Cartesianism in England," *SP,* XXVI (1929), 356–374.

──────. "The Microscope and English Imagination," *Smith College Studies in Modern Languages,* XVI, No. 4. Northampton, Massachusetts, 1935.

──────. *Mountain Gloom and Mountain Glory: The Development of the Aesthetics of the Infinite*. Ithaca, New York: Cornell University Press, 1959.

──────. *Newton Demands the Muse: Newton's "Opticks" and the Eighteenth Century Poets*. Princeton: Princeton University Press, 1946.

──────. "The Telescope and Imagination," *MP,* XXXII (1935), 233–260.

Nitchie, Elizabeth. "Longinus and the Theory of Poetic Imitation in Seventeenth and Eighteenth Century England," *SP,* XXXII (1935), 580–597.

Noack, Friedrich Ernst. *Die bürgerlichen Züge in Addisons "Cato."* Berlin: Funk, 1940.

Northrup, Clark Sutherland. "Addison and Gray as Travellers," *Studies in Language and Literature in Celebration of the Seventieth Birthday of James Morgan Hart*. New York: Henry Holt, 1910. Pp. 390–439.

O'Connor, D. J. *John Locke*. London: Penguin, 1952.

Odell, George C. D. *Shakespeare from Betterton to Irving*. 2 volumes. New York: Scribner's, 1920.

Ogden, H. V. S., and Margaret S. Ogden. *English Taste in Landscape in the Seventeenth Century*. Ann Arbor: University of Michigan Press, 1955.

Papenheim, Wilhelm. *Die Charakterschilderungen im "Tatler," "Spectator," und "Guardian," ihr Verhältnis zu Theophrast, La Bruyère und den englischen Character-Writers des 17. Jahrhunderts*. Beiträge zur englischen Philologie, XV. Leipzig: University, 1930.

Pinto, V. De S. "Was Hobbes an Ogre?" *Essays in Criticism,* VII (1957), 22–27.

Pottle, Frederick A. *The Idiom of Poetry*. Ithaca, New York: Cornell University Press, 1941.

Quinlan, Michael A. *Poetic Justice in the Drama: History of an Ethical Principle in Literary Criticism*. South Bend Indiana: Notre Dame University Press, 1912.

Robertson, J. G. *Studies in the Genesis of Romantic Theory in the Eighteenth Century*. Cambridge: University Press, 1923.

Robinson, Herbert Spencer. *English Shakespearian Criticism in the Eighteenth Century*. New York: H. Wilson, 1932.

Rosen, Robert. "A Relational Theory of Biological Systems," *Bulletin of Mathematical Biophysics,* XX (1958), 245–260.

Sabine, George Holland. *History of Political Theory*. Revised edition. New York: Henry Holt, 1950.

Saintsbury, George. *A History of Criticism and Literary Taste in Europe*. 3 volumes. Edinburgh and London: Blackwood, 1900–1904.

Saudé, Emil. *Die Grundlagen der literarischen Kritik bei Joseph Addison*. Weimar: R. Wagner, 1906.

Sayce, R. A. *The French Biblical Epic in the Seventeenth Century*. Oxford: Clarendon Press, 1955.

Schueller, Herbert M. "Literature and Music as Sister Arts: An Aspect of Aesthetic Theory in Eighteenth-Century Britain," *PQ,* XXVI (1947), 193–205.

234 THE CULTURAL MILIEU OF ADDISON'S LITERARY CRITICISM

Sherburn, George. "Pope and 'The Great Shew of Nature'," *The Seventeenth Century: Studies in the History of English Thought and Literature from Bacon to Pope*, ed. Richard F. Jones. Stanford: Stanford University Press, 1951. Pp. 306–315.

Shorey, Paul. *What Plato Said*. Chicago: University of Chicago Press, 1933.

Smith, Andrew Cannon. *Theories of Nature and Standards of Taste in England, 1700–1790*. Chicago: Private edition, 1933.

Smithers, Peter. *The Life of Joseph Addison*. Oxford: Clarendon Press, 1954.

Snow, A. J. *Matter and Gravity in Newton's Physical Philosophy: A Study in the Natural Philosophy of Newton's Time*. London: Oxford University Press, 1926.

Southern, Richard. *Changeable Scenery, Its Origins and Development in the British Theatre*. London: Faber and Faber, 1952.

Spence, Joseph. *Anecdotes, Observations and Characters of Books and Men*, ed. S. W. Singer. 2nd edition. London: J. R. Smith, 1858.

Spingarn, Joel E. *A History of Literary Criticism in the Renaissance*. 2nd edition. New York: Columbia University Press, 1925.

Stephen, Sir Leslie. *History of English Thought in the Eighteenth Century*. 3rd edition. 2 volumes. London: John Murray, 1902.

Stewart, Keith. "The Ballad and the *Genres*," *ELH*, XXIV (1957), 120–137.

Stolnitz, Jerome. " 'Beauty': Some Stages in the History of an Idea," *JHI*, XXII (1961), 185–204.

——. "On the Origins of 'Aesthetic Disinterestedness'," *JAAC*, XX (1961), 131–143.

Stone, George Winchester, Jr. "Shakespeare in the Periodicals, 1700–1740," *Shakespeare Quarterly*, II (1951), 221–231.

Strauss, Leo. *The Political Philosophy of Hobbes*, trans. Elsa M. Sinclair. Oxford: Clarendon Press, 1936.

Stromberg, Roland N. *Religious Liberalism in Eighteenth-Century England*. London: Oxford University Press, 1954.

Summers, Montague. *The Restoration Theatre*. London: Kegan Paul, 1934.

Summers, Silas E. "Addison's Conception of Tragedy," *College English*, VIII (1947), 245–248.

Sutherland, James. "The Last Years of Joseph Addison," *Background for Queen Anne*. London: Methuen, 1939. Pp. 127–144.

Swedenberg, H. T., Jr. "Rules and English Critics of the Epic," *SP*, XXXV (1938), 566–587.

——. *The Theory of the Epic in England, 1650–1800*. University of California Publications in English, XV. Berkeley and Los Angeles, 1944.

Sykes, Norman. *Church and State in England in the XVIIIth Century*. Cambridge: University Press, 1934.

Tate, J. " 'Imitation' in Plato's *Republic*," *Classical Quarterly*, XXII (1928), 16–23.

——. "Plato and 'Imitation'," *Classical Quarterly*, XXVII (1932), 161–169.

Taylor, A. E. *Plato, The Man and His Work*. 6th edition. London: Methuen, 1949.

Thorpe, Clarence DeWitt. "Addison and Hutcheson on the Imagination," *ELH*, II (1935), 215–234.

————. "Addison and Some of His Predecessors on Novelty," *PMLA*, LII (1937), 1114–1129.

————. "Addison's Contribution to Criticism," *The Seventeenth Century: Studies in the History of English Thought and Literature from Bacon to Pope*, ed. Richard F. Jones. Stanford: Stanford University Press, 1951. Pp. 316–329.

————. "Addison's Theory of the Imagination as 'Perceptive Response'," *Papers of the Michigan Academy of Science, Arts and Letters*, XXI (1936), 509–530.

————. *The Aesthetic Theory of Thomas Hobbes*. University of Michigan Publications, Language and Literature, XVIII. Ann Arbor, 1940.

————. "Two Augustans Cross the Alps: Dennis and Addison on Mountain Scenery," *SP*, XXXII (1935), 463–482.

Trevelyan, George Macaulay. *England under Queen Anne*. 3 volumes. London: Longmans, Green, 1930–1934.

Tuve, Rosamund. *Elizabethan and Metaphysical Imagery*. Chicago: University of Chicago Press, 1947.

Tuveson, Ernest. *The Imagination as a Means of Grace*. Berkeley and Los Angeles: University of California Press, 1960.

————. "Locke and the Dissociation of the Ego," *MP*, LII (1954–1955), 159–174.

————. "Space, Deity, and the 'Natural Sublime'," *MLQ*, XII (1951), 20–38.

Voegelin, Eric. *Order and History: Volume Three, Plato and Aristotle*. Baton Rouge: Louisiana State University Press, 1957.

Walcott, Fred G. "Dryden's Answer to Thomas Rymer's *Tragedies of the Last Age*," *PQ*, XV (1936), 194–214.

Walcott, Robert. *English Politics in the Early Eighteenth Century*. Oxford: Clarendon Press, 1956.

Walker, Ernest. *A History of Music in England*. 3rd edition, revised and enlarged by J. A. Westrup. London: Oxford University Press, 1952.

Wallerstein, Ruth. *Studies in Seventeenth Century Poetic*. Madison: University of Wisconsin Press, 1950.

Walmsey, D. M. "The Influence of Foreign Operas on English Operatic Plays of the Restoration Period," *Anglia*, LII (1928), 37–50.

Ward, W. R. *Georgian Oxford, University Politics in the Eighteenth Century*. Oxford: Clarendon Press, 1958.

Warren, Austin. *Alexander Pope as Critic and Humanist*. Princeton Studies in English, No. 1. Princeton, 1929.

————. "Literary Criticism," *Literary Scholarship: Its Aims and Methods*, ed. Norman Foerster. Chapel Hill: University of North Carolina Press, 1941. Pp. 133–174.

Wasserman, Earl R. *Elizabethan Poetry in the Eighteenth Century*. University of Illinois Studies in Language and Literature, XII, Nos. 2–3. Urbana, 1947.

————. "The Inherent Values of Eighteenth-Century Personification," *PMLA*, LXV (1950), 435–463.

————. "The Pleasures of Tragedy," *ELH*, XIV (1947), 283–307.

Weinberg, Bernard. "The Poetic Theories of Minturno," *Studies in Honor of Frederick W. Shipley*. St. Louis, Missouri: Washington University Press, 1942. Pp. 101–129.

Weinberg, Bernard. "Robertello on the Poetics," *Critics and Criticism, Ancient and Modern,* ed. Ronald S. Crane. Chicago: University of Chicago Press, 1952. Pp. 319–348.

———. "Scaliger versus Aristotle on Poetics," *MP,* XXXIX (1947), 337–360.

Wellek, René. "The Conception of Evolution in Literary History," *For Roman Jakobson: Essays on the Occasion of his Sixtieth Birthday,* compiled by Morris Halle and others. The Hague: Mouton, 1956. Pp. 653–661.

———. *A History of Modern Criticism: 1750–1950, The Later Eighteenth Century.* London: Jonathan Cape, 1955.

———. "Literary History," *Literary Scholarship: Its Aims and Methods,* ed. Norman Foerster. Chapel Hill: University of North Carolina Press, 1941. Pp. 91–130.

———. *The Rise of English Literary History.* Chapel Hill: University of North Carolina Press, 1941.

———. "Theory of Literary History," *Travaux du cercle linguistique de Prague,* VI (1936), 173–191.

———, and Austin Warren. *Theory of Literature.* 2nd edition. New York: Harcourt, Brace, 1955.

Wheatley, Katherine E. "Addison's Portrait of the Neo-Classical Critic," *RES,* n.s. I (1950), 245–247.

White, H. O. "Thomas Purney, A Forgotten Poet and Critic of the Eighteenth Century," *Essays and Studies by Members of the English Association,* XV (1929), 67–97.

Wilkins, A. N. "John Dennis and Poetic Justice," *N&Q,* IV (1957), 421–424.

Willey, Basil. *The Eighteenth Century Background: Studies on the Idea of Nature in the Thought of the Period.* New York: Columbia University Press, 1953 (reprint of the 1940 edition).

———. *The Seventeenth Century Background: Studies in the Thought of Age in Relation to Poetry and Religion.* London: Chatto and Windus, 1949 (reprint of the 1934 edition).

Williams, Basil. *The Whig Supremacy: 1714–1760.* Oxford History of England, XI. Oxford: Clarendon Press, 1942.

Williamson, George. "The Restoration Revolt against Enthusiasm," *SP,* XXX (1933), 571–603.

———. *The Senecan Amble: A Study in Prose Form from Bacon to Collier.* Chicago: University of Chicago Press, 1951.

Wimsatt, William K., Jr. "Rhetoric and Poems: The Example of Pope," *English Institute Essays, 1948,* ed. D. A. Robertson. New York: Columbia University Press, 1949. Pp. 179–207.

———, and Cleanth Brooks. *Literary Criticism: A Short History.* New York: Alfred Knopf, 1957.

Winton, Calhoun. "Steele, the Junto, and *The Tatler* No. 4," *MLN,* LXXII (1957), 178–182.

Wolf, A. *A History of Science, Technology and Philosophy in the 16th & 17th Centuries.* London: Allen and Unwin, 1935.

Wood, Paul Spencer. "Native Elements in English Classicism," *MP,* XXIV (1926), 201–208.

Worsfold, William. *The Principles of Criticism: An Introduction to the Study of Literature*. New York: Longmans, Green, 1902.

Wright, C. H. C. *French Classicism*. Cambridge, Massachusetts: Harvard University Press, 1920.

Yolton, John W. "Locke and the Seventeenth-Century Logic of Ideas," *JHI*, XVI (1955), 431–452.

———. *John Locke and the Way of Ideas*. London: Oxford University Press, 1956.

Zobel, Arthur. "Darstellung und kritische Würdegung der Sprachphilosophie John Lockes," *Anglia*, LII (1928), 289–324.

Unpublished Theses and Dissertations

Anderson, Augustus Edwin. "Theories of Fancy and Imagination in English Thought from Hobbes to Coleridge." Ph.D., Vanderbilt University, 1953.

Beers, Cora Lee. "Longinus and the Disintegration of English Neo-Classicism." Ph.D., Stanford University, 1940.

Bond, Donald F. "Theories of the Imagination in English Literary Criticism of the Seventeenth and Eighteenth Centuries." Ph.D., University of Chicago, 1934.

Doering, J. F. "Joseph Addison as Literary Critic." Ph.D., University of Ottawa (Canada), 1944.

Elioseff, Lee Andrew. "English Empirical Philosophy and Addison's Literary Criticism." M.A., New York University, 1957.

———. "The Cultural Milieu of Addison's Literary Criticism." Ph.D., New York University, 1960.

Hamm, Victor M. "The Imagination in English Neo-Classical Thought and Literature." Ph.D., Harvard University, 1935.

Hathaway, Baxter Levering. "The Function of Tragedy in Neo-Classical Criticism." Ph.D., University of Michigan, 1940.

Kallich, Martin. "The Association of Ideas and Critical Theory in Eighteenth Century England: A History of the Psychological Method in English Criticism." Ph.D., The Johns Hopkins University, 1945.

Marcus, Mitchell. "Joseph Addison as Literary Critic." Ph.D., Stanford University, 1950.

Morris, Robert Lee. "Joseph Addison's Literary Criticism." Ph.D., Iowa State University, 1931.

Sawyer, Robert Graham. *"If Atticus Were He . . .* A Study of the Relations between Addison and Pope." Ph.D., New York University, 1952.

Toub, Kasena. "Criticism and Satire of Italian Opera in England: 1656–1728." M.A., New York University, 1938.

West, Dorothy Irene. "Italian Opera in England (1660–1740), and Some of Its Relations to English Literature." Ph.D., University of Illinois, 1938.

INDEX

Abercromby, David: on wit, 187 n.

"Account of the Greatest English Poets, An" (Addison) : criticism of Milton in, 51, 52

Addison, Joseph: on ballads, parodied by Wagstaffe, 65; admires Boileau, 40; *Cato,* 77; *Cato* and the Augustan virtues, 67; the love theme in *Cato,* 77–78 and n.; on true and false critics, 27; admires Descartes, 147–148, 151; and divine-right theory, 133 and n.; education of 43; on enthusiasm, 105–106, 107; on the imagination, 180–181; range of interests of, 42–43; on Le Bossu on heroic poetry, 54; on mental activity, 152 and n.; on imitation of Milton's poetic style, 51–52; on Milton's politics, 51; on moral and fable in heroic poetry, 58–60; response of, to mountain scenes, 112–114, 114 n.; originality of, as a critic, 192–193; on Philips's pastorals, 127 n.; philosophical optimism of, 147 n.; faith of, in natural philosophy, 145, 146 and n.; on natural philosophy, 45–46; Platonism of, 207–208; and Dennis debate on poetry and tragedy, 88–92; early poetry and criticism of, 44–45; early reading of, 44; as a political figure, 130 n.; prospects of, for religious career, 105 n.; religious moderation of, 105–107; influence of, on Thomas Purney, 184 n.; scepticism of, about science, 145; MSS of, on the sublime, 99 n.; reactions of, to Dennis on the sublime, 98–99; on tragic passions and sentiments, 61

—, debts of: to Dryden and Dennis re *Paradise Lost,* 51; to Dennis, re Milton criticism, 62 n.; to English empiricism, 195–199; to Hobbes for tragic theory, 90–92; to Hobbes and Locke, 154–162, 173, 174 ff.; to Le Bossu, 61; to Locke summarized, 196–197; to Rapin and Le Bossu on

heroic poetry, 49 ff.; to Roscommon, 51

Aden, John M.: on Dryden on imagination, 173 n.

Aeneid: 52, 70; Addison and Le Bossu on, 54

aesthetic distance: 180

affective criticism: 6, 10; of art and nature, 162; Bacon's influence on, 148 and n., 151; and argument from *consensus gentium* on the ballads, 69; rejected by Dennis, 73; English beginnings of, 74; and evaluation, 11; Hobbes's and Locke's influence on, 156; and the imagination, 161; and Addison on the pleasures of the imagination, 13; of pastoral, 124–125, 126, 126 n., 139, 141; Purney, 8, 184 n.; in evaluation of Dennis, 101; of tragedy, 88

allegory: in heroic poetry. SEE heroic poetry

Allen, B. S.: on landscape painting, 118 n.

ancients and moderns: battle of, 108 and n.; relative value of, 6

Answer to Davenant (Hobbes) : on imagination, 171

Antigone (Sophocles) : Blackmore on, 54

Aristotle: 38; appeal to authority of, 86; on catharsis, 11 and n.; Farquhar on, 37; on imitation of the painful, 187; on the infinite, 109–110, 110 n.; on artificiality of language, 165, 166; on conceptualism and language, 166; on nature as "coming-into-being," 160; the rationale of criticism of, 9; Rymer cites, 80; rules of, for tragedy, 49

art: as mirror of life, 15

Arte of English Poesie, The (Puttenham) : 21, 165

Art of English Poetry, The (Bysshe) : on the rules, 37

Art of Rhetorique, The (Wilson) : 21